SICILY

Also in the Series

SICILY

A Cultural History

JOSEPH FARRELL

Interlink Books

An imprint of Interlink Publishing Group, Inc.
Northampton, Massachusetts

First published in 2014 by
INTERLINK BOOKS
An imprint of Interlink Publishing Group, Inc.
46 Crosby Street, Northampton, Massachusetts 01060
www.interlinkbooks.com

Library of Congress Cataloging-in-Publication Data
Farrell, Joseph.
Sicily : a cultural history / Joseph Farrell.
    pages cm
Includes index.
ISBN 978-1-56656-952-1
1. Sicily (Italy)--History. 2. Sicily (Italy)--Civilization. I. Title.
DG866.F28 2014
945'.8--dc23
                            2014002426

Cover images: Leonardo Corradini/istockphoto
Illustrations: Wikipedia Commons; Lambert (Bart) Parren/istockphoto p.1, Peeter Viisimaa/istockphoto pp.7, 38, anzeletti/istockphoto p.15, Giovanni Rinaldi/istockphoto p.159, Nathan Gutshall-Kresge/istockphoto p.279; maps by Sebastian Ballard

Printed and bound in the United States of America

To request our complete 48-page full-color catalog, please call us toll free at
1-800-238-LINK, visit our website at www.interlinkbooks.com, or write to
Interlink Publishing 46 Crosby Street, Northampton, MA 01060
e-mail: info@interlinkbooks.com

Contents

To Ciaran, Elliot, Euan and Katie, my grandchildren.
The hope of the future, the heirs of a ruined past.

"Perhaps the deepest nostalgia I have ever felt has been for Sicily, reading Verga. Not for England or anywhere else—for Sicily, the beautiful, that which goes deepest into the blood. It is so clear, so beautiful..."

D. H. Lawrence

"I am drawn by an irresistible attraction to the fair levels and richly verdured heights of Sicily. What a country! a shadow of Eden, so as at once to enrapture and to make one melancholy. It will be a vision for my whole life."

John Henry (Cardinal) Newman

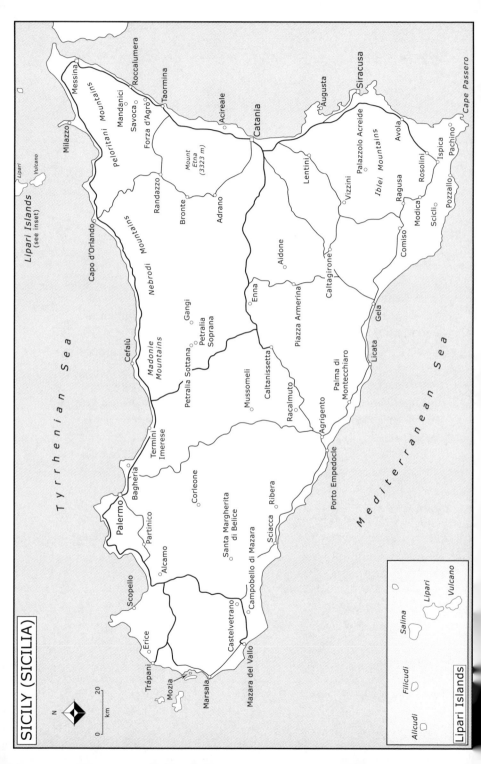

Preface and Acknowledgements

When a British football team was playing in some European competition in Calabria, in the toe of Italy, a reporter sent to cover the match wrote that as he walked around Reggio Calabria he was conscious of being sufficiently close to Sicily to make him keep his hand on his wallet. More recently, in a piece on the Leveson Enquiry into relations between journalists and politicians in Britain, a columnist remarked that these were two groups with a Sicilian-like capacity for holding grudges.

It is hard to establish the roots of this negative image of Sicily, but while it has been pervasive and tenacious, fortunately it has not led to people boycotting the island, which is visited by growing numbers of tourists every year. Certainly some will remain in the resort areas in Cefalù or around Taormina and will seek little contact with the island or its inhabitants. This is a pity, but if they can be persuaded to venture further afield they will discover the charms, delights and surprises that Sicily has to offer.

It is tempting to introduce Sicily with a series of questions of the "Did you know?" sort. Did you know that Sicily is the biggest wine-producing region of Italy? Did you know that sugar was introduced into Europe via Sicily by the Arabs? Or, on a different level, did you know there are more Greek temples in Sicily than in mainland Greece? Did you know that many of the famous tales of Greek mythology are actually set on the island? Did you know that the sonnet was invented by Sicilian poets? Did you know Sicily was ruled by Arabs for over two centuries? Did you know that the Normans invaded Sicily in 1061, five years before William the Conqueror crossed the English Channel to establish Norman power in England? Did you know that you can find churches in Sicily in the same style as some country churches in England? Did you know that Baroque architecture is beautiful, in spite of what sniffy art histories write? Did you know that Lord Nelson had an estate in Sicily, where he hoped to retire with Lady Hamilton after Napoleon was defeated? Did you know that it was merchants from Yorkshire who invented Marsala wine? Did you know that the British-American fleet which invaded Sicily in 1943 was the largest ever assembled? Did you know there is more to Sicily than the mafia, and did you know that only a tiny percentage of Sicilians are members of that pernicious body?

This book sets itself the ambitious aim of giving an insight into the totality of Sicilian life and experience. Sicily has changed nature and identity at many points in its long history and prehistory, and the main surprise for curious visitors is the discovery of just how rich and varied Sicilian history and civilization are, and, since there is more to the good life than the enjoyment of art and architecture or the knowledge of who ruled when and how well, how attractive life in Sicily can be. The seas and the landscape are beautiful, the cities can be fascinating, but freedom from the pinched Puritanism of northern Europe means that Sicilians have always appreciated the joys of the table. The aim, then, is to take in not only the history of other times as it can be seen in the many impressive temples, castles, churches and palaces all over the island, but also the attractions of today, including the distinctive cuisine and the many good wines to be savoured in Sicily. As it happens, that cuisine also demonstrates the richness of the island's history, with traces of Greek, Arab, Norman and Spanish influence.

The book is divided into two parts. The first six chapters are a general introduction to Sicily, focusing on its image, its daily living, its history and culture, on the way it has been portrayed by its own writers, as well as on how it has been seen by the travellers who have visited it over the centuries. The remaining chapters are a travelogue, a journey around the island from Messina to Messina. The cities, the main repository of history, are fascinating, but so too are many towns and villages. The landscape is varied. It is fierce, sun-scorched and arid over large swathes of central Sicily but in other areas, especially the two huge Regional Parks which cover the Madonie and the Nebrodi mountain ranges, it is cool, even cold in winter, with a variety of wild life and fauna which entice bird-spotters and animal lovers from all over Europe. And the need to provide a portable volume means there are many more places to discover. Sicily is a welcoming place.

લ⁄૭

I am grateful above all to Rossana Dedola for initial encouragement with this project and for putting me in touch with the publisher. James Ferguson has been the ideal editor. Among those who have helped with suggestions and enlightening conversation I would like to mention Vincenzo Barbarotta, Gaetano de Bernardis, Vito Catalano, Sergio and Carlo

Mastroeni, Tom Baldwin, Peter Brand, Dario Tomasello, Allan Cameron, Marina de Stefano and Andrew Wilkin. I could never have completed this work without the patient and loving assistance of Maureen, who read every word several times.

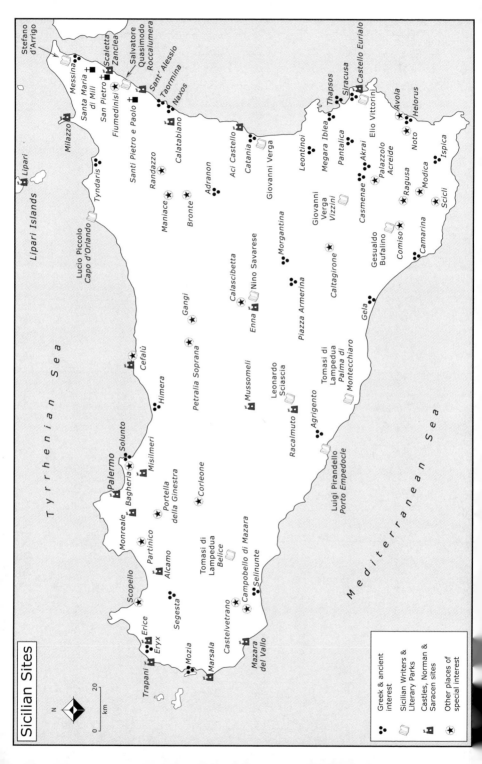

Sicilian Sites

N

km
0   20

Tyrrhenian Sea

Mediterranean Sea

Lipari Islands

Stefano d'Arrigo

Messina
Santa Maria di Milì
San Pietro
Scaletta
Zanclea
Salvatore Quasimodo
Roccalumera
Sant' Alessio
Taormina
Naxos
Milazzo
Lipari
Fiumedinisi
Santi Pietro e Paolo
Randazzo
Calatabiano
Maniace
Bronte
Adranon
Aci Castello
Catania
Giovanni Verga
Lucio Piccolo
Capo d'Orlando
Tyndaris
Cefalù
Himera
Gangi
Petralia Soprana
Calascibetta
Nino Savarese
Enna
Morgantina
Leontinoi
Giovanni Verga Vizzini
Piazza Armerina
Caltagirone
Thapsos
Megara Iblea
Pantalica
Siracusa
Castello Eurialo
Akrai
Casmenae
Palazzolo Acreide
Avola
Helorus
Noto
Ispica
Modica
Ragusa
Scicli
Camarina
Comiso
Gesualdo Bufalino
Gela
Elio Vittorini
Palermo
Solunto
Monreale
Bagheria
Misilmeri
Partinico
Alcamo
Scopello
Erice
Eryx
Segesta
Mozia
Trapani
Marsala
Castelvetrano
Mazara del Vallo
Campobello di Mazara
Selinunte
Belice
Tomasi di Lampedua
Portella della Ginestra
Corleone
Mussomeli
Leonardo Sciascia
Racalmuto
Agrigento
Tomasi di Lampedua
Palma di Montecchiaro
Luigi Pirandello
Porto Empedocle

Greek & ancient interest

Sicilian Writers & Literary Parks

Castles, Norman & Saracen sites

Other places of special interest

Chapter One
THE CULTURES OF SICILY
THE ROSEBUD QUEST

There is a temptation, perhaps stronger in the case of Sicily than of any other place, to search out a "rosebud" factor. This was the last word spoken by the protagonist of Orson Welles' masterpiece, *Citizen Kane,* and being uttered on the point of death was taken as some Delphic key capable of unlocking the strivings and aspirations which had goaded Kane all his life. Of course, it did nothing of the kind. It transpired that the word was the name given to a favorite plaything from which Kane had been separated at the moment of his removal from home.

Is there a "rosebud" factor which could open out the rich complexities of Sicilian life and culture? The prosaic fact that there is not has not inhibited the poetical quest. Vincent Cronin, author of *The Golden Honeycomb,* one of the most lyrical and penetrating books on Sicily, made out he was on a quest for the honeycomb which legends say was crafted by Daedalus when, after losing his son Icarus on their winged flight from Crete, he landed in Sicily and, as the supreme scientist-artisan of ancient

Europe, offered a honeycomb of gold to the goddess Venus of Erice. More recently, both the eighteenth-century French pamphleteer Paul-Louis Courier, an officer in Napoleon's army frustrated by the lack of a favorable wind to carry the troops across the Straits of Messina, and the contemporary American writer, Mary Taylor Simeti, imagined that the elusive rosebud factor was the seizure in Sicily of the maiden Persephone by the Lord of the Underworld. More ambitiously Goethe, who completed his travels in Italy with a visit to Sicily, wrote that Sicily was "the key to everything." Everything! More modestly, the Australian culinary journalist Brian Johnston saw the core object of his quest as the ideal Sicilian *cassata*. Curiously, some of those engaged on a quest have combined love of Sicily with a haughty contempt for Sicilian people. Cronin found them "lacking in vigour and self-reliance," while Philippe Diolé, author of an idiosyncratic book which examines Sicily from the perspective of a diver, concludes that "on the whole, the race lacks zest."

Visitors project onto Sicily their own beliefs and fears. The most recent image, of a land of endemic corruption, of ritual killings, and of a mafia-polluted society, is the most impoverished of all, but Sicily is a land of extremes where the best and worst of the human race have flourished. It has been the Mecca of many celebrated travelers and commentators. Patrick Brydone from Coldstream in Scotland smoothed the path in the eighteenth century when as traveling preceptor he extended the Grand Tour by venturing south of Naples and writing a book, *A Tour to Sicily and Malta*, which was immediately translated into several languages and which his illustrious successors carried in their pockets, sometimes with the intention of publishing rancorous rebuttals of what he had written. The great names who wrote about Sicily have included, in addition to Goethe, Henry Swinburne, Edward Lear, John Henry Newman when still an Anglican and long before he was made Cardinal, the artist Jean Houel, the novelist Alexandre Dumas *père* who stayed on his yacht while Garibaldi and his Thousand overran Sicily, the historian Gregorovius, Guy de Maupassant, Samuel Taylor Coleridge, D. H. Lawrence, and E. M. Forster as well as numerous minor novelists and thriller writers who found Sicily and its associations an ideally colorful or sinister background for their tales. Before them all, there had been the Greek poets, most notably Theocritus, the inventor of pastoral verse, and the Arabs, rulers of the island for centuries, whose poets sang of the charms of Sicily and whose travelers, including the great geographer Mohammad al-Idrisi, described those charms in enthralled detail. Today's Sicilian writers are fascinated by their own land and its multi-layered history, but they will be considered separately. At this point, it is enough to say that their view tends towards the jaundiced, although that is often the tone writers and intellectuals everywhere find most appropriate for expressing a frustrated love for their native place. I recall going to visit Leonardo Sciascia, a great writer and Sicilian to the core, and asking him why it was that the depiction of Sicily by its writers was so grim. *Perché la realtà Siciliana è pessima*, he replied, and the translation—"Because Sicilian reality is appalling"—loses the force of the onomatopoeic, snake-like hiss with which he dragged out the twin *sses* in the superlative *pessima*. As regards the history and culture of Sicily, there are two main interpretative approaches which can be described as *Sciasciano* and *Gattopardesco*, the second taking its name from *Il gattopardo,* the Italian title of Tomasi di Lampedusa's great novel (*The Leopard*). Both authors provide in their works extended, introspective meditations on Sicily, but Lampedusa's is founded on a notion of an essentially unchanging Sicily, afflicted by a "summer as long and as grim as a Russian winter," defying history and drifting in accordance with inner imperatives which successive waves of invaders have struggled to comprehend and have failed to dominate, while Sciascia's view is of an island subject to competing historical forces and changes. I love Lampedusa's novel (as Sciascia did not) but I am myself a *Sciasciano*. How can one be Sicilian, what does it mean to be Sicilian and why is Sicily as it is, Sciascia asks continually, obsessively. Sicily has been a center of civilization, or civilizations, from ancient times, but when did Sicily become Sicily? In the view of Sciascia's friend and fellow novelist, Vincenzo Consolo, "Arab culture left such a deep imprint on the island that it can be said that Sicilian history begins when it is grafted onto the island."

The most penetrating judgement on the nature, roots, complexity, and dilemmas of Sicilian culture was made by Giuseppe Antonio Borgese, a Sicilian writer forced into exile for his anti-fascist views. He spent many years in America and wrote some of his books in English, giving him the advantages of both proximity and distance. In a celebrated article, he declared that "Sicily is an island which is not island enough." It is a deceptively simple and necessarily enigmatic judgement. Sicily has a strong sense of its own selfhood, but has at the same time an ill-defined identity, made up of varying, competing elements. At a cultural level, the island has always been open to the trade in ideas as well as in merchandise from elsewhere in Europe, France, and Spain in particular, but also from Africa. Leoluca Orlando, the veteran politician and current mayor of Palermo, known for his unbending honesty and hatred of the mafia, has always been fond of describing Sicily as a bridge-head between Christian Europe and Islamic North Africa. Its geographical position was decisive for its development and left open two possibilities—of being an island at the center of the Mediterranean or else an offshore island of Italy. At various points, it has been constrained to take one or other of these roles. As an island, it was too big to be ignored but yet too small to dominate. Conquerors came and went, and their attitude to the Sicilian people varied on a spectrum from indifference to contempt, but they were compelled to take them into account to an extent which later European imperialist rulers of African or Asian colonies were incapable or unwilling to do. They all left their mark, but only one indigenous class, the aristocracy, was given a share in government when the ultimate rulers were in France, Vienna, Madrid, London (briefly), or Naples.

IDENTITY AND TRADITIONS

Identity is a nebulous concept, and many of the identities which have been most tenaciously fought over are often the most ill-defined. Freud railed against the "narcissism of tiny differences," but the issue of these differences, tiny or not, cannot be ignored. There is, all Sicilians will agree, a Sicilian tradition expressing a Sicilian sense of self, part of a wider European culture but specific and separate from the wider Italian identity, even if now not wholly distinct from it. The Sicilian tradition is autonomous but not totally self-enclosed, similar to the traditions of Catalonia, which once ruled in Sicily, or Ireland, which did not. Of all the distinguishing marks of Sicily's culture, the most powerful is a sense of an existential and historical precariousness, a belief or fear that civilization is fragile, that happiness and success have to be grasped when available but that their attainment is exceptional, since all that is good is transitory and perishable. Both historical and natural forces in all their ferocity have been unleashed on Sicily. They combine to make the sense of peril and fragility omnipresent and to reinforce the precarious mindset. It is a mentality which underlies the novels of the Catanese writer Giovanni Verga and the theater of Luigi Pirandello, Sicily's greatest writers.

An identity is expressed most cogently in works of art, and there is an anomaly to be noted here. Sicily has not been strong in every field of the arts. In music, at least in classical music, it has produced only one undisputed genius, Vincenzo Bellini of Catania, whose operas such as *I Puritani* or *Norma* are part of the standard canon of every western opera house, but he never lived in Sicily as an adult. He left the island when he was seventeen, and did not return in his lifetime. The city fathers campaigned to have his body brought back and now he is entombed in a grand sepulchre in the cathedral. The city's opera house is named after him, but his relations with the city were not close. The island is featured in other operas such as Verdi's *Sicilian Vespers* or the twin one-act works, Pietro Mascagni's *Cavalleria rusticana* and Ruggero Leoncavallo's *Pagliacci*, now irreverently nicknamed *Cav* and *Pag* by opera administrators. The first was inspired by a short story by Verga. An examination of popular music would yield a richer harvest, and the instrument known in Italian as the *scacciapensieri*, and in English as the Jew's Harp, is frequently used. The word Jew here has nothing to do with Jewishness, but is a corruption of "jaw," since the simple instrument is circular with a protruding lever and is played by being placed in the jaw and strummed. It does not permit great variety of sound, but has the hypnotic effect of a zither.

There is an element of injustice in Sicily's limited presence in art history. It is true that there are towns in Tuscany or Lazio which have produced more artists than the whole island, but there are also masters whose work has, inexplicably, not traveled. *The Triumph of Death* in the Regional Art Gallery in Palermo is a masterfully executed work of art, and there is also an infinity of canvases and frescoes by Sicilian painters in churches and palaces, and some of these, such as those produced by Antonello Gagini, are of a high if unrecognized aesthetic standard. There is one painter of undisputed genius, Antonello da Messina. One of his Madonnas is in the National Gallery in London, but his masterpiece, *The Smile of the Unknown Mariner*, is in a gallery in Cefalú. Antonello was an example of the cosmopolitan Sicilian, and was the conduit by which the achievements of Flemish art became known to the Venetians and helped shape their art. His impact was enormous, and his delicate, gentle canvases are to be ranked with the best of Renaissance work.

In modern times, Renato Guttuso has been widely admired for his vivid canvases of Sicilian life. He was for much of his life a member of the Communist Party, and was driven by a conscientious need to depict and contribute to the improvement of the lot of the Sicilian peasantry. His paintings are a commentary on social conditions, but he never descended into mechanical propaganda or socialist realism. Guttuso was tied to the traditions of his native Sicily, and on one occasion went so far as to say that even when he painted an apple, Sicily was there. He never painted an apple, but he did some wonderful still lifes. He upset both the Church and the fascist regime with his 1941 painting *Crucifixion*, which was not a religious portrait but a protest on behalf of suffering people everywhere. One of his best known works, *Vucciria*, is a huge, sprawling but disciplined, beautifully structured canvas of buyers and sellers in Palermo's biggest street market. The center of the work shows a generously proportioned Sicilian woman with a basket of produce, while all around her are the brightly colored stalls with fruits, vegetables, fish, and meat. Much of his work is in a converted palace in his home town of Bagheria.

The oratories of Palermo, and other churches around the island, exhibit a school of delicate stucco works which have few equivalents in other countries and which reached a climax of perfection with Giacomo Serpotta. It is strange that the fame of the works of this seraphic, delicate genius has not traveled beyond Sicily, but perhaps it can be explained by the uncommon *genre* in which he worked. In any case, the discovery of this marvelous artist will be one of the joys of travel in Sicily.

It is in literature that Sicily expresses its genius. Only Tuscany among Italian regions surpasses the historical achievements of Sicilian writers. In the late Middle Ages it was the home of the first school of Italian poetry, which Dante decreed should be known simply as the "Sicilian School," a name which he explicitly stated should never be varied at any future date. The poets were courtiers at the brilliant court of Frederick II, and included the king-emperor himself. The island has produced two Nobel Prize winners, the playwright Luigi Pirandello and the poet Salvatore Quasimodo. The list of great Sicilians over the nineteenth and twentieth centuries includes many of the leading names in Italian literature: Giovanni Verga, Federico De Roberto, Luigi Capuana, Luigi Pirandello, Salvatore Quasimodo, Lucio Piccolo, Leonardo Sciascia, Gesualdo Bufalino, and Vincenzo Consolo. There are others, and the visitor may be surprised at the numbers of that quintessentially Italian institution, the "literary park" dedicated to the cultivation of individual writers, that are to be found around the island, although not all these parks are especially fertile.

THE STONES OF SICILY

Travel in Sicily offers the imaginative traveler the opportunity to reconstruct the history of the island in unexpected ways. Perhaps to a greater degree than in other countries, it can also be traced in stones, in landscape, and in cuisine. Of cuisine more later, but man's insensitive behavior towards the environment has meant that the land which Romans called "the granary of the empire," and which the Arabs lauded for its ample waters is hard to visualize nowadays. The passage of various conquerors can be traced in places now out of the way, and in buildings which have uses unintended by the original occupants. There is an insatiable need for public buildings since there are three tiers of government (town or city council, province, and Region) attending to the needs of Sicilians, or simply multiplying in accordance with the imperatives of bureaucracy everywhere, and in consequence a growing demand for space for officials and elected members. Successive phases of history are already illustrated by

Isnello's thirteenth-century castle overlooks modern urban sprawl

the fact that the Sicilian Regional Assembly meets in Palermo in the Palace of the Normans overlooking Piazza Indipendenza, while the President of the Region has his official residence in the nearby D'Orleans Palace.

No other part of Europe can have so many castles, some ruined, some converted, some abandoned, and some available for any enterprising individual with a bright idea. The same could be said of monasteries. The sheer number of such successive conquests, or civilizations, may come as a surprise. Cultural consciousness in Sicily is a reckoning with history. Fabrizio, Prince of Salina and protagonist of *The Leopard*, drew attention to the diverse civilizations which had made the island their home, even if uninvited. In a dialogue with an envoy of the House of Savoy who had come to offer him a seat in the newly united Kingdom of Italy, the prince explained his decision to decline the offer:

> We Sicilians have become accustomed by a long, a very long hegemony of rulers who were not of our religion and did not speak out language, to split hairs. If we had not done so, we would never have coped with Byzantine tax gatherers, with Berber Emirs, with Spanish Viceroys. Now the bent is endemic, we're made like that... We are old, very old. For over twenty-five centuries we have carried the weight of superb and heterogeneous civilizations, all from outside, none made by ourselves, none that we could call our own. We are as white as you are, and as the Queen of England; and yet for two thousand five hundred years, we've been a colony. I don't say that in complaint: it's our fault. But even so we're worn out and exhausted.

The prince blamed the inertia of the Sicilians for their position as a "colony," and based on that tormented history his doubts as to the wisdom of those who hoped to "channel Sicily into the flow of universal history." He went on:

> Anyway, I've explained myself badly; I said Sicilians, I should have added Sicily, the atmosphere, the climate, the landscape of Sicily. Those are the forces which have formed our mind together with and perhaps more than the alien pressure and varied invasions: this landscape which knows no mean between sensuous sag and hellish drought; which is never petty, never ordinary, never relaxed, as should be in a country made for rational

human beings to live in; this country of ours in which the inferno round Randazzo is a few miles from the beauty of Taormina Bay: this climate which inflicts on us six feverish months at a temperature of 104 … this summer which is as long and as glum as a Russian winter and against which we struggle with less success.

Fabrizio began with the Arabs, and ignored the more ancient civilizations, the Carthaginians, the Greeks, and the Romans. Not all these regimes remained foreign impositions, *pace* the Prince of Lampedusa. Some adapted and integrated, making Sicilian culture the fusion of all these diverse civilizations, and its history the sum of all these incoming peoples. Some were welcomed and domesticated but others were always resented or detested. There are solemn tomes on Sicilian nobility which distinguish between Norman, Angevin, Catalan, and Spanish families, and there are ordinary Sicilians with blonde or red hair who boast of Norman ancestry, although there may be in some cases less dignified explanations. Novelists like Sciascia and Consolo reveled in the flux and diversity of the Sicilian past.

Not every civilization, or conquering force, has left evidence of its presence, or perhaps it would be more accurate to say that not all such evidence has been allowed to survive. The Greeks have left splendid temples and theaters, at Selinunte, Segesta, Siracusa, or Agrigento, so that there are more Greek temples in Sicily than in the whole of mainland Greece. On the other hand, there is surprisingly little trace in stone of the Roman Empire, which lasted for centuries. There are the wonderful Roman mosaics at Piazza Armerina, there were important modifications made to Greek theaters, such as Taormina, but astonishingly little else. The Arab heritage is more ambiguous. No genuine Arab-style buildings remain, although the Moorish, Saracen, or Arab lifestyle was not eliminated by expulsion as happened in Andalucía. Arab craftsmen were still welcome on the island and contributed to that style known as Arab-Norman, which could only have emerged in the melting pot that was Sicily. Having overthrown the caliphate, the Normans were keen to imitate the Arabs in various ways. The institution of the harem pleased Norman kings. On a different level, the Church of San Giovanni dei Lebbrosi (St. John of the Lepers) in Palermo flaunts the kind of red dome common in Middle Eastern mosques, while the construction of such pleasure palaces as

La Zisa in Palermo imitates Arab customs and styles. There is no shortage of Norman castles, some in a precarious state, like the castle in Aci Castello which clings to a rock over the sea and looks down on the populace as they take their evening promenade.

A WORD ON THE BAROQUE

The Baroque style would deserve special mention on account of its seeming omnipresence, even if architecture were not the art in which, together with literature, Sicily excels. The Baroque is not the only style encountered in Sicily, although acknowledgement of the stupendous Arab-Norman and of the so-called "Catalan-Gothic" styles is often grudging in both guide books and academic monographs. Medieval Gothic is, like Baroque, an international style with intriguing local variations. The Normans changed the nature of Medieval Gothic in England, and their main contribution in Sicily, apart from the many castles, were the magnificent cathedrals of Monreale, Palermo, and Cefalú. The later Catalan imprint is if anything more pervasive, and here it could be noted that although the ruling house of the time has always been identified as Aragonese, the accompanying architecture has maintained the name Catalan. Both designations refer to the same people and period. There are many Catalan-Gothic churches, with Santa Maria dei Miracoli (Our Lady of the Miracles) in Palermo only one example among many, and many palaces, of which there happen to be several splendid examples in Siracusa.

But let us render due homage to the dominant Baroque. There is a need for some critic capable of altering received perspectives on Baroque styles as John Betjeman did with Victorian architecture in England. The Baroque style in architecture and painting is an acquired taste for twenty-first century observers, particularly for those whose views have been formed, perhaps unconsciously, by northern Protestantism, but it is a taste worth acquiring. To many it can seem heavy, overbearing, too opulent, unduly florid, and even vacuous, sinful in its excess, tasteless in its lack of restraint, and totally overloaded in its fear of the undecorated corner. In Baroque churches, not an inch can be left under-colored or unenhanced by the presence of a fleshly angel, of a smiling saint, or of a curlicue or motif which has no justification other than embellishment as an end in itself. The more favorable view of this vision of art is that it is founded on unbounded creativity. Baroque artists were not satisfied with one central

The Cathedral of San Giorgio in Modica: a cry of joy after the tragedy of the earthquake

vision and fringes only meagerly sketched in so as not to create a distraction, as with Caravaggio. Baroque art is founded on the willingness to distract, to arouse wonder, to refuse to leave a speck free, to demand full concentration of the mind on the parts as well as the whole. Since there are so many outstanding examples of Baroque art and architecture all over the island, it would be a pity if visitors were to deny themselves the opportunity to delight in the extravagance of façades, church interiors, palace staircases, city gates, archways, and balconies designed in the ages in which Baroque was the dominant architectural and artistic language.

There is no sense in seeking too narrow or precise a definition of exactly what is meant by the term Baroque. The definitive work on the subject, simply titled *Sicilian Baroque*, was written by Anthony Blunt, once Sir Anthony until his spying activities for the Soviet regime were uncovered and he was stripped of his knighthood. Mr. Blunt fights shy of providing too close a definition or too restrictive a description, and we will be happy to defer to his authority. The Baroque was a genuinely pan-European movement, emerging in Rome, spreading to Turin and Naples in Italy, becoming particularly strong in southern Germany and such Central European cities as Prague as well as in the Iberian Peninsula, and thus in some Latin American countries, notably Mexico. It is an additional truism that the Baroque emerged as a reaction to, and development of, Renaissance styles, so it may be viewed as curious that while the mainstream Renaissance by-passed Sicily, the Baroque established itself and made itself as much a native plant as imported botanical species such as sugar cane and tomatoes.

There is no one single Baroque common to the whole island, and indeed natives of Catania will bridle in indignation at any suggestion that Catanese Baroque is indistinguishable from that of the nearby Siracusa, let alone from the Baroque styles of Palermo. By the same token, it is not only experts who will point to a development of Baroque styles over the period in which the style flourished. Only an incautious fool would attempt to put precise dates to the emergence and disappearance of cultural phenomena in any field, so we will say that the age of the Baroque was an uncommonly lengthy one, covering approximately the two centuries from mid-sixteenth to mid-eighteenth century, at which time taste switched towards the neoclassical. Baroque was not, of course, an exclusively architectural style, but one which, more than any other movement before or since, could be expressed in all the arts, poetry, painting, music, and sculpture. In Sicily there was also a lively, creative school of stucco artists. Only those with the most entrenched antipathies and prejudices can fail to be moved by these exquisite, touching miniature sculptures.

The Baroque corresponded not only to the private taste of artists and commissioning patrons, but was also the style preferred by the Catholic Church in the defensive, nervous climate of the Counter-Reformation. Sicily did not feel the impact of the Reformation, but was deeply marked by the dark pessimism and repressive policies of the Counter-Reformation. In the two centuries when the Baroque held sway, much occurred in Sicily and the island was, as is recorded elsewhere in this volume, brought under the control of different powers, Spain and Austria being the most significant. Both of these were countries where the Baroque flourished, and it may be, as Blunt tentatively suggests, that styles specific to those countries can be detected in Sicilian buildings at the appropriate times. The leading architects were Sicilian, but the later exponents of the art had traveled and had been influenced by developments in Naples and Rome.

The central point is that there is something essentially religious in the style and not only in the churches, but the mood was not open or expansive. The Council of Trent had decreed that all ecclesiastical art should have a didactic purpose to assist the teaching of supernatural doctrine to the illiterate. This objective was hardly new or revolutionary, since St. Augustine had been of the same view, but it was advanced with particular force in the Counter-Reformation/Baroque age. In spite of these considerations, what will first strike the viewer is the ostentation, the flamboyance, the theatricality, the delight in prettified ornamentation, the fantasy, the élan, the opulence, the extravagance, the unrestrained imaginative release, and decorative impulse which mark many manifestations of the Baroque in Sicily even more strongly than elsewhere in Europe. However, this exuberance is not synonymous with indiscipline. The Baroque gives free rein to a complex architectural code of whorls, curves, flourishes, frescos, cavities, domes, and broken pediments. It has often been said that it is intrinsically theatrical, but it would be equally valid to point to its operatic quality. There is a melody to Baroque architecture at its best, which makes it sing. In ecclesiastical architecture it was at the far extreme from the more sober Gothic.

There are, of course, examples of Baroque architecture, especially in Catania, which show more measured qualities, but whatever form it assumed the Baroque swelled beyond the boundaries fixed for it elsewhere in continental Europe. Sicilians have identified the Baroque as *their* style, as laying down the approach to life, art, and creativity which most clearly distinguishes them and helps define their identity. No doubt there is an element of self-aggrandizement in taking to themselves a style which gives free rein to inventiveness, but putting together the terms Baroque and Sicilian as though the one expresses something of the basic life philosophy held by the other has become something of a cliché. In poetry and fiction, the Baroque is a commonplace tag which many Sicilian critics and writers have found convenient to express the literary playfulness, verbal elaboration, descriptive fancifulness, deliberate incongruities, or even obscurities which may indicate depth of thought or may simply indicate a mannered delight in style for its own sake. It was no accident that the twentieth-century poet Lucio Piccolo gave his first published volume of verse the title *Baroque Songs,* or if his younger contemporary, the novelist Vincenzo Consolo, chose to write in a style which critics have identified, to his delight, as Baroque. In Consolo's words:

> The Baroque was more than the fruit of a historical coincidence. That fanciful and crowded, tortuous and abundant style is, in the Sicily of nature's continuous earthquakes, of the infinite historical upheavals, of the daily risk of loss of identity a yearning of the soul against the anxiety of solitude, of the indistinct, of the desert, and against the vertigo of annihilation.

Blunt identifies three moments: an early vernacular which he dismisses as "frankly provincial and often naïve," a later wave influenced by Roman trends and a final moment where architects applied lessons they had learned in other disciplines, such as mathematics or the new theories of perspective, as they traveled around Europe. The Jesuits, the order most associated with the culture, spirituality, and ideology of the Counter-Reformation, were zealous promoters of architectural and decorative Baroque, as can be seen in their two main churches in Rome, the Gesú (Jesus) and the Sant'Ignazio (St. Ignatius), but the same extravagance, perhaps even multiplied, is evident in the Chiesa del Gesú (Church of Jesus) in Palermo. Like the

Baroque *putti* idling and playing: doorway on Palazzo Biscari, Catania

Church of San Benedetto (St. Benedict) in Catania, it is designed in a style which can induce vertigo in the unwary. No space is left uncovered, and no ornamental device from wrought iron to marble sculpture has been ignored. Biblical stories or lives of the saints and the activities of *putti*, devout or mischievous angels, are inlaid in the marble or drawn in frescos on the ceiling or walls. This is art employed to demand assent, not to stimulate questioning. However, for all his/her vertigo, the sensitive visitor will be overwhelmed by the power of the vision implicit in such a vista. The potential for overwhelming the faithful is largely the point of such a construction and is, at least in part, the response the creators wished for.

The great practitioners worked all over the island, and it will be good to look for the signature of such men as Giovanni Battista Vaccarini, Tommaso Napoli, Vincenzo Sinatra, the Gagini family (perhaps especially the founding patriarch Domenico Gagini) as well as Andrea Palma, and Rosario Gagliardi. These are not necessarily names to conjure with outside Sicily, but they deserve applause and recognition. The Baroque, as we will have occasion to remark at the appropriate places, is the style used in such diverse structures as the Quattro Canti (Four Corners) in Palermo, where the two principal thoroughfares cross, in the façade of the cathedral of Siracusa, in the villas of Bagheria as well as in many churches and palaces in out-of-the-way villages all over Sicily.

Chapter Two
WOUNDED BY HISTORY
SICILY'S TROUBLED PAST

Many Sicilians regard Sicily as a land wounded by history, and certainly it can seem that the map of the island is dotted with battlefields, massacre sites, and invasion beaches as Mediterranean or European powers fought for control of this strategic crossroad, or, when no external enemy threatened, different indigenous groups fought for supremacy. Perhaps no other land has seen the arrival of so many conquerors and invaders, or been colonized by so many incomers, leading to heated debates on the nature and depth of consequent social or psychological changes on the inner being of Sicilian peoples. Sicily has been home to the great languages, religions, and cultures of Europe and North Africa—the Greek, the Latin, the Arab. The powers which have ruled from early times and for varying periods of time include early Sicels and Sicanians, Phoenicians, Carthaginians, Greeks, Romans, Vandals and Goths, Byzantine-Greeks, Arabs, Normans, Germans, Angevin-French, Catalan-Aragonese, Spanish Habsburgs, Piedmontese, Austrians, Spanish and Neapolitan Bourbons with a brief interlude during the Napoleonic war when the British were in *de facto* control, and all this before the landing by Garibaldi and his Red Shirts which many Sicilians regarded as a further invasion by northern Italians. To this should be added waves of mass or minority migration, for instance from Lombardy, North Africa, France, Spain, or nineteenth-century England, all of which have added to the complex DNA of the population.

Sicilian pre-history was already ancient when Thucydides dedicated part of his classic work on the Peloponnesian War, written probably around 413 BC, to the Sicilian Expedition, the naval attack by Athens on Siracusa. In a section conventionally given in English the significant title "Sicilian Antiquities," he confesses his ignorance of the quasi-mythical peoples who first inhabited Sicily and writes of them with a resigned scepticism that scarcely conceals his discomfort at reconciling such skimpy, dubious information with his demanding views of the responsibilities of a historian:

It is said that the earliest inhabitants of any part of the country were the Cyclopes and the Laestrygonians. I cannot say what kind of people these were or where they came from or where they went in the end. On these points we must be content with what the poets have said and what anyone else may happen to know. The next settlers after them seem to have been the Sicanians, though according to the Sicanians themselves they were there first and were the original inhabitants of the country. The truth is, however, that they were Iberians who were driven out by the Ligurians from the district of the river Sicanus in Iberia. The island, which used to be called Trinacria, was in their time called Sicania after them, and they still live up to the present time in the western part of Sicily. After the fall of Troy, some of the Trojans escaped from the Athenians and came in ships to Sicily, where they settled next to the Sicanians and were called by the name of Elymi.

Even if archaeologists have subsequently enriched our knowledge, later historians have largely had to accept what Thucydides wrote. There were three peoples: the Sicanians, the Sicels who gave Sicily its name, and the Elymians, whom he believed to be descended from the Trojans. Traces of all three races are to be found in archaeological sites. The Elymians

Pre-historical Pantalica: the mysterious, haunting graves and shrines in a lonely spot where some defeated people took refuge

inhabited Segesta, where their city walls can still be seen, as well as Eryx (modern Erice) where they may well have been founders of the cult of the goddess who was Astarte to them, Aphrodite or Venus to the Greeks and Romans, and who was replaced by the Catholic figure of the Madonna. The Sicanians possibly originated in the eastern Mediterranean, but our knowledge of them is complicated by the fact that their history merges with the Greek myths of Daedalus. Although in the flight from Crete, Daedalus's son Icarus flew too close to the sun and fell into the sea which still bears his name, Daedalus himself found refuge with King Kokalos of the Sicanians. The Sicels on the other hand retained some kind of identity even after the coming of the Greeks, and in the fifth century BC Ducetius, whose name is remembered in the town hall in Ragusa, led an ultimately unsuccessful anti-imperialist struggle. The mysterious "oven" tombs in the cliffs at Pantalica or in the Cava d'Ispica in the east of the island may indicate the place where the Sicels found refuge after the arrival of the Greeks.

The first Greek colony was Naxos founded in 734 BC, next to the modern town of Giardini on the eastern coast under Taormina. The independent city-states of mainland Greece founded their own colonies in the east and south, so the origins of such Sicilian cities as Siracusa, Agrigento, Gela, Lentini, Catania, and Messina are entirely Greek. Siracusa, of Corinthian origin, surpassed even Athens in power and prestige. Agrigento was founded in myth by Daedalus and populated in history by people from Gela, which was in its turn settled by colonists from Crete and Rhodes. There are in Sicily the ruins of countless Greek towns, not to mention temples and theaters. Many great figures of Greek verse (Theocritus), thought (Empedocles), and science (Archimedes) were natives of Sicily, while Aristotle drew up a now lost constitution for Siracusa and Plato acted as consultant to the same city's government.

However, Sicily was also colonized by the Carthaginians, who were in their turn part of the Phoenician diaspora. Their main settlements were Solunto, the island of Mozia and the city that would become Palermo. The history of the classical period is a doleful tale of incessant warfare between Carthaginians and Greeks or indeed between Greek and Greek, with accounts given by the Greek historians of sieges, battles, massacres of defeated armies, and whole cities sold into slavery. The decisive encounter between Greek and Carthaginian took place in 480 BC at Himera, on the north coast near modern Termini Imerese, when the Greeks defeated the

Carthaginian army led by King Hamilcar I. It was not the complete end, for in 409 the king's grandson Hannibal Mago sacked the town and slaughtered some 3,000 men on the spot where his humiliated grandfather had thrown himself onto the flames.

The final defeat of the Carthaginians was accomplished by the Romans, but only after three Punic Wars. Although these wars are best remembered for Hannibal's feats in bringing elephants across the Alps into Italy, the theater for the first two was Sicily. By 241 BC Sicily could be regarded as a Roman possession, but the process was completed only in 212 when Siracusa, which always held out longest against enemies, was taken in the course of the Second Punic War. The island suffered terribly during the hostilities since both sides practiced scorched earth tactics. Sicily was one of the spoils of war and had the honor of being the first of the Roman imperial provinces. Roman rule lasted for centuries, but it is curious how little physical evidence of the empire has remained, certainly nothing to compare with the aqueducts or amphitheaters of Spain, southern France, or North Africa. The luxury villa at Casale, near Piazza Armerina in the south of the island, with the beautiful mosaics including the so-called "room of the bikinis," is the main exception. The Romans also made alterations, mainly insensitive, to the layout of certain Greek theaters like those at Taormina and Tindari, so that in their final form they are Roman amphitheaters. Sicily's status as "granary of the Roman Empire" meant that its inhabitants had to ship shares of their crops to Rome. Individual cities paid tributes, taxes and tithes, but the *pax romana* was of no small value to an island which had undergone such strife. Under Rome, the Sicilians continued to be largely Greek-speaking, but there is no way of knowing if there was any alienation between them and their Latin-speaking rulers. The consul Verres attained historical notoriety by plundering the island of its artistic treasures and extorting money from the populace, as we know from the speeches of Cicero, who prosecuted him, but he may have been an exception. Generally, however, the imperial age is a curiously obscure period in which little relating to Sicily was recorded by the great Roman historians.

The Roman era ended in the mid-sixth century, but Rome's grip on Sicily had long since weakened. The empire had been split between the West, ruled from Rome, and the East whose capital was Byzantium (Constantinople, or modern Istanbul). If Sicily was still politically under Roman rule, its affinities with Greek-Byzantine culture were strong. The barbarian invasions by Germanic tribes, who had established a base in North Africa, began in 440. As ever throughout history, Sicily became a target because of its central geographical position and because of its agricultural resources. In 468 the Vandals took control, but this lasted only eight years, when they were succeeded by another Germanic tribe, the Goths. Their rule was ended by the Byzantine general Belisarius, hero of a novel by Robert Graves, who led a successful invasion in 535 in furtherance of a scheme by the Eastern Emperor Justinian to reunite the divided empire. Sicily became a province of Byzantine, and for a brief period of five years from 663 the Emperor Constans II made Siracusa his capital, although he was personally hated and the costs of maintaining his court did the city little good. There was no mass immigration from the East, but the impact of Byzantine culture and art on Sicily was lasting. Icons, mosaics, and architectural styles can be seen in churches, palaces, and castles all over the island, with the Martorana in Palermo only one outstanding example. Subsequent Arab and Norman rulers were willing to incorporate Byzantine styles and motifs into their own favored art forms, as can be seen in the cathedrals of Cefalú and Monreale.

THE CALIPHATE: ARAB RULE

The next invaders were the Arabs or Saracens. In his *Decline and Fall of the Roman Empire* Edward Gibbon writes that the advance of the Muslim Arabs was swifter than that of any army since the days of Alexander. The first Arab raid on Sicily took place in 651, but the real invasion got under way in 827 when Arab forces landed at Mazara in the south-west. The campaign to subdue Sicily lasted over seventy years, and was a *fait accompli* only with the capture of Taormina in 907. The Arabs were no more a unified force than any other occupier, and Arab rule in Sicily passed through three dynasties: the Aghlabids, the Fatimids, and the Kalbids. In 948 Hassan al-Kalbi declared himself Emir of Sicily, but there were rival emirates in Enna and Siracusa. Sicily became fully integrated into the Muslim world but since the Koran advocated tolerance of the peoples of the Book, Muslims, Jews, and Christians lived side by side in mutual tolerance. Certainly the latter religious groups were relegated to the status of *dhimmis*, which made them liable to special taxes and land dues, but there was no large-scale persecution.

The Arabs were always stronger in the west of the island, and it was they who finally and definitively made Palermo the capital. The modern form of the name is derived from Arabic (Balern), but so are the names of many Sicilians towns—Caltagirone, Alcamo, Racalmuto, Misilmeri being random examples. Administratively, the island was divided into three, the Val di Mazara in the south-east, the Val di Noto, and the Val Demone, the largest unit which covers more than half the island. (Val comes not from "valley," but is the Arabic for "province.") This arrangement was maintained until Sicily was integrated into the Kingdom of Italy in the nineteenth century, but it remains alive in the island's culture, as does a division of the island into a Greek east, dominated by Siracusa, and an Arab west, whose center is Palermo. The other peoples who passed through the island have not left such a deep imprint on the mindset of writers and artists.

Arab travelers enthused about the fertility of the fields and the plentiful supply of water, as well as about the wealth created by international trade. Later Arab poets such as Ibn Hamdis write plaintively from exile in Tunisia about the loss of the beauties of Sicily, and pine for return. The Arabs were great builders, and contemporary travelers record that there

A nineteenth-century lithograph of San Giovanni degli Eremiti, Palermo:
Arab architecture for Norman masters

were more than three hundred mosques in Palermo alone. In spite of that, not a single Arab building of any importance has survived. There are many extant castles but they were without exception so restructured and redesigned by successive rulers as to be unrecognizable as Arab fortresses. It is easy to be deceived by the domes and cupolas that can be seen in such churches in Palermo as San Giovanni degli Eremiti (St. John of the Hermits), where the architecture and the garden around the church recall similar buildings in Andalucía or Morocco, but these were the work of Arab craftsmen working for Norman masters. Similarly, the beautiful, now delicately restored, palace of La Zisa in Palermo may have an Arab name and appearance, and may even be inspired by oriental ideals, but it too was Norman. Depictions of scenes of Arab life turn up in some unexpected places, none more so than the sensuous belly dancers who can be detected by the keen eyes in the mosaics in the royal chapel, the Cappella Palatina (Palatine Chapel) in Palermo.

These are only tantalizing glimpses, but the impact of the Arabs on Sicily was deep. They changed the nature of Sicilian agriculture, improving irrigation techniques, introducing sugar cane, planting orange groves, importing melons and dates from Persia, and introducing cotton, and thus expanding the textile industry. Until the disappearance of the industry in the 1960s the head figure in the tuna fishing operation always bore the Arab name, *rais*. Their impact on Sicilian cuisine, too, was profound, and manifests itself in the most unexpected ways. It is fondly imagined that Marco Polo brought back from China the inspiration for a food which became spaghetti, since it has some resemblance to *zha jiang mian,* but this is a fantasy, however pleasing. There are accounts of pasta from early times but the decisive ingredient is the durum wheat which the Arabs imported from North Africa. Sicilian cuisine without pasta is unimaginable, but so would it be without the tomato which was yet to arrive from the New World.

George Maniakes (d. 1043) led an invasion of the island in 1038 in an attempt to re-conquer it for Byzantium. He defeated the Arabs in 1040 in a battle near the Castello di Maniace, named in his honor and later part of the estate given to Lord Nelson, but his triumph was short-lived, for he was recalled soon afterwards in disgrace to Byzantium. A new, unlikely power from the North, the Norman, was on the point of asserting itself.

1061 AND ALL THAT: THE NORMAN KINGDOM

"The establishment of the kingdoms of the Normans in Naples and Sicily is an event most romantic in its origin, and in its consequences most important both to Italy and the Eastern Empire," writes Edward Gibbon. Even a generation immune to the romance of arms cannot fail to be overwhelmed by the sheer scale and improbability of the Norman achievement. Descendants of Viking raiders who settled in the region of France to which they gave their name, the Normans expanded, or exploded, all over Europe in the mid-eleventh century. It will astonish visitors from England or northern France to find in Sicily the same style of ecclesiastical architecture familiar in their home countries. To add to the implausibility of the romance, the leadership was provided by the eight brothers of one family, the Hautevilles, all born in Normandy, who Italianized their name to Altavilla. Theirs is an epic adventure. The story which has them going on pilgrimage to the shrine of St. Michael the Archangel in Monte Gargano in Puglia and there being invited to help expel the Saracens from the south of Italy has the savor of pious legend, but may well be founded on fact. The whole complex, fascinating history cannot be recounted here, but briefly the first Normans appeared in southern Italy around 1016. Under Robert Guiscard, they secured control of Calabria, Puglia, Basilicata, and Campania, before turning their attention to Sicily. Robert concerned himself with the mainland, but he aided his brother Roger when he was invited by one of the warring but decidedly ill-advised emirs to come to Sicily in 1061. Five years before William the Conqueror undertook the Norman Conquest of England, Roger, known in Sicilian as Ruggero, invaded Sicily.

As with the Arabs centuries earlier, the conquest of Sicily was gradual but was complete by 1091. The Norman rulers guaranteed freedom of religion to their subjects, allowing the Muslims to be judged by Sharia Law and the Jews by their own courts. Sicily was in the eleventh and twelfth centuries what America aspired to be in the twentieth, a mosaic of races—Norman, Arab, Byzantine-Greek and Lombard (who came in the train of the Normans). Liberty of conscience was granted to all. Although theoretically subject to his brother, in practice Sicily under Count Roger was united and independent for the first time in its history. This situation was regularized when his son Roger II, who came to power in 1112 at the age of seventeen, was crowned king in Palermo in 1130. Under Roger II,

Christ crowns King Roger II, a mosaic in Monreale Cathedral

Sicily became the major power in the Mediterranean, even for a time conquering overseas territories in Tunisia and Albania and taking control of all Norman lands in southern Italy. Roger was succeeded by his third son, William the Bad, who died in 1166 to be succeeded by William the Good.

There was no mass immigration from Normandy, but the elite of knights and lords made Sicily unquestionably European, or "Latin," after centuries when the island had been Greek or Arab. They introduced the feudal system, which had the advantage for the Hauteville-Altavillas of allowing them to exercise control over the realm through a tightly knit group of men, even if it had less benefit for the serfs. The Normans created one of the first modern states in Sicily, with a centralized administration whose functionaries were drawn from the most talented of each race and who conducted their business in three languages. Poets, including many Arabs, were welcome at their courts, provided they used their talents to sing of the glories of the reign. Roger II employed the brilliant Arabic scholar, Muhammad al-Idrisi, regarded as the first geographer of modern times, to draw a map of Europe and to write a treatise on its countries. The Normans engaged Arab craftsmen to decorate their churches and palaces. The spectacular beehive ceilings in the cathedral in Monreale and in the Palatine Chapel were their work, and if the phrase "Arab-Norman style" is now an art-history cliché, it is worth stopping to wonder over the union of distant cultures it implies and which could have been achieved only in Sicily. Byzantine artists too were still resident in Sicily or were summoned from Constantinople to add their contribution and help create in Palermo a globalized art-style.

The Norman overlords, although initially supported by the papacy against Muslim rule, had to contend later with the claims of the Pope in both the spiritual and temporal spheres. Hostility to Islam did not prevent the Norman monarchs from succumbing to the temptations of the oriental lifestyle. William I was described by the great historian of Muslim Sicily, Michele Amari, as a "baptized sultan." He began work on La Zisa, the Arab-Norman pleasure palace in Palermo, but had to leave it to his son and heir to see it completed. Both men, good Catholics though they professed themselves to be, kept harems and dressed on ceremonial occasions like Byzantine monarchs or oriental sultans. The court was open to influences, positive and negative, from East and West, from both the flaunting exhibitionism of the emperors in Byzantium and the power-haunted pretensions of German rulers who styled themselves Holy Roman Emperors.

The Normans disappeared from Sicilian history as rapidly as they had appeared, but theirs was a glorious chapter. William the Good had no direct heir and committed the mistake of compelling his aunt, Constance, to marry the German Emperor Henry VI, meaning that on his death in 1189 the throne passed into German hands. (The marriage did nothing for the happiness of Constance, but the happiness of female royals was not a consideration in those times.) The Norman claimant Tancredi resisted for a time, but both he and his son died within months of each other, leaving the way clear for Henry to take uncontested power in 1194 and to carry off the treasures of Sicily to embellish his court in Germany. Henry inaugurated the dynasty of the Hohenstaufen family, known to history as Swabian (*Svevo* in Italian) from the district on the borders of Bavaria and Switzerland where they originated. It is hard to avoid the conclusion that

Henry's main achievement was to father Frederick II, identified then and later as *stupor mundi* (the "stupefaction of the world" in G. K. Chesterton's translation), who ascended to the throne when he was three years old. He was a true cosmopolitan, fluent in five languages, and if he had in his veins Norman, German, and Sicilian blood, he was wholly Sicilian.

The accession of Frederick ushered in a new golden age. Palermo was his capital, but he campaigned in Italy, France, and Germany, and went on crusade to the Holy Land where, to the annoyance of the pope, he displayed his diplomatic rather than military gifts. The principal titles he acquired allowed him to style himself King of Sicily, King of Jerusalem, King of the Germans (official title, King of the Romans), and Holy Roman Emperor. Dante was unsure about him, and praised him in one book as a paragon of the chivalric virtues, but in the *Divine Comedy* consigned him to the circle of hell reserved for heretics. There were doubts about his orthodoxy during his lifetime, and after running foul of the papacy he was excommunicated several times.

He was one of the greatest rulers in European history, and a man of all-round genius. An enlightened ruler, he drew up a legal code and imposed the rule of law. He continued the Norman policy of tolerance, having Saracens as his personal bodyguard and Jews among his counselors. However, faced with revolts from the Muslim population, he had them removed to Puglia, so that mosques disappeared from the Palermo cityscape, as did the tradition of Arab-Norman architecture and design. At Frederick's court a school of poetry developed and he himself wrote love verses. It was this school that invented the sonnet. Frederick wrote a treatise on hunting with falcons, which is regarded as the first work of ornithology in Europe. He is buried in the cathedral in Palermo and his palace nearby is now a luxury hotel, Palazzo Conte Federico, but it still displays his coat of arms on the exterior.

Frederick's reign was the last time Sicily was fully autonomous. After a period of turbulence the pope chose Charles of Anjou as successor and crowned him king in Rome in 1266. The Angevin interval was an unhappy time and is remembered mainly for the rebellion which ended it, the so-called Sicilian Vespers of 1282. Charles made Naples his capital, and his soldiers and nobles on the island behaved with arrogance and exploitative greed, causing resentment among Sicilians. The traditional story of the origin of the revolt is that it was provoked by the insolent behavior on

Easter Sunday of a French soldier towards a Sicilian woman outside the Church of Santo Spirito (Holy Spirit), which is still standing inside a cemetery on the outskirts of the city. Bitterness against the French was widespread, meaning that one spark was all that was needed to cause revolution, so the story may be true. The rebellion spread quickly, and those French soldiers who did not manage to flee were massacred.

SPANISH VICEROYS

There followed a period of turbulence and anarchy. The crown was offered to Peter of Aragon, but there was no agreement between the contending parties and his accession ushered in the dire period of the Ninety Years War between the Aragonese and Angevins. Sicily at one point had two kings, one from each side, and was ruled for a time by a king who attracted the name of Frederick the Simple. This situation was only brought to an end in 1372 with a peace treaty signed in Avignon, the then residence of the popes. The treaty introduced rule identified as Aragonese, although the dominant force was Catalan. The Duke of Barcelona had become King of Aragon, and preferred to style himself king rather than make do with the more modest title of duke. As a consequence of the settlement Sicily's status was diminished. The first viceroy was appointed in 1415, and if he made Palermo the administrative center, power now lay elsewhere, in Spain.

In 1469 the crowns of Aragon and Castile were united under Ferdinand and Isabella, the "Catholic Monarchs," and the impact of their crusading zeal was felt in Sicily. The following centuries have been routinely portrayed as dark times for the island as it labored under an obscurantist Spanish regime, but it should be said that there is now a revisionist school which challenges this view. Even so, the condition of Sicily was determined by the affairs of Spain. The Muslims having been already removed from Sicily to mainland Italy, the Jews were expelled in 1492, as they were in Spain, and the Inquisition established in 1513. The fifteenth and sixteenth centuries were the age of the Renaissance and of the Reformation in northern Europe, but the new learning, the new art, the new theater, the new poetry, indeed the whole cultural moment passed Sicily by. On the other hand, Sicily was exposed to the worst excesses of the Counter-Reformation.

In the Mediterranean basin the new factor was the rise in power of the Turks after their seizure of Constantinople in 1453. Sicily as a whole was threatened by Turkish fleets, and its coastal towns were in addition tormented by corsairs and pirates from North Africa. The island also became the base for the Christian counter-offensive. It was from Messina that the Christian fleet sailed in 1453 for the decisive Battle of Lepanto against the Turks. However, later that century, the overall centrality of the Mediterranean in world affairs was irreversibly undermined by the discovery of the Americas and the switch in trade towards the Atlantic. Spain's new empire in the Americas led to indifference towards Sicily and meant that the standard of life of the people was under continual threat. There were many riots in cities, put down with ferocity. In international diplomacy, Sicily became a mere bauble to be passed around in diplomatic or military exchanges between the great powers. In the Treaty of Utrecht of 1713 Sicily was presented to the Duke of Savoy, who did not want it, and in 1720, after a war in which Sicily was despoiled by the armies of Spain and Austria, the island was swopped for Sardinia and passed into Austrian control. The Austrians were on the losing side in the next war, the War of the Polish Succession, and power over Sicily again changed hands. The Spanish Bourbon, Don Carlos, ascended the throne and had himself crowned in Palermo as Charles III in 1735, the last coronation to take place in Sicily.

The king then took up residence in Naples, establishing the Bourbon Kingdom which became known later as the Kingdom of the Two Sicilies. The dynasty remained in power until Sicily was incorporated into the United Italy in 1860. Initially Charles made a promising start, appointing as viceroy Domenico Caracciolo who had lived in Paris, was a friend of Voltaire and an adherent of the new Enlightenment thought. In this he was unique, since the Enlightenment was another European cultural movement which did not take root in Sicily. Caracciolo abolished the Inquisition in 1782, but made the mistake of trying to reduce the number of days devoted to the celebrations of the feast of Santa Rosalia, causing the people to turn against him. He already had little support among the nobility, and Sicily had no bourgeoisie. He was removed from power and was succeeded by mediocrities.

The turmoil caused by the French Revolution and subsequent Napoleonic Wars caused all European monarchies to tremble. When Napoleon's armies reached Naples in 1806 and dethroned Ferdinand I, the Bourbons (*Borboni* in Italian) took refuge in Palermo. Sicily avoided invasion by French armies, both the army of Revolutionary and Napoleonic France. Leonardo Sciascia pointed to the paradox that while Sicily had suffered from a long line of hostile invaders it missed the one set of invaders who might have had a favorable impact, since the French would have brought the advantages of European Enlightenment ideas. King Ferdinand in exile thoroughly disliked Sicily, although not as heartily as his wife, Queen Carolina, but their safety there was guaranteed by the British fleet under Lord Nelson, when he was not conducting in Naples and Palermo his famous affair with Lady Emma Hamilton. The Sicilian Parliament was recalled, but Sicily in this period was under the *de facto* control of Britain, with the Whig-inclined Lord Bentinck acting as viceroy. In the teeth of royal and aristocratic opposition, he introduced progressive policies, and under his aegis feudalism was finally abolished in 1812.

PAINFUL MODERNITY

The Bourbons returned to the throne in the post-Napoleonic Restoration, and their reactionary policies caused hardship and unrest in Sicily. There had never been an Industrial Revolution in Sicily, unlike in Milan, Turin, or Bologna, and the only industry on any scale was sulphur mining, which exacted a terrible human cost. Only one local family, the Florios, showed genuine entrepreneurial flair, but they floundered after two generations. However, English businessmen arrived to introduce other types of manufacturing activity, from Marsala wine to insurance companies and soap production, and they integrated to some extent in Sicilian society. Their beneficial work included the expansion of the road network, since there had been before their arrival only one good road, from Palermo to Messina. Some consideration was given in books, in debates in the House of Lords and even in some Sicilian pamphlets to the idea of making Sicily a British colony, but it gained only minority support and in any case the Risorgimento, the process of unification of the divided Italian peninsula, was gathering strength. There was a major rebellion in the island in 1830, and for a brief period in 1848 Sicily declared its independence. Both movements were put down brutally, but in 1860 Garibaldi landed at Marsala with his Red Shirts and ended Bourbon rule. There were some British warships anchored in the bay, and the level of support from Britain is still the subject of discussion among historians. Garibaldi declared himself dictator of Sicily, and incorporated Sicily into the new United Kingdom.

A federal settlement which many, not only in Sicily, considered the best structure for a country with Italy's multiple identities, was not granted. Piedmontese law superseded ancient Sicilian law.

Their new fellow countrymen discovered that Sicily and the south were beset with problems of poverty, banditry, and underdevelopment. The dominant fact of political, economic, and social life in the newly united kingdom was the division between what was seen as a European, advanced north and an impoverished, backward south. Cavour, the prime minister at the time of Garibaldi's invasion of Sicily, believed that Sicilians spoke Arabic. The Sicilian economy was overwhelmingly dominated by agriculture and the Italian Parliament was more concerned with the industrialized regions of the north. Corruption in political and financial circles became rampant in official circles in Sicily, and the mafia emerged as a force. It was said at the time that unification brought two things to Sicily: taxation and conscription. Many Sicilians found themselves fighting in the front line against the Austrians in the First World War, and for millions of Sicilians emigration offered the only escape.

Sicily was as loyal to fascism as any other part of the country, and as dismayed as any by the progress of the Second World War. When North Africa and the Mediterranean became major theaters of war, Sicily suffered more than mainland Italy from Allied bombing campaigns. Marsala, Trapani, Palermo, and Messina were all major targets. The island was invaded in 1943 and fighting, especially in the east, was fierce, as the German forces put up more resistance than had been anticipated and the Allies were weakened by ego-battles between British and American commanders. The reception accorded the Allied troops in Sicilian cities has become part of legend, but there can be no doubting the relief and the warmth of the welcome. Nor can there be any doubt over the part played by Allied forces in re-establishing the mafia. The suppression of the mafia had been one of Mussolini's successes, and knowingly or not, the Allies facilitated its re-emergence.

The new constitution drawn up after the Second World War set up in Sicily a parliament with a Special Statute which gave it, like four other regions, greater devolved powers than those accorded the ordinary regions. The Regional Assembly sits in Palermo in the former palace of the Norman kings, but opinions are sharply divided over its success. It has been the scene of corrupt practices and petty infighting, and many members have

"When this lousy war is over": Allied soldiers fraternizing with the ex-enemy

been guilty of collusion with the mafia. However, the standard of living of the population has improved more in the decades since 1945 than in previous centuries. There is no comparison between the pictures of villages with dirt tracks, main-street hovels, ill-fed children, and unhygienic conditions and the same places with renovated buildings, good roads, and modern educational and health facilities.

Meanwhile, the prosperity of European Sicily has made it an attractive magnet for would-be immigrants from Northern and sub-Saharan Africa as well as from Asian countries, and this has created wholly new problems, especially for Lampedusa, the small Mediterranean island which is the first port of call for dangerously overcrowded boats packed with desperate refugees. These immigrants may point to a new multicultural history, but they are also a reminder of Sicily's past relations with Africa as well as with Europe.

Chapter Three
MORALS AND MANNERS
SICILIAN SOCIETY AND TASTES

In spite of preconceptions, life in Sicily today will no longer seem initially so distinctive and *different* to modern travelers as it did to those of previous generations. This will come as a relief or a disappointment, depending on individual expectations, for the distinctiveness of culture of other times often overlapped with poverty, whose manifestations appeared picturesque only to those who did not have to endure all its facets. Visitors returned with excited tales of carts painted with scenes from the battles and duels of knights from the days of Roland and Charlemagne, of quaint customs on local feasts, of colorfully dressed women in remote villages where Greek or Albanian was still spoken, of menacing men, of dark atmospheres in certain quarters of cities, but also of goatherds in cities selling milk freshly taken from the flock which accompanied them, of pursuit by child beggars, of families living in cave dwellings, and of town roads which were dirt tracks. There was a richness to a peasant culture which has disappeared but the words written in 1922 by D. H. Lawrence after his residence on the island should be an antidote to any undue nostalgia for some mythical golden age:

> The island is incredibly poor and incredibly backward. There are practically no roads for wheeled vehicles, and consequently no wheeled vehicles, neither carts not carriages, outside the towns. Everything is packed on asses or mules, man travels on horseback or on foot, or, if sick, in a mule litter. The land is held by the great landowners, the peasants are almost serfs. It is as wild, as poor, and in the ducal houses of Palermo even as splendid and ostentatious as Russia.

Travelers with some knowledge of the language or with pre-arranged access to Sicilian society would talk of codes of honor, of acts of ritual violence, of family feuds, of sexual jealousies, of the unpredictable passions of a people endowed with an exotic quality categorized as the Latin Temperament, and of the restrictions placed on women of all ages.

The main, and wholly welcome, change is that yesterday's poverty is only a memory. Sicily today is a wholly different place, which is not to say that today's society is ideal or that stories told in other times were without foundation. Globalization means that Sicilians dress in the same denims and T-shirts, wear mini-skirts, eat at MacDonald's, drink beer which was once unfamiliar in a wine-producing land, drive the same car, buy Nike trainers, watch the same Hollywood films, have access to CNN and imported TV shows, listen to the same music, and read the same books as their counterparts elsewhere. Those with delicate feelings may complain about the loss this process entails and worry about homogenization of cultures and identities. They may also deplore the forests of satellite TV dishes which have sprouted alongside Catalan-Gothic bell-towers and cathedral domes, and will, with more justice, unite in denouncing the sheer tastelessness of some of the high-rise flats which defile the skyline of the historic centers of some cities, with the lovely cities of Noto and Ragusa being notable sinners in this respect.

There have been many factors responsible for the greater affluence and wider changes in Sicily, including land reform, more equitable distribution of resources, improved educational opportunities, better welfare facilities, and international travel, but perhaps the greatest reform has been wrought by feminism, which has forced a change in attitudes that is still underway. Women today would no longer accept the restrictions their forebears endured. A member of the Intelligence unit of the British Army recalls being based in 1944, in Agrigento to root out fascist officials. After the completion of his mission, he did not go back to the city for some forty years. During his return visit, he and his wife stopped for a drink in a bar outside Agrigento where he was astonished by the sight of a sports car drawing up, a young woman dressed in T-shirt and shorts getting out, lighting a cigarette and entering the bar, unaccompanied, to order an *espresso*. Such a sight is utterly unremarkable now but was regarded by the officer as the symptom of a revolution in social mores. Such liberated conduct would have been unthinkable in the Sicily of the 1940s, and in preceding centuries.

Once women were expected to stay at home, except when going to church, a situation which in both life and fiction encouraged inventive ways among the young to make contact with each other *en route* to Sunday mass or out of sight of their elders and chaperones. A woman who slept with a man before marriage was "dishonored" and would not be accepted by any other suitor. The same officer recalled an illuminating incident. A young woman named Angelina had run away with an Italian soldier, who had then tired of her and abandoned her. She tried to commit suicide and was rescued by some British soldiers, who were given the strictest orders not to touch her. She knew her conduct had dishonored not only her but the whole family, and indeed when she was eventually able to return home it transpired that her sister's fiancé had left her because of the shame caused by Angelina's behavior. Angelina had to be rescued from the violent wrath of her sister, but her own future was irredeemably compromised. She made a temporary arrangement by setting up home with an American officer, but when he left her and Sicily, she had no future other than prostitution.

The only resolution for a woman who had "surrendered her chastity" to a man was either violent revenge by the men in the woman's family or marriage to the guilty male, but this latter had paradoxical consequences. A couple who wished to marry but who were prevented by family pressure could resort to the *fuitina,* a one-night elopement. They might spend the night chastely, but public perception of compromised chastity was everything. Marriage was the only remedy, but since that was the result the couple had wished for in the first place, the *fuitina* was an accepted means of circumventing patriarchal pressures. These practices seem as grotesque to today's youth as wearing corsets and stays.

The restriction on women appearing in public also led to the odd and seemingly non-chauvinist fact that men had to do the shopping. For many a *paterfamilias,* a visit to the market preceded going to work. This way of life has gone but it is still surprising for women visitors to go to towns like Palma di Montechiaro or Bronte and see in the piazzas and around the cafés groups of men, only men, sitting huddled over card tables, chatting, staring, or simply sitting with not a woman in the company or in sight. The Sicilian male could, and sometimes still can, behave in ways which will seem alarming, threatening, or pestering to women. Foreign women, including those of a certain age, may find it unpleasant to circulate on their own not because they are at any greater risk of major sexual violence than elsewhere, but because they face being stared at, commented on, invited to partake of hospitality, and perhaps followed by packs of sniggering youths. Leonardo Sciascia spoke of the "terrible matriarchy" of Sicilian society, and while that may have been the reality of domestic life, public life was, and to a large extent still is, deeply *machista*.

Although there are still areas of the big cities which are extended slums and where people live in decrepit buildings, the grinding poverty of other days has been eradicated. The Italian 1960s "economic miracle" led to a growth in prosperity and was the other major driving force behind the revolution in society. The European Union has poured funds, many of which have regrettably been squandered or embezzled, into agricultural and industrial projects, meaning among other things that Sicilian wine and citrus fruits have found international markets. Since the war, re-building has taken place on a vast scale, although here too the mafia creamed off much of the earmarked cash, and some of the new housing estates and unregulated office building programs, especially in Palermo, are an eyesore. The infrastructure of roads and motorways has been expanded, including the aesthetically pleasing but curiously designed *autostrada* on stilts which cuts across the island from Catania to Palermo. Another major improvement which brought Sicily into line with life elsewhere has been the general availability of water in houses. There still are droughts over summer, but the once common shortages or the sight of queues at public wells is a thing of the past. It may seem banal, but this change altered the way of life as much as any seemingly radical social or political reform.

Sicily today is, then, familiar and unfamiliar, modernized and un-changing, and it is so to mainland Italians as much as to travelers from abroad. The visitor will arrive in an out of the way town and find an Aragonese castle in the central piazza, will stumble across a Norman church by the side of a lesser traveled road, will see red Muslim-styles domes over a Christian shrine, will find a Baroque church of breathtaking beauty in a village, will enter an updated hotel and discover a Catalan stair-case in its heart, will catch a glimpse from the motorway of a solitary Greek temple on the horizon, will happen on a procession or the celebrations of the patron saint of a run-down district of a city, and will stop and wonder.

The history, the culture, the things that make Sicily Sicily (to adapt a phrase used in another context by Walter Scott) will be discussed later, but let us pause first over some of the irritations and delights which are part of daily life in Sicily.

MATADOR DRIVERS

Sicily today is endowed with excellent, scenic motorways like the A19 which cuts across the island from Catania to the Tyrrhenian Sea, joining up some 100 kilometers from Palermo with the N113, a motorway which runs across the north of Sicily from the capital to Messina. There is also the splendid N114 which proceeds down the eastern coast from Messina and which has recently been extended as far south as Siracusa. Only the latter requires the payment of a toll. There are dark tales as to why the majority of motorway kilometers in Sicily are free, with the generally accepted theory being while most motorways on the mainland are managed by private companies, the Sicilian motorways are publicly owned and so free of charge. The darkness lies in the fact that the mafia, through its links with political budget-holders, was allegedly involved in encouraging state involvement in the allocation of contracts.

The everyday difficulty for travelers lies in the lack of road signs, or the difficulty of interpreting the few there are. There is an exasperating tendency among the sign-makers to erect one sign at some distance from the desired destination, inviting the keen tourist to go in a certain direction, only to find him or herself abandoned at the next turn or fork in the road. This trick is common in both cities and country. In other cases, there will be no sign at all, or possibly one for traffic coming from one direction but not the other. An example is the ancient Greek site of Megara Iblea, a town celebrated by poets and historians of antiquity, and not only for its famous honey. The sign on the N114 is situated at the exit point from the *autostrada*, carefully positioned to make it impossible for anyone traveling even at moderate speed to turn off. The solution would seem to be to exit at the next opportunity and turn back along the same motorway, but there are no signs for motorists coming from the south. Those tenacious enough to persevere will discover that off the motorway the signs vanish entirely, except for the odd, romantically rusting sign hidden in bushes which serves to indicate where a road to Megara once ran. Enquiries in local shops will be met with looks of nostalgia or compassion as elderly residents reminisce about roads closed under Mussolini, and remember days in their youth spent strolling along paths and joyfully clambering over Greek ruins, but they cannot quite recall when the roads were allowed to decay or the signs to disintegrate, and are regretfully unable to help. Road signs in Sicily are a disgrace.

Traffic in Palermo on a street going towards the cathedral, but built for carriages

Order is not the most prominent attribute of Sicilian life at any level, even if it is a quality sought with the energy once expended in the hunt for the Holy Grail, and one which the elders will nostalgically recall as having existed once, even if the exact epoch cannot be placed. Traffic disorder is a minor manifestation of a habit of mind. Driving in cities presents specific challenges. It is on city roads that the war of each against all is waged on a daily basis, and where Sicilians exhibit that indifference to laws, including the laws of common sense, which is part of their inheritance from centuries of foreign domination.

The sheer volume of cars in Palermo or Catania, each one belching fumes, pawing at traffic lights like a bull facing a matador, snaking into impossible or imaginary spaces between hostile vehicles, defying oncoming traffic, and disregarding pedestrians, is itself upsetting to an outsider, whether behind a wheel or on foot, particularly because the streets are narrow and the parking chaotic. The German poet and pundit Hans Magnus Enzenberger once wrote that in southern Europe chaos fends off anarchy, but in Sicilian cities both these satanic forces joust endlessly. The fundamental instrument in Sicilian driving is not the steering wheel, the clutch, or the brake but the horn. Streets are a cacophony, and drivers will feel obliged to alert others to their presence by generously sounding the horn from a distance if another car is seen to be considering exiting from a side-road, or from close-up if the gladiator-driver is considering over-taking. These are gestures of self expression rather than of annoyance, and it is a matter of good sense to familiarize oneself with the various tones of a Sicilian car horn.

Parking presents different problems. No Parking signs are subject to especially subtle interpretation, and the law is routinely ignored by locals but can be applied arbitrarily, so visitors would be advised to obey it to the letter. Cars are parked obliquely on the pavements, making walking along a street awkward, and when they are parked on the road, double or even treble parking is not uncommon. Crossing a road requires firm nerves, and the rule is similar to that given to mountaineers: look straight ahead, ignore the surroundings, and when embarked move with a pace which suggests indifference or self-control. Traffic lights bring the added danger of the vendors of paper handkerchiefs, sponges, cigarette lighters, as well as child beggars and people who will wash the window screen uninvited. Any driver who thinks his life is at risk inside a car should consider the sur-vival prospects of people like these who spend their days leaping about from lane to lane as the signals change.

Religious Feasts

The inner nature of Sicilian religious belief is complex and idiosyncratic. Leonardo Sciascia wrote that Sicilians were Catholics who had never been fully Christianized. The Church is still a substantial power, even if secu-larism has expanded in Sicily as elsewhere in Europe, but the enigma which will puzzle observers concerns the private and public application of Chris-tian morality. It is a matter of surprise to discover the number of *mafiosi* who were also good Catholics, and who will indeed demand as a sign of power and prestige roles of honor in public ceremonials, such as carrying platforms with scenes from the Passion of Christ on Good Friday. This is not a simple matter of hypocrisy, but of a complex intellectual and moral schizophrenia which sanctions the division of the conscience into closed, non-communicating compartments. Of the two Greco brothers who were prominent mafia bosses in the 1970s, Michele was known as "the Pope" for his scrupulous observance of religious duties. Bernardo Provenzano, a

39

later boss and vicious killer, was in hiding for decades and communicated with his followers by means of hand-written messages in which orders for mafia business were interlaced with encouragements to ethical living and with quotations from the Bible. Provenzano's Bible intrigued magistrates after his capture when they studied the verses underlined and the notes in the margin to see if he was using a code. They decided that he was not, and that Provenzano was according to his own lights sincere in his piety. He may have been self-deluding, but that is another story.

The irreverent suggestion has been made more than once that Sicilians saw the Supreme Being as a Godfather rather than as a God or a Father. The Madonna and the saints occupy a prominent position in worship, but the patron saints of individual towns have to show their mettle if they are to retain their position. They are not guaranteed a job for life, or for eternity. The original patron saint of Palermo was Santa Cristina, with some help from Santa Ninfa, but the outbreak of plague in 1624 suggested that these two were not up to the job, so they were ousted in favor of St. Rosalia, whose remains had been discovered shortly before on Mount

Religious procession

Pellegrino. The occurrence of some pestilence has normally presented a severe test and many saints did not pass muster. St. Rosalia herself had been patron of Vittoria, but was dethroned in favor of St. John the Baptist. In Castronovo, St. Vito took over from St. Lawrence, and even more astonishingly, in Montelepre Christ replaced his Mother, Our Lady of the Rosary. Other saints were more enduring. St. Agatha is still invoked in Catania whenever Mount Etna threatens. Her statue is carried around the city and even up the mountainside.

In few parts of Europe are there so many public manifestations of what was once belief and may now be folklore. Mayors, counselors, high-ranking police officers, and public officials, whatever their party affiliation and whatever their personal belief or disbelief, will turn up to march alongside priests and bishops and will even argue over the right to carry statues and sacred images on the solemn days of the liturgical calendar. Such days include the universal feasts of the Church, Good Friday, and Corpus Christi in particular, but also local saints' days as established by tradition. Traditional costumes are worn, rites are observed, linguistic formulae now unintelligible are uttered, and processions led around streets and across piazzas back to the churches which the participants may not have visited since the corresponding time the previous year.

Each village and each district of the big cities put on such ceremonials which now attract crowds of curious spectators. Municipal authorities encourage them under a heading now called "religious tourism," as distinct from the more worldly variety. Holy Week is marked in different ways in many cities. On Palm Sunday in Piana degli Albanesi, the bishop rides into town on the back of a donkey. There are Good Friday processions all over Sicily, with scenes from the Passion of Christ re-enacted, and men in white habits walking along a route which recreates Christ's *via crucis*. The procession in Erice is especially notable, with the police band providing mournful music, while in San Fratello "Jews" are still pursued around the streets. On Easter Sunday in Enna, the meeting between the risen Christ and the Virgin Mary is the climax of a search which has the woman representing Mary wandering sorrowfully but hopefully through the town.

The best-known festivities for patron saints take place in the cities, but these are not necessarily the most interesting. The feast in honor of St. Rosalia in Palermo is stretched out over three days in mid-July, although there is also a lesser feast in September. Brian Johnson writes that during the Festival of St. Rosalia, "snails are dipped in garlic and parsley sauce and eaten as a street snack." The celebrations for St. Agatha in Catania are on 3-5 February, while the feast of St. Lucy in Siracusa falls on 13 December. There are two peculiarities to this feast. Observants are required to abstain from wheat-products including bread and pasta but are free to indulge in meats, fish, and sweets of all kinds. It also coincides with the Nobel Prize ceremonies in Stockholm and the two cities now exchange young women who take part in the celebrations of the host cities. St. James is the patron saint of Caltagirone, a center for the production of ceramics. The 142 steps of the Staircase of Santa Maria del Monte (St. Mary of the Mountain) are permanently, wonderfully decorated by ceramics inlaid into the individual steps, and for the *Luminaria*, as the 24-25 July celebration of the feast of St. James is known, flowers and lamps are laid on the steps up which the statue of the saint is carried after a tour round the town.

There is no philosophy more inimical to the Sicilian mindset and way of life than the sour Puritanism of northern Europe. Their Catholicism was always lax and leisurely, far removed from the harsher forms of the same religion as practiced in Ireland or Poland. The creed may be the same but practice differed widely. Religious ceremonies, even pilgrimages to sacred spots like Tindari, end with eating and drinking. There are special sweets for particular feasts. Marzipan originated in the Orient, possibly in Persia, and it too came to Sicily with the Muslim invasions but was quickly domesticated and used in imaginative recipes and given unexpected forms, especially in convents. The convent beside the cathedral in Palma di Montechiaro still produces the sweetmeats celebrated in *The Leopard,* and men, apart from descendants of the noble house of Salina, are still not allowed in, although they can enjoy the sweets. The torture to which St. Agatha of Catania was subjected involved cutting off her breasts, and the commemoration of this barbaric act sanctions a mixture of the sensual and the spiritual which appeals to the Sicilian mind and leaves outsiders bemused. On her feast day breast-shaped marzipan sweets, sometimes topped with a cherry suggestive of an over-ripe nipple, are sold in Catania along the route of the sacred procession in honor of the saint. Palermo has its own *frutta martorana,* named after the convent of the Martorana in the city center. This sweetmeat can be molded and colored to resemble fruits, but is also given pseudo-religious but overtly erotic form pleasing to the Sicilian male. Breasts feature largely. Some convents around the island still make their own marzipan, although the good sisters are today more restrained in the forms they view as compatible with their chaste calling. However, accounts from other days give a different impression of fleshly longings sublimated into indecent shapes which would have made their Irish counterparts blush.

The effort expended and the expertise gained by cloistered nuns in the making of such luxuries has amused and puzzled many commentators, including Mary Simeti Taylor, the doyenne of writers on Sicilian cuisine:

> The universal if questionable cliché of the frustrated female consoling herself with a box of chocolates or a cream-filled éclair has little application here, since the bulk of the pastries were given away. The pastries that the nuns produced, like the bread made for Saint Joseph's day, offered women of very restricted lives a rare outlet for creativity, and both would provide interesting material for the study of the relationship between women, food and religion. I can only venture to suggest that what was originally a humble offering of one's own labour, considered proper for a woman vowed to poverty, maintained this air of suitability and propriety even when it became quite out of hand.

The St. Joseph table is one custom which emigrants took with them to the United States. Traditionally, families invited the poor of the neighborhood to share their meals on 19 March, the feast of St. Joseph. In contemporary America, Catholic parishes, particularly in districts with a high Sicilian-American population, still organize such events to raise money for charitable causes.

In Sicily, Christmas and the Day of the Dead (2 November) are also occasions for indulgence. Given the nature of the feast, the second date may cause raised eyebrows, but this feast was once the occasion when children were packed off to bed early for the same reason as were children elsewhere on Christmas Eve. Gifts would be delivered that night, but the bearer of these gifts was not some elderly man in a red outfit, but deceased members of the family who descended on ropes from heaven and left their bounty at the foot of the children's beds. Children were not always reassured by adult promises that the returning dead were benevolent, but the gifts were real and marzipan sweets were *de rigueur*.

CUISINE AND COFFEE

Food, recipes, and styles of cooking are always and everywhere indicative of history and culture, but perhaps especially so in Sicily. Even those whose visit to Sicily is motivated by highly earnest cultural considerations are happy to widen their search or deepen their experiences, so many will recognize the reaction of Brian Johnston, an Australian travel writer, although perhaps in reverse order.

> I went to Sicily a casual visitor, keen to hunt down cassata and learn more about cooking, and found myself seduced by the island's neglected beauty and passionate people... Sicily's greatest treasure is its remarkable cuisine. Every dish is a culinary clue to this island of marvels and magic, full of eroticism and fervent religion, history and culture. In Sicily, there's glorious seafood, pasta glistening with tomato sauce and olives, and pastries galore. Then there's cassata, the ultimate Sicilian dessert, a baroque extravaganza of sponge cake and sweet ricotta, lavishly decorated with marzipan and candied fruit.

The less sybaritic who are attracted initially by Sicily's history and art, and who remain unable to accept the excited judgment that the food is the

The Vucciria market in Palermo, the most famous of the three in the city

island's "greatest treasure" in the face of competing wonders, will rejoice in the discovery of the island's culinary traditions and present delights. Here too the Arab influence is conspicuously strong. The list of products they brought to the island, and thus to Europe, includes sugar, almonds, dates, apricots, artichokes, cinnamon, oranges, pistachios, pomegranates, saffron, sesame, and spinach.

It was not that the Arabs invented Sicilian cooking, for the ancient Greeks left testaments to their enjoyment of Sicilian fare. In *The Republic,* of all unlikely places, Plato has Socrates sing the praises of "the refined Sicilian cuisine." Travelers in the eighteenth century were amazed at the quality and quantity of food served at official meals. Patrick Brydone wondered if one could eat as well anywhere in the world as at the table of the Bishop of Agrigento, and indeed in ancient times Agrigento was famed for its hedonistic life-style. Siracusa too was celebrated for the excellence of its chefs. Sicily is, for better or worse, a land of excess or perhaps of indulgence, not only at table. Sensuality is not exclusively sexual.

Although they nowadays merge, every Italian region had two parallel culinary traditions—the popular and the aristocratic—which might correspond to a distinction between cuisine and cooking. Paradoxically, although the poor were obliged by poverty to eat as they did, popular cuisine is now relished by snobbish foodies. However, some Sicilian dishes in this tradition are probably best approached with circumspection even by the more adventurous gourmet anxious to immerse himself in local ways. *Stigghiola* is a poor man's haggis, made with the intestines of lamb, but without the addition of the oats which are intrinsic to the Scottish variety. It entered popular cuisine for the same reasons as did its Scottish counterpart, that a poor people cannot afford the luxury of discarding any part of a beast which is edible, even if revolting. Central components of *musso* are the lips of a cow or bull, while *quarume* makes imaginative use of the ears and innards of the beast: *frittola* is very similar with the addition of a sprinkling of saffron. These dishes are readily available in small restaurants or at those benches by the roadside, normally near markets, where an enterprising cook stands beside a steaming pot plying his trade. Sausages employ a range of ingredients and those made with a rare species of boar, the *suino nero* which roams wild in the Nebrodi mountains, is especially prized.

Two traditional fast foods worth sampling are *pane e panelle* and the *arancina*. The *pane* is simply a bread roll which encloses the *panelle,* flat, square, batter-covered fritters made of chickpea flour. The *arancina* is a kind of rice ball whose orange color comes from the breadcrumb cover and is commonly oval-shaped but is sometimes, even if not produced in convents, given the teasing form of a breast. It has a piece of meat or cheese in the center. Potato croquettes, known in dialect as *cazzilli*, are an excellent accompaniment, and if washed down with a glass of strong wine, perhaps white or red Rapitalà, any selection of these simple foods will provide a lunch fit for a king, or at least a prince.

Pasta can be regarded as the great Sicilian contribution to world cuisine, once again of Arab origin. In *The Leopard,* when the Prince is newly arrived at his country estate and has, as tradition requires, invited his tenants and retainers to dinner, an event disrupted in 1860 by the arrival of the gorgeous Angelica, there is an audible sigh of relief, almost a cheer, from the guests when the first course turns out to be genuine, tried-and-tested spaghetti and not some new-fangled *potage* from France. Risotto, being made with rice grown in northern Italy, was not native to Sicily. The division between pasta and risotto eaters has been much discussed since the rise of the secessionist Northern League, and ardent League supporters, airily convinced of the profound cultural differences between the two halves of Italy, often find themselves, when pressed for examples, able to refer only to the spaghetti–risotto divide as the supposed unbridgeable dyke. It is in any case much less marked nowadays.

Pasta is rarely served in Sicily with a meat sauce. Fish and seafood—shrimps, cuttlefish, mussels, squid, crabs, and lobsters—give a distinctive tone to the accompaniment. *Pasta con le sarde* is a delicacy of the west of the island, with the *sarda* a bigger and much drier variety of sardine, but the finished dish has an addition of variable quantities of pine nuts, raisins, fennel, and oil. Vegetable sauces, with many regional varieties, are common. *Fusilli alla siracusana* is made with cauliflower and ricotta cheese, while broccoli, eggplant, pistachios, or French beans are alternatives which give more color. *Pasta a picchi pacchi* is irresistible, not only because of its curious name; which probably simply means fresh. Basil and tomatoes are the essential ingredients and thereafter cooks can give their imagination free rein. Anchovies are helpful in this dish, garlic optional, and an appearance which pleases the eye even more than the tongue essential. *Spaghetti alla norma* is another dish whose etymology arouses controversy. The Catanians claim it as theirs and say the name derives from the heroine of the eponymous opera by Vincenzo Bellini, while others believe the derivation comes from a demand for something which corresponds to established "norms," a plate in other words which respects tradition and expresses an abhorrence of innovation. Catanian imagination has also likened it to Etna, since it is fondly believed that the colors of the dish reflect the dominant colors of the volcano—red (tomatoes) for burning lava, black (eggplant) for hardened lava, green (basil) for the vegetation on the lower slopes, and finally white (salted ricotta cheese) for the snow at the peak.

Another reminder of the Arab past is couscous, written *cuscus* in Italian, best savored in the west near Marsala or Trapani where the Arab impact has lingered longest. Once again, meat does not figure strongly in the Sicilian variant of this dish, although chicken is beginning to appear, but for the real thing the flour is lightly roasted, flavored with fish stock, and served with as many kinds of seafood as come to hand. There is a couscous festival at San Vito Lo Capo, which is situated on a northern promontory looking onto the Aeolian Islands.

The Sicilian masterpiece is the *caponata,* a dish which arouses the normally hesitant patriotism of Sicilians and has inspired visiting food writers to heights of lyrical excess. The preparation of this dish requires a vigorous battering of the prime materials. The key ingredient is the aubergine, or eggplant, of which there are two kinds available in Sicily, the standard elongated variety and a more rounded, multi-colored sort. Thereafter, other items may include green olives, onions, garlic, artichokes (which may replace the eggplant), capers, which grow wild in Sicily, and tomatoes, but the flavor is given by the discriminating use of lemon juice and basil and then, decisively, by the addition of the right quantity of vinegar and sugar, as well as by the removal of the garlic at a carefully timed moment. The exasperating problem in attempting to reproduce this recipe is that the best cooks rely on experience or work by instinct and are incapable of communicating precise quantities or timings to the aspiring neophyte.

Nothing in Sicily is served plain. Fish dishes, particularly of swordfish or tuna, are commonly given the names of the cities where their sauces supposedly originate, but the differences between the tomatoes, olives, and herb served as *alla palermitana, alla catanese,* or *alla messinese* are not substantial. Other fish more common in Mediterranean waters include *spigola* (bass), *orata* (sea bream), *pesce di San Pietro* (John Dory). These translations are approximate since these are fish found in the Mediterranean and are only distant cousins of their Atlantic counterparts. *Sarde a beccafichi* is an elaborate fish dish, although a *beccafico* is a plump bird known to Anglophone ornithologists as a "fig-eater." Sardines top and bottom provide a kind of sandwich which supposedly resembles the bird, and some fastidious chefs even twist one end to make it look like a bird's tail. The filling can vary with the brio of the cook, but pine nuts, bread crumbs, anchovies, raisins, olives, various herbs, and lemon juice are the common ingredients.

It may come as a surprise that the Sicilians have such a sweet tooth, but there are *pasticcerie* whose windows display the same lush richness and variety of cake as comparable shops in Vienna. Once again, we have the Arabs, with their introduction of sugar to Sicily, to thank for this abundance. By the tenth century the Sicilians were growing sugar in sufficient quantities to be able to export it, but they kept a fair bit for imaginative use at home. *Cannoli*, once reserved for consumption during Carnival, have lost all religious associations and are now a common dessert or accompaniment to coffee. The word means "tubes" and the round containers are finished off with a filling of ricotta or goat's cheese and an admixture of tiny particles of fruit. As with so much else, there is a great deal of rivalry over size and quality. The town of Mineo claims primacy for quality, but then so does Erice, while Piana degli Albanesi claims to produce for daily consumption, and not for special occasions, the biggest *cannoli* in Sicily.

The *cassata*, with or without the qualification *siciliana*, is the queen of desserts. Its origins are disputed, with historians divided over Roman, Arab, and Norman claims. In these more benighted days it can be purchased commercially as ice-cream in a triangular shape with bits of dried or synthetic fruit inserted, but this is not the traditional form of the cake. The Arabs did not actually invent or import ice-cream, but they did devise sherbet. Recipes abound but the instructions they give are the bluntest of culinary tools, for a list of ingredients will mention sugar, cheese, flour, and a touch of ice-cream but omit the essential elements—the whimsy and imagination of the cook. Anyone reading that it is a sponge cake flavored with fruit juice and liqueur, with ricotta, vanilla, candied fruit, and perhaps ice-cream added before it is given a marzipan covering, then decorated generously with architectural whorls, tiny rosettes, or fetching inserts, the whole emerging in various colors and not only the customary green and white, would have the appetite whetted but will have only a pale sense of the actual *cassata*. It is one of the many products of the Sicilian imagination which conventionally draw the description Baroque on account of the elaborate forms they assume. The *cassata* is often a kind of public sculpture, to be admired for the riot of color and delicacy of structure before being savored as a gastronomic masterpiece. And there are regional variations in accordance with local feasts and the characteristics of local saints.

Sicily has always had a greater acreage of vineyards than any other Italian region, and has an ancient tradition of wine-making. Its wines and wine production are celebrated by Robert V. Camuto, an American journalist and travel writer, in his book, *Palmento*.

> The story of Sicilian wines is a long one: Homer mocked it; Pliny the Elder exalted it; Arab and Muslim conquerors more than tolerated it. The British merchant John Woodhouse "discovered" it in the sherry-like wine of Marsala at the end of the eighteenth century. And the French and the Italians coveted Sicilian wine when phylloxera ravaged their vineyards at the end of the nineteenth century. Today vestiges of that last golden age are the *palmenti*—traditional stone wineries with massive wood lever presses that for the most part lie abandoned across wine-growing Sicily. Made obsolete by newer technology or deemed illegal for commercial use by European regulations, the old structures have been given over to brambles or recycled into *agriturismo* bed-and-breakfast or modern wineries.

These "old structures" can be hard to locate but are fascinating places to visit. Until recently, Sicily viewed its own wines as modest products, fit mainly to give body to wines grown elsewhere, but the quality of Sicilian wines has improved enormously in recent years. Since each district has its own characteristic wine, the choice is very wide. Improvement has gone hand in hand with greater commercialization and the increased use of oenological technology, but there are many wine-producers who continue production in ways hallowed by traditions dating from the Romans. Some newcomers also shun modern ways.

It is legitimate to wonder why with such a rich native choice of grapes, some Sicilian winemakers have taken to planting and bottling Chardonnay,

Cabernet, Merlot, and Syrah, wines which are already ubiquitous on the world market and have no connection with Sicily. Most Sicilians still drink local wine, or *vino della casa* (house wine) in restaurants, and many will go to their grave without having ever tasted a vintage. There is no reason not to follow their example. Surprises will include dry white wines served with peaches floating in the flask. A more traditional sweet wine is Malvasia, whose native abode is the island of Lipari.

Some Sicilian wines are easily available in supermarkets around the world, and that is not a coded way of saying they are to be shunned. Corvo wines both white and red have famously declined to seek the government guarantee of the DOC (Denominazione di Origine Controllata) label, but the standard they maintain is more than acceptable. Other readily available wines include Regaleali and Rapitalà, especially the white in both cases. It is hard to go wrong with Inzolia or Catarratto grapes. Zibibbo, a good, strong sweet wine, is now identified with Siracusa, and the famous Marsala wines need no introduction to British drinkers, for reasons discussed in a later chapter. The dominant wine in the south-east is the Nero d'Avola, whose production is no longer restricted to its home base around the lovely town of Avola, but the sheer abundance has, as with Chianti or Valpolicella, made standards difficult to police. For complex reasons beyond the grasp of anyone not at home in that uncertain borderland where Sicilian viticulture meets political maneuvering, most Nero d'Avola wines do not qualify for the protective DOC categorization but have to be content with the less reliable IGT (Indicazione Geografica Tipica). However, the search for a reliable producer is as valid a reason for visiting this region as the desire to see the Baroque architecture of the towns. Although the deep red Nero d'Avola is the most commonly sold, and even mis-sold for as little as one euro a bottle, there are lighter rosés which are tantalizing and pleasurable. Avola is also very proud of its almond crop, and there is a sweetish almond-flavored wine, *vino alla mandorla*, available. At its best nero d'Avola is a big, generous wine, as challenging as the best of Bordeaux, to be savored in the evening when the day's work is done.

There is everything to be said for exploration and experimentation, and as part of the greater commercial awareness of modern winemakers, there are now wine trails (*strada del vino*) in different parts of the island. Producers are not quite as ready to offer samples as their Australian or

Californian equivalents, but they are anxious to advertise their wares and welcome visitors. The seven existing trails are the Alcamo trail, the Marsala trail which takes in the island of Pantelleria where Moscato is produced (but there is also a separate Moscato trail in the east centerd on Noto and Siracusa), the Nero d'Avola trail, which has to make special provision to include the similar but richer Cerasuolo from Vittoria, the Inzolia trail, the Etna trail, and finally the Malvasia trail on Lipari.

Coffee is another of those aspects of daily living which is both familiar and unfamiliar. Italian coffee has now conquered the world, making *cappuccino* universally available, and there is no need to pay heed to those tales about it being drunk only before midday. The question of *espresso*, called simply *caffè* elsewhere in Italy but known as *caffè ristretto* in Sicily, is slightly more complex. In Sicily coffee is taken stronger, shorter, and more concentrated than anywhere else on earth. It does not have dregs at the bottom, like Turkish coffee, but it is a pitch black in color, bitter in taste, should cover only the bottom of the cup, and is in principle refreshing, even if its harshness represents a challenge for outsiders. The litmus test applied by Sicilians is to add a spoonful of sugar, watch to see if it floats on the surface rather than sink: if the sugar floats, the coffee is dense enough to drink. It is safer to ask for a *caffè lungo*, which will have more water and be more easily palatable. *Caffè ristretto* has been made into an alternative symbol for the island by Leonardo Sciascia when he sought a colorful way of expressing his fear that all Italy was taking on the worst characteristics of Sicily. Just as geographers believed that the line of the desert was moving north, so too, Sciascia believed, was the "line of the *caffè ristretto*."

Ice-cream can be taken here with a croissant or a brioche, making an interesting and refreshing sandwich. In Catania ice was once transported down from the top of Mount Etna, and sold to the benefit of the Church, since the archbishop had a monopoly on the sale. Sherbet was an Arab import, and *granita* was invented from the combination of ice and sorbet. This fairly solid drink can become delightfully addictive, and comes in a dizzying variety of fruit flavors, from the more conventional orange and lemon to the more select myrtle, almond, or even basil. It can be taken along with, or even instead of, breakfast, can be consumed as a dessert, enjoyed as a snack, savored along with a brioche, or can even be sipped on its own as a refreshment in the summer heat. For best effect it has to be consumed fairly rapidly before it melts into a sweetish, sticky liquid. The delights of the table have always been part of the Sicilian experience, to be indulged and savored with the other wonders of the island.

Chapter Four

THE IMAGINED ISLAND

SICILIAN WRITERS

Sicilian literature has strong local roots, in the sense that Sicilian writers tend to draw on their knowledge of their home town, as frequently to lambast it as to celebrate it. This does not make their minds or imaginations provincial, nor does it impose on them some narrowness of vision, any more than Dickens was made provincial by allowing his imagination to roam mainly in London, Balzac in Paris, or Joyce in Dublin. Metropolitan critics, whether the metropolis is London, Paris, or Rome, write slightingly of those whose stage is some location far removed from the venue of operatic first nights and publishers' cocktail parties, but imaginative probing of human behavior or keen observation of manners and mores can take place in any setting, whether a capital or a village. The contemporary writer, Maria Attanasio, has found for her novels and stories gripping, arresting material with universal relevance in the past and present events in her home town of Caltagirone. *Of Concetta and Her Women,* not yet available in English, deals with the struggles of a proto-feminist to have a women's section established in the local, supposedly revolutionary, Communist Party, and the comedy and drama will be appreciated, perhaps ruefully, well beyond the town.

This local attachment and celebrity, even if the celebrity is often accorded only post-mortem, is reflected in the series of institutions known as "literary parks," which do not have the greenery and flower beds associated with parkland but are initiatives established to foster and encourage knowledge and appreciation of a writer from a particular district. There are several such parks at various points of the island, all with specific headquarters in one locality but with a reach to other areas associated with, or embellished and enhanced by, the writer's imagination. These parks are dispersed all over Sicily, so a traveler of a dedicated literary bent could see much of Sicily by zigzagging from one to another. If such a person were to read the novels, plays, and poetry as he or she meandered, they would also have access to enriching visions of life. In a straightfoward list the existing parks are in honor of Stefano d'Arrigo in Messina, Salvatore Quasimodo in Roccalumera, Giovanni Verga in Vizzini and Catania, Elio Vittorini in Siracusa, Nino Savarese in Enna, Gesualdo Bufalino in Comiso, Tomasi di Lampedusa in Santa Margherita di Belice and Palermo, Luigi Pirandello near Agrigento, Leonardo Sciascia in Racalmuto, and Lucio Piccolo in Capo d'Orlando. These bodies are managed to different standards, have varying levels of access, and differing types of exhibition.

Not all these writers enjoy international renown, although a surprising number do, and whatever their differences of outlook all would agree that they belong to a tradition which is unashamedly Sicilian. Most would subscribe to the notion expressed by Leonardo Sciascia in the title of a book-length interview, *Sicily as Metaphor*. Sicilian literature has characteristics specific to it, but draws from world literature and in turn deepens comprehension of, and compassion for, the emotional and intellectual predicaments of the human animal everywhere. Any attempt to identify the Sicilian contribution risks degenerating into a quest for the "rosebud factor" mentioned in the opening chapter, but perhaps the one overriding element underpinning and permeating Sicilian writing is a sense of existential, social, and political precariousness. This characteristic is produced by the historical vicissitudes and unpredictable natural calamities which have beset the island, and which finds expression in an all-pervading, fatalistic belief that all generations are equidistant from barbarism, that light is inevitably threatened by encroaching darkness, that the skin of civilization is fragile, that law is an instrument of the powerful and justice unattainable, that culture and civilization are temperate zones surrounded by areas marked *hic sunt leones,* and that regression and collapse from any temporary happy state are inevitable. The gunshot that rings out in the piazza of a previously peaceful town at the opening of Sciascia's *The Day of the Owl*, murdering the honest building contractor as he prepares to commute to work, can be taken as representative, but other instances of equal validity can be found in the great works of Sicilian writers.

It is not possible to discuss all writers, not even those who have parks devoted to their memory, but the one dedicated to Stefano d'Arrigo has many typical features. His fame rests on only one epic novel, *Horcynus Orca* (Killer Whale), and if the site in Messina is small, the invitation is to regard it as imaginatively taking in the neighboring stretch of the

Elio Vittorini, novelist and editor

Mediterranean where the sea journey towards Sicily which is at the core of his novel is set. Elio Vittorini was from Siracusa and his park is centered there. His best-known work remains *Conversation in Sicily*, an anti-fascist novel which Vittorini was inspired to write by disgust at the Spanish Civil War and yet in which he attempted to employ some of the techniques of opera. The work is also a search for roots, and Vittorini shares the common Sicilian desire to reflect on his homeland and to look beyond it, even if he wrote—self-deludingly—that the quest which makes up this work could have easily been set in Peru.

Ernest Hemingway was an admirer and friend of Vittorini and wrote an appreciative introduction to this novel, including the enigmatic judgment, "I care very much about Vittorini's ability to bring rain with him when he comes, if the earth is dry and that is what you need." He went on to explain that by rain he meant

> …knowledge, experience, wine, bread, oil, salt, vinegar, bed, early mornings, nights, days, the sea, men, women, dogs, beloved motor cars, bicycles, hills and valleys, the appearance and disappearance of trains on straight and curved tracks, love, honor… porcupine quills, cock-grouse drumming on a basswood log, the smell of sweet grass and fresh-smoked leather, and Sicily.

Sicily is certainly central to the author's concerns, and the rest may be attributed to creative reading by Hemingway.

Vittorini's sister married the poet Salvatore Quasimodo, who was awarded the Nobel Prize for literature in 1959, and whose literary park lies between Messina and Siracusa in the coastal town of Roccalumera. This "park" consists of some railway carriages parked beside a railway station where the poet's father was station master. Quasimodo's poetic output can be divided into two phases. Under fascism he wrote in a style described as "hermetic," a deliberately obscure, allusive style which was beyond the grasp of the censors, but in the post-war period he joined the Communist Party and opted for a more open, accessible style. In a celebrated essay he wrote that every poet had to choose a "hedge" which would establish the boundaries of his poetic homeland, and "my hedge is Sicily." One of his most celebrated pieces has only three lines, and is an arresting statement of precariousness:

> Everyone is alone on the heart of the earth
> Pierced by a ray of sun:
> And suddenly it's evening.

In Comiso, after the death of the writer, a native of the town, the Gesualdo Bufalino Foundation took over the grand, circular, colonnaded structure which was previously a fish market. Bufalino worked as a teacher and only emerged as a writer late in life. His prose is elaborate and stylish, perhaps "Baroque," but he drew criticism from fellow Sicilians for his preference for pure Tuscan Italian over any form of Sicilian diction. He combined acute, acerbic essays on Sicilian life with novels of whimsical imagination. One of most original, *Quid pro Quo*, is a crime story where the enquiry is led by the dead victim.

SICILY ARAB AND GREEK

These writers were all from the east of the island, and, as we have seen, there is a mildly held belief that in cultural terms even today Sicily can be divided into a Greek east and an Arab west, with Siracusa as the Greek city par excellence and several rivals, Trapani, Mazara del Vallo, or Palermo, put forward as "Arab" equivalents. The notion of such a divide lies behind some of the novels of Vincenzo Consolo but was articulated strongly before him by the writer Vitaliano Brancati, who hailed from Pachino in the deep south-east of the island. In a fine poetical flourish he wrote:

> From the Palermo gate entered the Arabs and with them subtleties and equivocation, the ego and non-ego, melancholy and mosaics. The subtleties and the melancholy ended up in Agrigento, in the head of Luigi Pirandello, with another part at Castelvetrano in the head of Giovanni Gentile. From the eastern gate, entered the Phoenicians, the Greeks, poetry, music, commerce, deceit, clowning and comedy: Stesicoro, Bellini, Di San Giuliano, De Felice, Rapisardi, Verga, Martoglio…

He added that he hoped for some encounter, some exchange between "these beings so distinct the one from the other." Not all these names will be familiar even to contemporary Sicilians, but Brancati's own reputation is growing, at least in his homeland. His novels are all set in eastern Sicily, and examine the sexual mores and fantasies of the Sicilian male, marked by an attitude he named *gallismo*, "cockery" in any sense the term will bear. His work is not easily exportable since although he was a shrewd social observer, to a greater extent than with other Sicilian writers his novels address the mindset and malaise exclusive to Sicily.

The greatest of the writers from eastern Sicily was the novelist Giovanni Verga, who was born in Catania in 1840 and spent his boyhood and much of his adulthood there. The main site of his park is Vizzini but the house on Via Sant'Anna in Catania where he was brought up now houses a museum in his honor. In spite of the fact that D. H. Lawrence admired him and actually translated three books of his works—*Little Novels of Sicily, Cavalleria Rusticana and Other Stories,* and the novel *Mastro-Don Gesualdo*—Verga has never attracted in the English-speaking world the readership his talents merit. In his introduction to the last novel, Lawrence, that great nomadic mind and imagination which could settle in any culture, wrote perceptively of Verga and of the Sicily he depicted:

> The Sicilians of today are supposed to be nearest things to the classic Greeks that is left to us: that is, they are the nearest descendants on earth. In Greece today, there are no Greeks. The nearest thing is the Sicilian, the eastern and south-eastern Sicilian… Gesualdo Motta might really be a Greek in modern setting, except that he is not an intellectual… He is

not a bit furtive, like an Italian. He is astute instead, far too astute and Greek to let himself be led by the nose. Yet he has a certain frankness, far more than an Italian. And far less fear than an Italian. His boldness and queer sort of daring are Sicilian rather than Italian, so is his independent manliness… isolated the people too have some of the old Greek singleness, carelessness, dauntlessness. It is only when they bunch together as citizens that they are squalid.

Sicilian pundits too have made the point that it is only when Sicilians gather in associations, like mafia gangs or political parties, that problems arise.

For Giovanni Verga, as with other writers, Sicily itself is the main subject of his fiction. Verga left Sicily in 1865 first for Florence and then for Milan, but the fashionable novels he published did not please him and he changed tack to depict the daily life of the Sicilian peasants. He was attracted to *verismo*, the Italian version of European naturalism, and aimed to produce a cycle of five novels to portray every section of society, in broad imitation of Balzac's *Comédie Humaine*. The overall title was to be *The Cycle of the Defeated*, but in the event he produced only two, *I Malavoglia* (in English, *The House by the Medlar Tree*) and *Mastro-Don Gesualdo*. These were set in villages near Catania and gave a harsh, bitter portrait of the efforts, invariably unsuccessful, of men to escape from the grind, labor, and poverty that marked their lives. The next novel was to be *The Duchess of Leyra*, but he found he could not think himself into the mindset of the aristocracy and so was never able to complete the book. Nor could he redirect his creative energies, so he did not write another novel over the following decades of his life.

Verga's letters are evidence of an unhappy, depressed man, weighed down by a sense of failure. While he reworked some of his earlier writings and produced new short stories and plays, he could not focus on the fictional cycle he regarded as his life's mission. He was made a senator of the newly united Kingdom of Italy, was praised by his contemporary Luigi Pirandello, but declined to attend public festivities in his honor. He died in 1922 after a stroke. In Italy he is regarded as ranking with the great European Victorian novelists, and his neglect elsewhere is inexplicable.

Agrigento and its surrounding area produced two writers of exceptional talent: Luigi Pirandello, born in a district called Caos, and Leonardo

Sciascia, born in Racalmuto. Pirandello reveled in the irony of the name of his birthplace. "I am a child of chaos," he wrote, while Sciascia said that Racalmuto was the ideal observatory from which to view the world. Both are buried in the towns where they were born. In the main street in Racalmuto there is a statue of Sciascia, one hand in pocket the other clutching a cigarette, not on a pedestal but at the level of shoppers and passers-by. His tomb bears the enigmatic epitaph: We Will Be Mindful of This Planet.

Pirandello lived in Rome for most of his adult years and traveled widely, but his remains were brought back to his childhood home, which still stands in splendid isolation in the countryside overlooking the sea. It is now the museum of the literary park, and although it has relatively few exhibits, it does make an effort to recreate the imaginative universe where Pirandello's characters had their being. He requested in his will that he be cremated and that nothing at all of him be left, but his ashes were brought back and buried under a pine tree in the garden. Perhaps his wishes were honored more fully than he had hoped, since the pine tree was blown down a couple of years ago, and the ashes reinterred in a wall.

In his lifetime Pirandello was probably more admired abroad than at home, and in 1934 was awarded the Nobel Prize. He joined the National Fascist Party in 1924 and never gave up membership although he became progressively disillusioned with Mussolini and refused to write "fascist" plays. His reputation is linked principally to his dramatic works, but he was forty before he came to the theater and prior to that had published novels, volumes of short stories, essays, and poems. His best-known plays remain *Henry IV*, *Right You Are (If You Think So!)*, and *Six Characters in Search of an Author*, all tantalizingly demanding intellectual works with a vein of comedy only in the second. *Six Characters* caused a riot outside the theater in Rome where it was premiered in 1921. The baffled, outraged audience pursued him along the street with cries of "Idiot, clown!"

Some critics divide his output into two phases, an early "Sicilian" phase which includes plays written in dialect and stories drawing on Sicilian culture and folk beliefs, and a later "European" period in which he advanced quasi-philosophical notions of personality, truth, and the clash between "life" and "form." He himself described as myths the plays written from 1928 onwards, *The New Colony*, *Lazarus*, which was premiered in English in Huddersfield, and the unfinished *The Mountain Giants*. On his deathbed, discussing the finale of that final play, he said he had "resolved everything with the pine tree." It was a very Pirandellian resolution. Whatever tag is attached to Pirandello, there is no doubting his abiding attachment to Sicily and his debt to the culture of the island, even in the formation of that complex of ideas on personality and truth known as *pirandellismo.* The debt is clearest in his earlier work, when he explicitly adhered to *verismo.* Some of the tales from this period are grotesque, such as *The Jar,* which tells of a workman called to mend a break in a large oil container but who manages to enclose himself inside the repaired jar and becomes an object of ridicule to the peasants who turn the event into a party and dance around him. Others tell of the impact of sexual jealousy, expressing itself not necessarily in spontaneous acts of violence but in ritual vengeance of the sort that the code of honor entails. Pirandello's sympathies are with the women of Sicily, notably in a short novel, *The Outcast Woman,* depicting the plight of a newly married woman thrown out of her house after a false accusation of adultery. *The Other Son,* a one-act play based on an earlier short story, features a woman criticized by the townsfolk for her romantic yearning for the two sons who have emigrated and abandoned her and her indifference to the loyal son who has stayed at her side. In the embittered monologue which is the climax of the piece she reveals that the loyal "other" son was born after her kidnap and rape by a brutal bandit gang.

The debate over whether the dilemmas and values expressed in his mature works like *Six Characters* are a sublimated expression of a purely Sicilian mindset or whether they are an aspect of wider European philosophical culture cannot be resolved. Pirandello had studied in Bonn and was familiar with German Idealist thought, but he was deeply rooted in a Sicilian folk culture which was itself highly sophisticated. He questioned the validity of any notion of truth, and concluded, especially in *Right You Are,* that truth is unattainable and can be no more than a purely individual outlook. He doubted the existence of one enduring personality in any human being, and said that all we know of ourselves or others are the masks we choose to wear or which are imposed on us. He came to believe that life was a basically unknowable, evolving force, fixed temporarily in a series of forms. Perhaps that relativistic mode of thought owed more to his Sicilian background than international critics allow. In no place on earth do individuals hold to so many conflicting notions of individual facts, or are they so divided over interpretations, as in Sicily.

THE TWENTIETH CENTURY

Racalmuto is in the same province as Pirandello's birthplace. It is a beguiling little town set in the heart of an area dominated in the nineteenth century by the sulphur industry which was controlled by the British and French. The name is Arabic in origin, apparently meaning "ruined village." The imposing castle was originally Norman but passed into the hands of the powerful Chiaramonte family. Although a small center, Racalmuto had the misfortune of being home to two noble families, the Chiaramonte and the Del Carretto, who were as quarrelsome as the Montagues and Capulets in Shakespeare's Verona. The village's former power station is now the Sciascia Foundation and center of the literary park which takes in sites possibly described in his novels as well as ex-sulphur mines, deserted farmhouses, and other places associated with the writer.

Leonardo Sciascia lived under the shadow of Pirandello, which is an uncomfortable place for a writer. His relations with his illustrious predecessor followed a predictable parabola of early rejection as Sciascia sought to find his own voice, of mature acceptance as he produced appreciative books and articles on Pirandello, and final submission in a posthumous

"I tried to recount something of the life of a town I love": memorial to Leonardo Sciascia overlooking Racalmuto

essay in which he proclaimed Pirandello to be "my father." Sciascia came to believe Pirandello's Sicily was the Sicily he too inhabited, but this was not a consoling realization, for he recognized the individual madness and collective insanity which featured so prominently in Pirandello's depiction of their common homeland.

Sciascia's life was outwardly uneventful, but in essays and newspaper articles he became embroiled in the principal controversies of public life in Sicily and Italy. He was elected in 1976 as independent counselor in the City Council in Palermo, and between 1979 and 1982 sat in the national Parliament in the ranks of the Radical Party. He wrote in 1979, "I have always taken an interest in politics, and always in an ethical sense," and those who enjoy categorizing novelists will file him as a moralist. His loyalty to Sicily was constant, but was often expressed as polemical anger at the defects, injustices, and endemic corruption of Sicilian society. A modest man, he made only one boast, that he was the first Sicilian to have given in *The Day of the Owl* a "non apologetic portrayal of the mafia phenomenon." As he would do in a series of novels such as *To Each His Own,* he used the structure of the detective story not to create a diverting whodunit, or not only for that purpose, but as a tool for the analysis of a corrupt society where leading figures in Church and state tacitly and constantly defended the mafia or denied its existence. The mafia is present in all his detective stories, but it undergoes in successive novels a process of transformation, evolving from the organized crime syndicate which operates in Sicily into an image for ruling elites in society, all societies. Increasingly, he saw all power as corrupt and corrupting, and democracy as a façade behind which powerful men plotted their own advantage. In Sciascia's detective stories, unlike those of Agatha Christie, whom he admired, the criminal is not brought to justice, for a mafia-infested society cannot provide justice. It was not, however, that Sciascia did not believe in justice, for he held tenaciously to the hierarchy of Enlightenment values. In an age of irrationalism, whose exponents included Pirandello, Sciascia was a rationalist whose great intellectual heroes were the *philosophes* of the French Enlightenment, especially Voltaire.

The writer celebrated in the literary park centered on the village of Santa Margherita di Belice in the center-south of Sicily is Prince Giuseppe Tomasi di Lampedusa, author of *The Leopard.* Being a member of the high Sicilian nobility, he had more than one dwelling place, but the palace in this town was the one he loved most, as he proclaims in his fetching memoir, *Places of my Infancy*. The Lampedusa family palaces demonstrated, as he was aware, the precariousness and fickleness of fate. In *The Leopard* the author steps out of the time frame of his novel to recount that the Palermo palace, the residence both of the author and of the novel's protagonist, would be destroyed in 1943 by a bomb manufactured in Pittsburgh, Penn. It is still in its ruined state in a back street, although there have been signs of recent activity inside its devastated shell.

The palace in Santa Margherita suffered a similar fate in January, 1968, after Lampedusa's death, when a massive earthquake razed whole villages in the Belice valley to the ground, leaving some 370 dead and thousands injured and homeless. The plight of those homeless was another symptom of governmental incompetence or indifference since years later the people were still "housed" in steel containers initially erected as a stop-gap measure. The palace itself was completely destroyed, and while the church and the houses in the village have been built in a modern style, the palace has been reconstructed in its original state, with a Baroque building on either side. However valiant and sensitive have been the efforts of the reconstruction workers, to see the palace as it was it is better to trust Lampedusa's loving, nostalgic, poetic prose.

> Set in the middle of the town, right on a leafy square, it spread over a vast expanse and contained about a hundred rooms, large and small. It gave the impression of a vast and self-sufficient entity, of a kind of Vatican as it were, that included state rooms, quarters for thirty guests, stables and coach-houses, a private theater and church, a large and very lovely garden, and a big orchard.
>
> And what rooms they were! Uncle Nicolò had the good taste, almost unique for his time, not to ruin the eighteenth-century salons. In the state apartments every door was framed on both sides by fantastic friezes in grey, black or red marble, whose harmonious asymmetry sounded a gay fanfare at everyone passing from one room to another... I would wander through the vast ornate house as in an enchanted wood.

The writer inhabited the past with no discomfort, so his memories evoke a wonderland for a boy "who loved solitude, who liked the company of things more than of people." Everything in the palace and the village—

"A kind of Vatican": the ancestral home of the Tomasi di Lampedua family in
Santa Marghertia di Belice

the garden, the cathedral, and the theater—enthralled him and he recalls
them all in excited reverie. "The evenings, oddly enough, we always spent
in the ballroom, an apartment in the center of the first floor with eight balconies looking out over the piazza and four over the first courtyard… gold
was the dominating note of the room."

The present building is on a smaller scale than the original. It faces a
piazza with no trees, and houses a museum containing the writer's letters
and manuscripts as well as copies of the novel in the many languages in
which it has been translated. On the top floor is a waxwork presentation
of the characters from *The Leopard* as they were incarnated by the actors
in Luchino Visconti's film. Fabrizio, Prince of Salina, will forever have the
brooding appearance of Burt Lancaster and Angelica the radiant beauty of
Claudia Cardinale. Scenes from the film are endlessly projected onto a
screen over Father Pirrone's head.

The novel is set in the decades after Garibaldi's landing at Marsala,
which ended both Sicilian independence and the rule of the aristocracy.
The new regime replaced the Neapolitan Bourbons with the House of

Savoy, absolute monarchy with a liberal parliamentary regime and brought Sicily into the United Italy whose capital was then Turin. When *The Leopard* was first published in 1961, the problem for many critics was not so much that the author had no truck with a traditional depiction of the Risorgimento as glorious and heroic—that cliché had been challenged long before—but that his history was viewed from the wrong end, from the perspective of the losing class, a class that deserved to lose. The aristocratic bias, however concealed by the elegant style and louche disillusion of the protagonist, stuck in the craw of left-wing commentators. The words spoken by Tancredi, the adopted son of the Prince of Salina, "If we want everything to remain as it is, everything has to change," have become the motto of conservatives all over Europe. Tancredi was of noble stock, but he decided to throw in his lot with Garibaldi and the insurgents, either out of youthful idealism or opportunistic cynicism. From the same mixture of motives, he breaks off his engagement to the prince's plain daughter and marries Angelica, radiantly beautiful and wealthy, even if vulgarly bourgeois. Sex and money are the new forces in society.

In addition to recording historical change and the response to that change, *The Leopard* is also a profound meditation on Sicily. The new government in Turin sends an envoy to offer the prince a seat in the senate of the new kingdom. The prince declines and recommends the new man, Calogero Sedara, Angelica's father and a former peasant whose wealth now outstrips the prince's, but the conversation between envoy and prince turns not on contemporary political issues but on the nature of the Sicilian character and of Sicilian history. Sicilians do not suffer from some inferiority complex, says the prince, recalling an English captain who came "to teach us good manners" but who could not succeed "because we think we are gods."

This fatalistic explanation of the woes of Sicily profoundly irritated Leonardo Sciascia, no admirer of the novel. In an early review he went so far as to say that *The Leopard* was a historical novel with no sense of history. The sense of timelessness, Lampedusa's suggestion that Arab imams, Norman knights, and Catalan adventurers had inhabited the same unchanging reality clashed with the alternative view that history was the determining force, that character did not exist outside or above history, that power and not climate or landscape created conditions of life, that fatalism was nugatory, and that the aristocratic class was to blame for many of

Sicily's ills. "A good novel, but too class-based to be a great one," was a judgment on *The Leopard* Sciascia once delivered to me. These are two great writers who compel readers to see Sicily through their eyes but who hold incompatible views, meaning that each reader or visitor will have to choose between Lampedusa's and Sciascia's approach to Sicily, its culture, and way of life.

The most idiosyncratic Foundation in Sicily is surely the Piccolo Foundation near the northern coast town of Capo D'Orlando, facing the Aeolian Islands. It was established in 1978, ten years after the death of the poet Lucio Piccolo, but is really a memorial to the three members of a deeply gifted but highly eccentric family, Lucio and his brother and sister, Casimiro and Agata Giovanna. This family too was of blue-blood and the three were first cousins of Lampedusa, who was a frequent guest in the villa. Originally the villa was a summer residence, but the Piccolo family fell on hard times and moved out of Palermo. The baroness, mother of the three, was a woman of some energy and restored the family fortunes by planting olive groves and orchards of oranges.

Lucio came to public attention before Lampedusa when he won a literary prize for his first collection of poems, *Baroque Songs*. He invited his cousin to accompany him to the prize-giving ceremony in San Pellegrino, where the formally dressed pair and their accompanying servant aroused the bemused curiosity of the cream of Italian literary life. When Lampedusa attained posthumous fame, the assorted critics and novelists struggled to produce recollections of him based on his one sortie into the literary limelight. Seemingly, he was less impressed by them and decided he could outdo them. On his return to Sicily, he set to writing *The Leopard*.

Lucio Piccolo and Lampedusa had a prickly relationship, and on one occasion Piccolo declared that while Lampedusa was a cousin of his, he was no cousin of Lampedusa's. He was a poet of delicate talent, who produced few collections of poetry and those often obscure and difficult. They were translated into English by the American Ruth Feldman, but family difficulties have meant that the works are not as easily available as their excellence merits. He was not the only talent in the family. Casimiro was a painter who preferred water colors to oils, and who drew his subjects from tales of goblins, leprechauns, and elves. He corresponded with W. B. Yeats on subjects related to Celtic mythology. He believed in the rebirth not only of humans but of animals, a notion which pleased a family who were devoted to their pet dogs, all of whom were given Arab names and are buried in a cemetery on the estate.

The sister, Agata Giovanna, was an internationally renowned botanist who gathered flora from all over the Mediterranean and who laid out part of the gardens in styles which owe much to wholly imagined Irish-Scottish landscapes. The house is stocked with ceramic and majolica vases, porcelain dolls, ivory miniatures, mechanical clocks, Chinese figurines, *art nouveau* lamps, and many etceteras collected according to please tastes which are patrician, cosmopolitan, and highly individualistic.

The novelist Vincenzo Consolo, whose poetic style owed much to his acquaintance with Piccolo, died in January 2012 and is buried in nearby Sant'Agata di Militello, where he was born. His wife has announced that she does not want any foundation or literary park in his honor, although the town council has set aside a couple of rooms in the local library as a somewhat inadequate commemoration of him.

Other writers, notably Sciascia, preferred not to leave the custody of their memory to enthusiastic admirers, and made their own provisions. Such may be the case with Andrea Camilleri, the colossally successful creator of the detective stories featuring Inspector Montalbano. Camilleri

The home of Inspector Montalbano in Punta Secca, near Ragusa, as featured in the highly successful TV series

was a theater historian and director in a drama college in Rome and, like Bufalino, emerged as a novelist only at an age when most men are contemplating retirement.

In commercial terms, he is the most successful novelist Sicily has produced. His sales figures in Italy and abroad are counted in the millions, helped by the highly successful television adaptations which have been bought up by companies around the world. The crime-infested town where the inspector operates, the fictional Vigata, is based on Porto Empedocle, where the writer was born. This district is plainly an ideal nursery of literary talent since both Pirandello and Leonardo Sciascia come from the same part of the island, and Camilleri proclaims himself as an heir to the central Sicilian literary tradition. He has written a biography of Pirandello, has produced historical novels based on events in Sicilian history, and his admiration for Sciascia, who inspired his crime novels, is unbounded. He may not have Sciascia's subtlety, philosophical range, or moral-social vision but his novels are more than escapist crime stories. His anti-mafia passion is evident in such novels as *Excursion to Tindari,* and other novels deal with the scourge of drug-dealing (*The Shape of Water*), enforced prostitution (*Wings of the Sphinx*), the plight of asylum seekers, legal or illegal (*The Snack Thief*).

Most of the filming has been done in the south-east of the island. The urban scenes have been shot among the beautiful Baroque splendors of Ragusa, and already the locations used are marked by placards with images taken from the TV series. Striking piazzas designed by Baroque architects and planners of genius are now better known for their use as background in chase scenes rather than for their historical or artistic importance. As is expected of the detectives in Spain and Italy who feature in what has become known as the "Mediterranean *noir,*" Montalbano is a refined gourmet, and cookery books of his favored dishes are readily available. The restaurants where Luca Zingaretti, who has played Montalbano since 1998, has dined while pursuing his enquiries or dallying away from the attentions of Livia, his patient girlfriend from the north of Italy, are careful to make his patronage known for literary rather than hard-headed commercial reasons, obviously. There are trails to caves in the hills and ancient burial grounds where sinister encounters have occurred. Perhaps in modern society, such memorials will do more to guarantee Camilleri's enduring fame than any foundation.

Chapter Five
MEN OF HONOR
A NOTE ON THE MAFIA

Film based on Sciascia's *The Day of the Owl,* the first non-apologetic work
featuring the mafia

Although Sicilians groan, rightly, at the automatic identification of Sicily
with the mafia, discussion of the topic cannot be avoided. There is more
to Sicily, there is a richer culture and history, they will protest, once again
with justice, but there is no denying the international awareness of the
Sicilian mafia. The word itself is now in use in every language.

Visitors to Sicily will be in no danger, and anyone who claims to be
able to detect a dark atmosphere created by an unseen, sinister presence
suffers from an over-fired imagination. One such was, surprisingly, Mario
Puzo, author of *The Godfather.* In an interview he told me he had visited
Palermo only once, and had gone round the city in a state of trepidation,
peering nervously around corners before venturing up a street. He need
have had no fear, and not only because *mafiosi* both in New York and
Palermo were avid readers and admirers of his novel. The mafia takes little

interest in visitors, although they may have some stake in the hotels where they stay.

To assist the understanding of this phenomenon, a couple of straightforward preliminary propositions can be set out. Firstly, there never was a good mafia: from the outset, the mafia was exploitative, hostile to the interests of its own people, and brutally violent. In consequence, all romance related to the mafia, not only when expressed in Hollywood films, is phoney. Secondly, not everything in Sicily is related to the mafia, but much, especially in the economic sphere, is indeed so related. A Palermo prosecutor once calculated that some 96 per cent of central and local government contracts were corruptly assigned, but this may be exaggerated. Thirdly, not all Sicilians are *mafiosi* but all *mafiosi* are Sicilian. Fourthly, the mafia is not an ancient organization, although the mentality which underlies the mafia is as ancient as Sicily, or at least as a recognizable and distinct Sicilian culture. Taken together, these propositions justify our curiosity about the links between Sicilian-ness, Sicilian history and culture on the one hand, and the emergence and survival of the mafia on the other.

There are three organized crime syndicates operating in southern Italy in the territory covered broadly by the ex-Bourbon Kingdom of Naples: the *camorra* in Naples and Campania, the *'Ndrangheta* in Calabria, and the mafia in Sicily. There is also in Puglia a body which calls itself the *Sacra Corona Unita* (United Sacred Crown), but this is a more recent phenomenon and is more related to criminal gangsterism than to mafia-style crime. The terminology already indicates the multi-faceted historical heritage of the south: the word *camorra* is of Spanish origin, and this body is older than the mafia; *'ndrangheta* is derived from the Greek word for man; the origins of the term mafia are disputed but the word is probably of Arabic origin and possibly meant "hiding place." The word *camorra* is still current, but the other two terms tend nowadays to be replaced by the expression *Cosa Nostra*, which originated in America and which, as every reader of *The Godfather* knows, literally means "Our Thing." Individual *mafiosi* can be referred to by insiders as "made men" or "men of honor." The concept of honor was once a central element of the code of the gentleman all over Western Europe and underlay such gentlemanly activities as dueling, but it had deeper resonances around the Mediterranean.

Individual mafia gangs, or groups of gangs, are sometimes referred as "families," another term seemingly re-imported from America. The original term for a mafia grouping was *cosca*, a Sicilian dialect word meaning artichoke. These terms are pregnant with unsuspected layers of meaning. Relations inside the gangs are often, but by no means exclusively, based on blood ties, and where they are not, the code of the *mafioso* compels him to operate on the basis of that trust which ideally exists inside a family. Similarly, as the leaves of an artichoke form one plant, so the semi-autonomous sections of a widely dispersed association make up one mystical body. However, in today's globalized society the current term is "clan." Similarly the leader is more likely to be called a "boss" rather than a *capo*.

DEFINITIONS

There are many definitions of the mafia, each emphasizing different aspects of the body. The most comprehensive is that given by Leonardo Sciascia in an introduction to his polemically anti-mafia novel, *The Day of the Owl* (1961):

> The mafia is a criminal association whose aim is the illicit enrichment of its members, which sets itself up as a parasitical intermediary between property and labour, between production and consumption and between the citizen and the state, enforcing its position by means of violence.

Such definitions tend to be dry and bloodless, where bloodshed is what people associate, rightly, with mafia crime. Sciascia highlights both the parasitical nature of the organization and the crucial fact that mafia crime is of its essence financial. It extorts bribes, trades in arms and drugs, offers "protection" which is in fact protection against itself, and insinuates itself into a position in the public sector where it can take a regular cut in public contracts, especially in the building industry, by threatening civil servants and employers. The mafia is not and never was some chivalric body concerned with the defense of Sicilian well-being or with the protection of the downtrodden. Its aim is the increase in wealth and ease of living of its members, even at the expense of those of similar background. It behaves like those strike-breakers whom trade unionists used to call "blacklegs," scorning and spurning people like themselves. It worships only power and strength, and its code justifies the abuse and exploitation of the weak.

The mafia has traditionally divided territory between its constituent gangs, so that mafia families are known by the area where they operate and which they control. This can lead to warfare, although internecine violence, while far from unknown, is comparatively rare. Cosa Nostra prefers peaceful conditions of non-interference from police and judiciary which allow it to conduct its "business" in an orderly, regular, profitable, and undisturbed style. There is a Palermo saying to the effect that when blood flows, the mafia is in trouble. The conditions of globalized capitalism and diminished border controls inside the EU facilitate money laundering and other mafia financial activities, and indeed there are now mafia companies which operate in legal sections of society. They enjoy, in the sober language of sociologists, the advantage of access to investment funding derived from illegal activities, whether drug smuggling, extortion rackets, or whatever, but the source of mafia power is violence and the threat of violence.

Astonishingly, there is also a definition provided by a mafia boss, Joe Bonanno, who was born and brought up in Sicily and became leader of the one of New York's "five families" which bore his name. He managed to stay out of prison until he was so ill-advised as to write an autobiography, *A Man of Honor*, which provided the FBI with the kind of information they had been unable to gather by surveillance. It also provides a self-serving but invaluable insight into the mindset of the mafia man. He never uses the word mafia, preferring the euphemism "tradition." Joe Bananas, as he hated being called, did his own unscrupulous, mendacious PR work in his book, but stripped of their gloss, the words he wrote have some truth:

> Picture, then, an assortment of relatives and friends who share a common Tradition, and who, although pursuing different activities (mostly legal and some illicit), do so within the framework of a Family because this enhances their chances of success. The Family members can be from all walks of life. Some of them have a high character and some have a low character. Some are rich and some are poor. Some are bad and some are good. To make this form of cooperation work, they have to give some allegiance to one man, the Father... The Father has to be somewhat of a universal man.

Bonanno tags himself "Father." The term "godfather" was invented by Mario Puzo in his novel of that name. Those with a "high character" have not yet been identified.

For many years it was part of political cant to deny the very existence of the mafia. "Mafia, what is that? A kind of cheese?" asked Gerlando Alberti, a prominent boss on his arrest in 1980. A particularly notorious example was provided by the late Cardinal Ruffini, Archbishop of Palermo between 1945 and 1967. In an interview with an American journalist he stated: "The mafia? As far as I know it is a brand of detergent." When the anti-mafia crusader Danilo Dolci brought the criminal activities of Cosa Nostra to international attention, Ruffini issued a pastoral letter condemning those guilty of slandering Sicily. According to his Eminence, these forces were three: the novel *The Leopard,* Danilo Dolci himself and the mafia. The prelate went on to explain that the mafia did not exist and was an enemy of Sicily only in the sense that it was a slanderous invention of detractors of the island. A more sophisticated variation of this approach consisted in pointing to criminality in London, Paris, New York, and elsewhere, and wondering why Sicily should be singled out for special execration. This notion can still be heard, although less frequently now that criminal bodies in the ex-Soviet bloc operate on a mafia rather than the common gangster model.

A common metaphor for the mafia is that of the "octopus" in reference to the spread and grip of its tentacles. Commentators wonder whether the mafia should be viewed as a shadow state within the state, or as an autonomous, surrogate state. The former view is more probable, and it is here that the fundamental difference between mafia and ordinary criminality lies. Common criminals are aware of being in the literal sense of the word "outlaws," that is, they operate outside the law, in opposition to the state, continually attempting to evade its representatives, the police. The mafia on the other hand attempts to gain impunity by infiltrating the institutions of society and battening on the body politic. It seeks recruits among public officials or elected members of legislatures, either among those who share a common culture or who can be coerced by threats or attracted by contract-skimming appeals to self-interest. Cosa Nostra operates by preference if not inside the law at least with the collusion of law-makers and law-enforcers. It is essential to keep reminding oneself that the vast majority of Sicilian people are not *mafiosi*, will never cooperate with the mafia but have to endure the consequences of its power. Nevertheless, the level of connivance and collusion between elected politicians and men of violence in Sicily has no equivalent elsewhere.

A blurring of boundaries between the powers that be and criminal life is not new, and as early as 1770 Patrick Brydone came across an instance. He was initially comforted when the Prince of Villafranca offered him an escort across the island but was later horrified to discover that the guards consisted of "the most daring, and hardened villains, perhaps that are to be met with upon earth, who, in any other country, would have been broken on the wheel, or hung in chains: but here they are publicly protected and universally feared and respected." Mafia collusion with liberal politicians in the decades following Unification and with Christian Democratic politicians in the post-war era was common, since these were the dominant parties and the mafia is only interested in power. The most notorious recent case involved Salvo Lima, eventually gunned down in 1992 in the streets of Palermo in revenge for his supposed betrayal of mafia interests. His father had been a "made man" and Lima himself had well publicized links with the faction led by the La Barbera brothers. The mafia controlled much of the voting in Sicily, and this helped Lima enjoy a highly successful career in politics as Mayor of Palermo and as member of the Italian and later European parliaments. His huge personal following among Sicilian Christian Democrats made his decision in the 1960s to ally himself with seven-time Prime Minister Giulio Andreotti a matter of mutual advantage. Thereafter Lima was known as Andreotti's "proconsul" in Sicily. He was the intermediary between mafia gangs and political life, and his murder was interpreted as a warning to Andreotti from mafia men dissatisfied with the recent, honest conduct of trials which had seen criminals jailed. Andreotti himself was later tried, and acquitted, for collusion with the mafia. The charge sheet against him included the allegation that he was in contact with the boss Totò Riina, and had even exchanged a kiss of greeting with him at a reception in a Palermo hotel. Marcello dell'Utri, the right hand man of Silvio Berlusconi in his business empire and a member of the Berlusconi government, was actually found guilty of collusion with Cosa Nostra. In some senses, the real capital of Cosa Nostra is Rome rather than Palermo.

HISTORY

The mafia is not an ancient body. It made its appearance in the mid-nineteenth century, and its notoriety spread in Italy and Europe after Garibaldi's landing at Marsala in 1860. This is not to suggest, as some disingenuous or dishonest apologists have done, that in some sense the mafia was imported from northern Italy. The word mafia first appears in the title of a dialect play premiered in 1863, *I mafiusi di la Vicaria*. The Vicaria was the Palermo prison, and the work is set inside the jail where political and common prisoners mingled. The play exemplifies an ideal code of mafia behavior and honor, but strangely the word *mafioso* appears only in the title, while the term used in the script is the older, Neapolitan term *camorrista*. The outline plot was given to the actor-author, Giuseppe Rizzotto, by an ex-prisoner and owner of a hotel where Rizzotto's company was staying, but the author overheard the word mafia in a street conversation and chose it as an appropriate catch-all term.

The mafia did not initially cover the whole of the island, but was restricted to a triangle in the west whose extremities were Palermo in the north, Trapani in the far west, and Agrigento in the south. The eastern cities of Catania and Messina were once mafia-free zones, but those happy days have gone as the grip of the mafia has spread over the island, and indeed over the country, the continent, and the world. One important difference between east and west lay in the pattern of land-holding. The east

The accused in a nineteenth-century mafia trial. The dress of the men in a cage-dock indicates the middle-class respectability of members of mafia clans

was mainly the area of small farms while the west was dominated by the *latifondi,* huge agricultural estates. In 1812 Lord Bentinck, quasi-governor of the island while the Neapolitan Royal Family was in exile in Sicily under British protection, abolished feudalism, allowing the feudal estates to be bought and sold. The law of unintended consequences meant that peasants lost such rights—for instance, pasture and wood-gathering—as they had enjoyed. In addition, in the nineteenth century aristocrats preferred to leave the land for Palermo, Naples, or Rome but had no wish to lose the profits of their estates. A new figure, the *gabellotto,* emerged, and he can be regarded as the forerunner of the *mafioso.* He was initially charged with collecting rent for the absentee landowner, but was quickly able to set himself up as an independent operator, often subletting land to peasant-farmers but worming himself into a position where he could both exploit the peasants beneath and, in some instances, threaten the lords above. The means he employed and the basis of his power were quite simply violence or the threat of violence. One of the first reports to confront the issue spoke of an "industry of violence." Such violence is not mindless vandalism, but is methodical and purposeful. In the jargon of our times "the state was absent"; in other words there was, in fact if not in theory, no police force of the sort which in other European countries was tasked with overseeing the rule of law. Associations of violent men gathered round the very members of society who would elsewhere be the pillars of society, lawyers, doctors, priests, and from these ad hoc groupings emerged mafia criminal activity.

Many Sicilians hold that the state is still absent. General Carlo Alberto Dalla Chiesa led the successful struggle against the Red Brigades and other terrorist groups in the 1970s, but was assassinated by the mafia very shortly after he was appointed prefect of Palermo and given responsibility for the anti-mafia campaign. He knew the island well, having been there as a young *carabiniere,* and recalled an instance when the chief officer in Palma di Montechiaro received threats from the mafia. Dalla Chiesa went to stroll about the town with him, not only to offer him reassurance but also to let the townspeople see that the officer was not isolated, that the state was not absent. Later Dalla Chiesa himself was certainly isolated and abandoned in the months before his killing in 1982.

Cultural-historical factors have played a part in the creation of attitudes behind the mafia. The history of Sicily has been a history of conquest and exploitation and this sequence of invasions has played a decisive part in creating the "distrust of the state" which is still a factor in the life of Sicily. As happened in Poland and in Ireland in similar circumstances, a gulf between "them" and "us" became culturally embedded. Life under alien rulers tends to make people retrench and withdraw from civic society into private circles, and to operate among those in whom unquestioned trust can be placed, normally the family. Joe Bonanno put it accurately when he stated that "traditionally a Sicilian has a personal sense of justice. If a 'man of honor' is wronged, it is up to him to redress that wrong personally." He would not turn to the state and its institutions.

Collaboration with the state and its agents, especially its law-enforcers, cannot be tolerated, a mentality expressed by the code of *omertà*. The word is derived from the Latin *homo,* meaning "man," so in its original sense the term means "manliness," but in its acquired sense *omertà* indicates the iron law of silence and non-compliance with police and authorities, whatever the circumstances. There are cases of men who served long prison sentences for crimes they did not commit rather than reveal to investigating officers the identity of the real guilty party. The Catanian writer Nino Martoglio wrote a poem which describes two *mafiosi* eavesdropping while a younger associate on the point of death is interrogated by the police whose aim is to find out who had inflicted his wounds. To the delight of the *mafiosi* listeners, he refuses to reveal what he knows, saying that if he survives he will execute justice by himself. "Bravo," say the mafia men, "*è un giuvini d'onore,*" he is a young man of honor.

DEVELOPMENT AND ORGANIZATION

Magistrates as well as scholars have spent much time debating the thorny issue of whether the mafia is of its inner nature an organization with a hierarchy of power and rites of initiation or whether it is something more intangible, more like a culture, a tacit code, a way of life which its adherents follow instinctively or unconsciously. The vulgar view, found in many cheap thrillers, was that there was an organized structure with a defined line of command, while the sophisticated view was that the mafia was of the air breathed in Sicily, belonging to the realm of culture, and almost thus a matter of unconscious instinct. This issue can be regarded as settled following the revelations of Tommaso Buscetta, a leading mafia figure who turned state evidence. And the sophisticates were wholly wrong. What became known as the Buscetta Theorem established that Cosa Nostra is one single organization, carefully constructed and rigidly hierarchical. At the grass-roots there are clusters of ten "soldiers" whose leader reports to a family, which is in its turn part of a *mandamento* or zone, rising to a regional commission and all subject to the island-wide *cupola* or supreme commission. There is one overall boss. The initiation ceremony requires a novice to hold in his hand a picture of a saint which is set on fire while he recites three times an oath: "may my body be converted into ashes like the holy image if I betray Cosa Nostra." Buscetta compared being admitted to Cosa Nostra to being ordained a priest: "You cannot stop being a *mafioso* any more than you can stop being a priest." Buscetta himself had been in the mafia since his youth and was a notorious killer and drugs smuggler who was given the admiring nickname the "boss of the two worlds" in recognition his activities outside Sicily in North and South America. He operated at the highest levels, but during the mafia wars of the 1980s he found himself on the losing side. This more than any sense of repentance may have encouraged him after his arrest to break the code of *omertà* and to collaborate with the magistrate Giovanni Falcone, who used Buscetta's evidence to prosecute 475 *mafiosi* in the 1986 maxi-trial. Later Falcone and another leading anti-mafia judge, Paolo Borsellino, were assassinated. Falcone and his wife were killed in 1992 when the car they were driving

Memorial marking the spot on the motorway between the airport and the city where Giovanni Falcone and his wife, Francesca Morvillo, also a magistrate, were assassinated on 23 May 1992 by mafia killers

was blown up on the motorway between Palermo airport and the city center. Borsellino was murdered later the same year in an explosion at a block of flats where his mother, whom he had been visiting, lived.

The mafia has survived because it has shown itself to be flexible and adaptable to developments in society. There have been three main phases, with an interlude under fascism. The mafia emerged as a rural phenomenon in the mid-nineteenth century, transmogrified in the 1950s into an urban organization, and has more recently converted to what could be termed international gangsterism. The mafia flourished first in the orange and lemon groves around Palermo but even then they were active in other spheres, including the financial, as was instanced by one of the first crimes which came to national attention. The banker Emanuele Notarbartolo had exposed corrupt dealings in the Banco di Sicilia and was murdered in 1893 while returning by train from Termini Imerese to Palermo. His actual killer was Giuseppe Fontana, a street-level mafia man, but the crime was ordered by Raffaele Palizzolo, a Member of Parliament. Politics, finance, and organized crime were always part of the mafia mix. To free the jury from the febrile atmosphere of Palermo, Fontana and Palizzolo were put on trial three times in different Italian cities, but were acquitted.

The transformation into an urban phenomenon was gradual, but was completed by the mid-1950s. It was certainly a *fait accompli* by October 1957 when a hugely important meeting of Cosa Nostra associates from both sides of the Atlantic took place in the luxury Grand Hotel et Des Palmes, in Palermo. Participants included Lucky Luciano and prominent figures from the "five families" as well as such local bosses as Genco Russo. This meeting brought to an end a murderous civil war between factions in Sicily, established closer links between the families in Sicily and New York and gave final form to the internal structures of Cosa Nostra in Sicily. It also made agreements for the manufacture and distribution of heroin. The pious notion that Cosa Nostra would not deal in drugs is nonsense.

Mussolini's regime was successful in suppressing the mafia, or at least in driving it temporarily underground. Historians point to a visit by the *Duce* in 1924 to Piana degli Albanesi (which he renamed Piana dei Greci), in the Palermitan hinterland, as the turning point. The mayor was one Francesco Cuccia, who used the title "don" which is given, however odd the combination may appear, to priests and mafia bosses. Mussolini visited the village and in one version of the story the don felt himself humiliated

79

by the *Duce*'s lack of prior respect and ensured that Mussolini found himself addressing an empty piazza. In another, he rebuked Mussolini for bringing his own bodyguard and told him that he would be perfectly safe under his protection. Mussolini was outraged, and when he returned to Rome he gave Cesare Mori, known as the "iron prefect," full authority to stamp out the mafia by any means he chose. Two totalitarianisms faced each other, and the minor totalitarianism lost out. Mori was able to employ methods, such as arbitrary arrest and even siege of villages, not available to a liberal democracy. Years later, Sciascia drew attention to the paradox that the regime which enslaved Italy brought freedom of a sort to Sicilians who saw the various "dons" and bosses in the dock, or else in prison, with or without the benefit of trial.

One of the most debated of all points in the squalid history of the mafia is the part played by the Allies in the restoration of mafia power after the Liberation. It is well established that there was contact in New York between the US navy and the American mafia. Some of the leading figures were first-generation Sicilian immigrants, most notably Charles "Lucky" Luciano, then in jail in New York. The American authorities had and have every good reason for keeping these contacts secret so we are in shadowy territory, but enough has come out to allow us to say that the American mobsters offered to make contacts with "reliable" Sicilian friends who would be of assistance to the invading army. This has given rise to the story of an American airplane which flew over Villalba and dropped a silk scarf with an embroidered L for Luciano as a signal to the illiterate don Calogero Vizzini to collaborate with the Allies, although presumably his brother, the parish priest, would have been able to read a more conventional message. This tale has elements of quaint folklore and may be unfounded, but as with all folklore it hides a deeper truth. There are well attested accounts of meetings between mafia bosses and Allied leaders. The dilemma remains. Did the Allied officers know what they were doing, or were they so focused on defeating the Germans, and shortly afterwards the new enemy, the Italian communists, that they did not mind dirtying their hands? The latter explanation is put forward as justification, but not all Allied officers were naïve.

AMGOT (the Allied Military Government for Occupied Territories) governed Sicily until 1946, and in that time the mafia reasserted its control, paid off debts in the only way it knew how, established links with the nascent Christian Democratic party as the most likely dominant political grouping, re-established its territorial networks, enforced protection schemes, and embarked on smuggling activities, initially in cigarettes and later in drugs. Some prominent *mafiosi* were able to present themselves as anti-fascist victims and were invited to take positions of power after the Liberation. Don Calogero Vizzini became Mayor of Villalba, a post he was able to combine with his role as supreme mafia boss in the whole island. Vito Genovese, born in Naples but an American resident after fleeing Italy ahead of the police, was employed as interpreter in the American army HQ. He was a known mobster and had even been a fascist sympathizer, suspected of having murdered an anti-fascist activist in New York on Mussolini's orders. He later became leader of another of New York's five families, but in 1943 he made good use of his position as "interpreter" to organize a black market network which was more efficient than the official distribution system for foodstuffs. Their control of the black market, exploited unscrupulously in a time of real hardship and even starvation, gave the mafia access to massive riches and a financial basis on which to rebuild. Lucky Luciano was freed in recompense for his services and deported to Italy, where he took up residence in Palermo. His part in establishing mafia power is incalculable.

Charles "Lucky" Luciano (1897-1962), mafia boss and manipulator of organized crime in New York and Sicily

Italian politicians at every level, some intellectuals and some church-men have been either dupes of organized crime or actively complicit. The Cardinal-Archbishop of Palermo, Ernesto Ruffini, has already been mentioned. The case of the Friars of Mazzarino, a group of Capuchins in the order of the gentle St. Francis of Assisi who were put on trial in 1960 on charges of extortion and intimidation, scandalized Italian society, lay or religious. However, there is another side. Mafia power and influence have been resisted by brave Sicilians, and an anti-mafia campaign is as old as the mafia itself. Corleone, a mafia-infested town made famous in Sicily by the number of killers it has produced and elsewhere by the name given to the boss played by Marlon Brando in *The Godfather,* was the center of peasant movements which were principally anti-landlord but were anti-mafia inasmuch as the mafia sided with the landowners. Placido Rizotto organized the peasants in their struggle for land in the immediate post-war years, but gunmen walked into Corleone in broad daylight and led him away. He was never seen again. One of his friends later lamented that if each of the villagers had picked up just one stone each, they could have defended him, but no one lifted a finger.

The mafia today wields a different kind of power but is still the malign and active force it ever was. The basis of its power is still violence and the threat of violence, and it still enjoys political protection. The switch to the use of the internet and IT technology does not mean that Cosa Nostra has abandoned its more modest day-to-day activities of bribery, protection rackets, coercion, and corruption. It can endanger honest politicians, judges, and policemen, and is a menace to the lives of ordinary people. Recently a *mafioso* was jailed for extortion from a man who was hiring out deckchairs on the beaches at Mondello, Palermo's resort. He was hardly in the super-rich category. Libero Grassi, a clothing manufacturer and owner of a small factory in Palermo, was killed in 1991 for refusing to pay protection money, known in dialect as *pizzo*. (The word originally meant "beak" and someone extorting cash was asking his victim to "wet his beak.") His death aroused public outrage and led to the establishment of the movement *Addio pizzo!* There are shops in Palermo with stickers in their doorways proclaiming their refusal to pay mafia protection money. Such daily heroism is rarely needed elsewhere in modern Europe but it is a sign of courageous resistance to the great scourge of Sicily.

Chapter Six
ARRIVALS AND DEPARTURES
THE BRITISH AND THE AMERICANS IN SICILY

"An Italianate Englishman, a devil incarnate," was the judgement of Pope Sixtus V. It rhymes better in Italian, and could apply to some of the Englishmen who have arrived in Sicily in the early days. Certainly, the British influence on Sicily has been minor compared to that of France or Spain, but it has been real and has manifested itself over the centuries in unexpected ways and places.

Gualtiero Offamiglio is not a name to be found in the registers of English parish churches, but the man concealed behind it was an Englishman, or at least an Anglo-Norman, who started life as Walter of the Mill and whose name was Sicilianized in 1168 when he became Archbishop of Palermo. He was responsible for the construction in 1184 of Palermo's cathedral, built to replace a previous basilica which had been converted into a mosque by the Arabs. Another contemporary and rival of Walter/Gualtiero was Richard Palmer, known locally as Palmieri, archbishop first of Siracusa and then of Messina. Walter's tomb is in the crypt of his cathedral, while Palmer's has survived the earthquakes and bombings which have reduced Messina's cathedral to ruins on several occasions, and can still be seen behind the organ.

Archbishop Walter presided at the marriage ceremony in Palermo in 1177 between William II of Sicily and Joan, daughter of Henry II of England. Joan was only eleven when she was wed and crowned queen. In spite of the common Norman heritage she may have been dismayed at the conduct of life in the Sicilian royal court, especially at her husband's harem. She bore him a child, Bohemond, who died in infancy, and she was widowed in 1189. On William's death she was imprisoned by his successor, Tancredi, who seized her dowry. The following year her brother, Richard the Lion Heart, arrived in Messina en route for the Crusades. Historians agree that he was fond of his sister, and he negotiated her release and the return of her possessions. Richard was accompanied by an English army, whose conduct caused the townspeople to revolt in protest, and Richard is remembered in Messina for the ferocity with which he put down the rebellion. He and King Philip of France decided to winter in the city, and any further problems could be ironed out in direct negotiation between them and Tancredi, since all three were native French speakers.

In later centuries Britain was a signatory to the great international treaties which saw Sicily casually shifted from one foreign dominion to another. Sicily was a far-off land of which the government in Westminster knew little, so interest in the island was superficial. This changed only when, in the late eighteenth century, the cultural, commercial, and military importance of Sicily was recognized. Culturally, Sicily was "discovered" in 1770 when Patrick Brydone became the first traveler to extend the Grand Tour south of Naples, and subsequently wrote the book which brought Sicily to the attention of all Europe. Three years later, John Woodhouse landed on the island. There is a touch of legend to the story of his arrival and even the actual year is disputed. Woodhouse was apparently forced to take refuge from a storm in the port of Marsala. King Roger had taken refuge in Cefalú in similar circumstances and founded a cathedral in gratitude for his deliverance. Mr. Woodhouse founded a wine-exporting business.

Marsala Barons

John Woodhouse was from Liverpool and was a businessman of the type routinely described as hard-headed. He had no interest in Sicilian culture or history, but he was free of all xenophobic prejudice and was impressed by what he found. He was initially interested in buying primary materials such as coral and almonds, but was also a visionary entrepreneur with an eye for the main chance. When he was introduced to the local wines, especially *grillo*, he was struck by the resemblance between their flavor and that of Madeira, which was already popular in Britain. He decided the wine of Marsala would sell at home but was aware of the famous difficulties affecting wines which are enjoyable on the spot but do not travel well. Perhaps drawing on techniques employed in Spain or Portugal for the production of port or sherry, he decided that added alcohol would allow Marsala to be exported and arrive with the same bouquet that it had had on departure. More than any other single man, John Woodhouse can be regarded as the "inventor" of Marsala wine.

Other brothers came to join him, and if they were not in any sense philanthropists, the "trickle down" theory of wealth expansion worked in this case and their activities and those of other English businessmen who came later benefited Sicily enormously. Woodhouse established in Marsala his first *baglio,* a dialect word meaning courtyard but which in the town acquired the sense of warehouse or wine-producing plant. Woodhouse's original *baglio* covered some seven acres and had at its center his own English-style residence. It was surrounded by defensive walls, a necessary safeguard in days when Barbary pirates still sailed the Mediterranean. The pioneering Woodhouses changed the face of the city of Marsala, building roads and expanding the harbor, thereby providing the communication infrastructure which would allow Garibaldi to land there with his Red Shirts in 1860 to topple the Bourbons. Woodhouse did not own vineyards, but oversaw the introduction into Sicily of the techniques which had been part of the agricultural revolution in Britain. There were no banking institutions in Sicily to speak of but the Woodhouses and later English families organized a system of advance payments and anticipatory loans which led to the establishment of a financial network.

Woodhouse did not enjoy a monopoly for long. In 1806, while the British army was in residence during the Napoleonic war, Benjamin Ingham followed his footsteps. His family were woollen manufacturers in Leeds, and Ingham too was the personification of the thrusting, entrepreneurial bourgeois for whom even Frederick Engels was compelled to express a grudging admiration. And yet perhaps his outward obsession with finance and commerce concealed a frustrated romantic. There is a well attested story that Benjamin, who was only 22 when he arrived in Sicily, fled Yorkshire after being jilted by his fiancée for whom love was not everything. She seemingly showed him the door when a ship in which he had invested heavily went down. He fetched up in Sicily, looked around at the opportunities, and decided that Woodhouse had shown the way forward, so somewhat cheekily he too set up a *baglio* in Marsala. His partnership with one John Lee-Brown ended in tears, or at least in the law courts with accusations of fraud and deception, and perhaps it was for that reason that Ingham made a decision Sicilians would fully understand: trust only your own family. He invited his sister to send out her eighteen-year-old son, William Whitaker. The Whitakers' later prosperity and power in Sicily was immense, but not due to poor William who died in 1818, four years after his arrival. According to one story, Benjamin Ingham communicated to his sister in Yorkshire the news of her son's demise in curt terms: "your son is dead, send out another one." The family gave credence to the tale but the letter with these forbidding words has never come to light, so the belief may be no more than a reflection of how the man's character was viewed. Another letter found after a clear-out of a house in Yorkshire shows him in a more humane, sympathetic light. In it he breaks the news more delicately and speaks highly of his late nephew. William's brother Joseph was duly dispatched to assist his uncle in the business and he became the patriarchal figure for an Anglo-Sicilian dynasty of great wealth and influence.

Benjamin Ingham and the three generations of the Whitaker family who settled in Sicily accumulated riches on a colossal scale. Ingham built more warehouses in Marsala as well as in Castelvetrano and Campobello di Mazara, but for his main residence he found Palermo more attractive than Marsala. He ventured into the world of finance, and also exported to Britain a range of products from soda ash to rags, the latter needed for the production of paper. Most significantly, when sulphur was discovered in the south of the island he diversified into mining and into the production of sulphur-derived acids. Sicily became the main source of sulphur in the world, and while sulphur-mining was the one activity practised on an industrial scale, the impact on those who worked in the mines was devastating.

The sulphur industry can be regarded as another of the scars not only on the landscape but on the historical consciousness of Sicily. Mines were to be found in places like Racalmuto and Agrigento, and accounts of the human cost are provided in the writings of Carlo Levi, Leonardo Sciascia, and even Luigi Pirandello. In *The Parishes of Regalpetra*, Sciascia describes piles of sulphur lying on the beaches waiting for export and also gives a moving account of the funeral of a miner whose health had been ruined by the inhalation of the noxious mineral. Pirandello was more ambiguous. His father had worked as a sulphur miner, while his wife's fortune was built on her ownership of a mine. The news that her mine was flooded and that she was ruined sent her into a state of insanity from which she never recovered. In a short story, *Ciaula Discovers the Moon*, Pirandello recounts the reaction of a young boy who had always been required to do night shifts when he was sent above ground after darkness and, to his wonder, saw the moon in the sky. The experience opened new vistas to him.

Ingham went into partnership in the sulphur business with two Sicilians, one of whom was Vincenzo Florio, Sicily's leading entrepreneur, and the venture was highly profitable. He expanded on a global scale, and was for a time owner of what is now Fifth Avenue in Manhattan. He also invested in the New York Central Railroad, but these stakes were sold off after his death by his imprudent heirs. The Anglo-Sicilian community, unlike their counterparts in the Raj, mixed with Sicilians both commercially and socially, where "socially" includes "sexually." Ingham set up house with the Duchess of Santa Rosalia, who already had four children by a previous marriage, but the two never married. His wealth allowed them to own several houses. They retained the villa in the *baglio* in Marsala and built a new one on the hills outside the city at Racalia, which is still standing. The most imposing residence was in Palermo in what is now the Grand Hotel et Des Palmes, built by Ingham in 1856. In Ingham's day the villa was surrounded by extensive gardens which stretched down to the sea, and the road in front, now Via Roma, was impressively named Via Ingham. The Anglican church facing the hotel was the private family chapel, joined to the palace by an underground walkway. Ingham was no aesthete and did not collect works of art, but the villa itself was a residence of aristocratic splendor, with a grand staircase and magnificent public rooms. Free of any need to ape English manors, he commissioned a building in contemporary Sicilian style surrounded by an English garden, highly fashionable in Italy at the time.

In 1851 Ingham retired and his company was renamed Ingham & Whitaker. By now he had three Whitaker nephews involved in what was very much a family concern, but on his death he left the company to Joseph Whitaker's second son William, whom he considered the best equipped for the task. Business historians talk of a "third generation syndrome," indicating that if the first generation of any family-run company displays originality, flair, vision, and enterprise, and the second the managerial nous to continue on well-trodden paths, the third commonly has neither and squanders the inheritance on more leisured or idle pursuits. So it was with the Ingham-Whitakers, although they were not merely drones or wastrels. The most interesting was Pip Whitaker, who developed an interest in ornithology and archaeology. He wrote the *Birds of*

Villa Malfitano, the palatial residence built in the 1880s to Pip Whitaker's specifications, now headquarters of the Whitaker Foundation

Tunisia, and made a remarkable collection of stuffed birds which is now in Belfast, no Sicilian body having been interested in acquiring it. The business in Marsala bored him, but he was fascinated by the off-shore island of Mozia, known in his time as San Pantaleo. He had the insight and erudition to conclude that this was the probable site of the lost Punic settlement of Motya, destroyed in 397 BC by the Siracusan tyrant, Dionysius. Although derided for this notion, he undertook systematic excavations and was fully vindicated. He bought over the whole island farm by farm, and Mozia is now a perfectly preserved site of inestimable historical and archaeological importance, although contemporary archaeologists are exasperated at Pip's unsystematic failure to record dates and precise locations of his discoveries.

He and his wife Tina lived in Palermo in the splendid Villa Malfitano, surrounded by parklands with plants from all over the world. It is now the headquarters of the Foundation named after him, established to pursue scholarship in classical history. There are several other Whitaker villas around the island, mainly in Palermo, once the property of different branches of the family. The palace in Via Cavour in Palermo suffered from Allied bombing but was rebuilt, with even the un-Sicilian greenery in the garden restored, and is still known as Villa Whitaker. It is the official residence of the Prefect of Palermo, and it is one of the curios of Palermo life that the villa of the first citizen has an English name which no good Sicilian can pronounce—Vitakre or Vittacare being common approximations. Villa Sofia, once the home of Joss and Effie Whitaker, is now a hospital, and although the once vast garden is now covered with medical buildings, the structure of the original villa is preserved inside the grounds. The Villa Sperlinga belonged to the same couple and was bought to provide tennis courts in what was then open country. It now houses the police drugs squad and is lost in a suburban housing estate. The Whitaker wine business in Marsala was wound up in 1928 when Mussolini made life for foreign-owned companies tricky. Life became even more difficult in 1940 when Italy entered the war against Britain, and any property remaining in Whitaker hands and not leased to Italian in-laws was confiscated, but later restored. The family's misadventures under fascism were symbolic of the way the fortunes of the British community rose and fell with the great events which shaped Sicilian and Italian history.

BRITISH RULE

Lord Nelson and his fleet operated in the Mediterranean during the wars with the French, and he docked several times in Naples, where he made the acquaintance, initially Platonic, of Lady Hamilton. The love affair of Horatio Nelson and Emma Hamilton has been told many times in novels and films, but it is not always appreciated that a large part of that relationship unfolded in Sicily. In 1798, when the French overran the south of Italy, Nelson escorted the beleaguered Bourbon rulers, together with ministers and courtiers as well as Sir William and Lady Hamilton to Palermo. By this time Nelson and Lady Hamilton were lovers, and in Palermo, together with the compliant Sir William Hamilton, they lodged in the Palazzo Palagonia.

In Sicily, Nelson and John Woodhouse became friends. The admiral had a refined palate and was pleased with the new wine, even writing to his commanding officer that it was "so good that any gentleman's table might receive it." He also deemed it fit for his sailors and placed large orders for his fleet. Even more importantly, he allowed Woodhouse to associate the Nelson name with the new wine. King Ferdinando had given Nelson the estate of Bronte, near Etna, in gratitude for his services, and the admiral, who had taken to signing himself Bronte Nelson, suggested to Woodhouse that he should name the wine Bronte Marsala. This is one of the earliest instances of celebrity sponsorship, but unlike modern footballers or film stars, Nelson received no recompense. The producers of Marsala also received a boost from Napoleon's imposition of the Continental Blockade, an embargo on trade with Britain. There were doubtless more serious consequences, but one result was that fortified wines could no longer be imported from Portugal or Madeira. The Anglo-Sicilians provided a substitute for the bibulous requirements of the British upper class in the form of Marsala.

In the late eighteenth century there was a network of Englishmen in the Kingdom of the Two Sicilies occupying positions of power unparalleled since Norman times. The prime minister was Sir John Acton, and Sir William Hamilton himself, British Minister in Naples, was a man of considerable standing in the Bourbon court. Sir William, a renowned antiquarian, does not deserve to be remembered only as a more or less willing cuckold, but history is not kind. Lady Hamilton became a great friend of Queen Carolina, sister of Marie Antoinette, whom everyone else detested. The royal family had to flee twice to Palermo, the second time in 1805 without Nelson, who had died at the battle of Trafalgar, and without Lady Hamilton who was back in London, but Sicily was still protected by the British fleet and army. At the peak of London's involvement there were up to 20,000 British soldiers on the island, ably commanded by a group of officers of high caliber such as Sir John Moore, later hero of the evacuation of his army from the Spanish port of Corunna (La Coruña) ahead of the pursuing French, and remembered in Thomas Moore's sonorous poem, *The Burial of Sir John Moore at Corunna*.

The period of British occupation lasted from 1806 to 1815. After Moore was recalled, his successor Lord William Bentinck was made not merely commander-in-chief of the army but given the title of Minister Plenipotentiary. Sicily was virtually a British colony and Bentinck *de facto* governor general. He was no favorite of the royal family, and it was he who was mainly responsible for the abolition of feudalism and for coaxing the monarch to accept a constitution with a bi-cameral parliament based on the British system of the Houses of Commons and of Lords. The constitution did not survive the departure of the British forces in 1815, but Bentinck's role in reforming Sicilian government was an important one.

Sicily's history could have become more closely entwined with that of Britain had moves to make Sicily part of the expanding British empire been successful. A Scottish farmer Gould Francis Leckie bought a farm near Siracusa which he worked in the years 1800-1807. He tried to improve local farming techniques and took a deep interest in Sicilian life, but his main concern was with Sicily's potential from a British point of view. He became friendly with Samuel Taylor Coleridge, then secretary to the Civil Commissioner of Malta, and with Charles Pasley, a Royal Engineer who first arrived with the army. Pasley and Leckie published books advocating "an insular empire" of the major Mediterranean islands, since these could be valuable for British trade and military purposes. "By the conquest of these [islands], Great Britain opens new fields of commerce, colonisation and riches to her own subjects," Leckie wrote. The idea of annexation was debated in the press and in the House of Lords, and in the dark days of reaction following the Congress of Vienna a Sicilian delegation came to London in the 1830s, but the policy found no favor in government circles in Westminster. In the event, Britain took possession of Malta and Cyprus but never of Sicily. History is not written of "what ifs," but in idle moments it is irresistible to wonder: what if Leckie and Pasley had had their way?

The British business community in Sicily continued expanding. In 1811 a petition to the Council of Trades and Plantations in London was signed by no fewer than 28 British firms, and it is likely there were others not represented. It was estimated that in the decades after the Napoleonic War some 40 per cent of Sicily's exports went to Britain and 32 per cent of its imports were made by British companies. A survey published in 1812 found that the British community was served by 32 consuls and vice-consuls. The Anglicans established several churches all over the island. William Sanderson, who had served with the army, returned in 1817 to set up in Messina a business in citrus fruit derivatives and in soap. He prospered on a royal scale, and built a palatial villa surrounded by the inevitable and beautifully laid out garden stretching down to the sea. His family too intermarried with well-to-do Sicilians and Anglo-Sicilians. Joseph Whitaker married Sophia Sanderson, after whom Villa Sophia in Palermo

John Henry (Cardinal) Newman, the most unlikely of travelers to Sicily. He went to study the classical civilization, but was entranced by the landscape and the people

is named. The Villa Sanderson in Messina is now the Villa Pace and is the property of the University of Messina.

English gardens would deserve a special mention of their own. There is still a *giardino inglese* in Palermo, although there is very little today which is especially English. A similarly named garden in Taormina is still largely laid out as it was designed by Florence Trevelyan. The nineteenth-century British community in Taormina was anything but commercially minded. The draw was the beauty of the town, its permissive morals, and the attractiveness of the local boys. More surprisingly, there is an English garden in Bagheria not far from the famed Villa Palagonia.

Visitors and travelers are too numerous to mention, but one of the most unusual was Cardinal John Henry Newman, beatified by Pope Benedict in 2011. He traveled over the island in 1832 on the only extended trip abroad he undertook in the ninety years of his life, and wrote his impressions in *My Illness in Sicily*, an intriguing if idiosyncratic work. The nature of his illness is not clear but was clearly serious, and he interpreted his recovery as a sign that God had work for him to do in England. On his return, he established the Oxford Movement to reform the Anglican Church. He was highly impressed by the care shown by his Sicilian servant when his failing health forced him to stop at Enna. He stressed that the servant had stolen *nothing* (Newman's emphasis) and had behaved with a dedication no English servant would have shown. Oscar Wilde came after his release from prison and Churchill after losing the post-war election.

WAR AND INVASION

Churchill was mainly if not totally responsible for the Allied decision to invade Sicily in 1943, the last time foreign troops marched over the island. British and American forces had fought together in North Africa, but the Americans were anxious to move the theater of war to mainland Europe. Churchill preferred to attack the Axis powers from the south, believing that it would be possible to conduct a rapid campaign which would disable Italy and fatally weaken Germany. He and Roosevelt met at Casablanca to decide on future strategy, and Churchill carried the day. General Eisenhower was put in overall charge of Operation Husky, the invasion of Sicily, with Montgomery commanding the British Eighth Army and Patton the American Seventh Army. Sicily was bombed mercilessly, with great damage

The aftermath of the Allied invasion in 1943. The arrival of the British-American forces was viewed then as a liberation, as symbolized by the military medic

to cities and immense loss of life in all parts of the island. The fleet assembled to carry the men across the Mediterranean was possibly the largest ever assembled for any invasion in history. The soldiers landed at various points along the south of the island, the Americans landing near Gela and Licata and the British slightly to the north near Siracusa.

Military historians are uniformly scathing in their accounts of the planning and conduct of the campaign, even if it was finally successful. Montgomery himself later admitted that "Husky planning (was) a hopeless mess." Patton and Montgomery ended up in what was termed a "horse-race" to see who could take Messina first. The Nazi officers, meanwhile, could not believe their luck when they discovered there was no plan to stop them escaping to the mainland. In the Sicilian consciousness the British contribution has been written out, and the invasion is regarded as a purely American enterprise, but to demonstrate the contrary there are cemeteries around the island where men of both armies are buried. Pictures of enthusiastic Sicilians greeting the armies, rejoicing over what was by then a Liberation, of tanks making their ponderous way up narrow streets in villages, of women throwing flowers to the soldiers can be seen in various towns, such as Vizzini. An exhibition in Catania's Le Ciminiere exhibition center depicts the course of the whole campaign, including the aerial bombing which preceded the naval landing.

AMERICA'S SICILY: DIASPORA AND MYTH

The principal trade between the United States and Sicily has been the trade in ideas and in cultures. The central fact of America's relations with Sicily was emigration and the Sicilian diaspora, but Sicilian culture had a presence, not always positive, in the mind of many of America's leading creative spirits. In the early decades of the twentieth century America represented the dream ideal for impoverished Sicilians, and later American cinema and popular music gave that dream a more identifiable form.

The invasion of Sicily in 1943 brought to the island vast numbers of American soldiers, many of Sicilian descent and able to converse in the various dialects of the people they met. Most of the diaries and reports written at the time focus, unsurprisingly, on tactical and logistical problems, on casualties and on the maneuvers of the Italian and German armies rather than on the ways of the Sicilians themselves, but there are some incisive if also curious passages provided by the most distinguished of all war reporters, the future Nobel Prize winning novelist, John Steinbeck. He records a conversation about Palermo with a captain with a vivid imagination and a firm grounding in classical literature. Steinbeck records the captain's words:

> You know what Palermo looks like. That great, big, strong mountain right beside the city and the crazy lights that get on it and then the city spilled down there at the base. It looks like Ulysses has just left there. You can really get the sense of Vergil from that mountain, from the whole northern coast of Sicily for that matter. It just stinks of the classics.
>
> Palermo is a pretty big city. The Airforce really did a job on the waterfront there. Buildings and docks and machinery and boats just blasted into junk. Except for the harbour and the waterfront, our bombers hadn't hurt it very much. The First and I walked up into the town. I tell you, there wasn't one living soul in that city. The population had moved right out into the hills and the troops hadn't come in yet. There wasn't a soul. You know those little painted carts the Sicilians have with scenes painted on them? Well, there were some of them lying on their sides and the donkeys that pulled them were lying there, dead too.
>
> Neither of us had thought to bring a flashlight. When we saw the dark coming, I think we both got panicky without any reason. We started to walk back to the waterfront and we kept going faster and faster and then we finally broke into a run. There was something about that town that didn't want us there after dark.

The famous photographer Robert Capa was on hand during the arrival of the American troops in Palermo and his vivid photographs, published in *Life*, of women clambering aboard tanks, of cheering crowds lining the streets, of bemused children gawking at unfamiliar sights, of soldiers with flowers round their necks, of officers reacting as phlegmatically as they could to embraces and kisses from Sicilian men established the enduring images of the event. In the Sicilian memory, the Liberation was an American not an Allied achievement.

The Second World War was followed by the Cold War, which meant that the US kept naval bases in Augusta and later a nuclear base in Comiso but, unlike in the case of Britain America's relations with Sicily have been determined not by a presence on the island but by the absence from it of the masses of emigrants who left Sicily to take up residence in the US. In the decades after Unification in 1860 Italians from all regions left Italy in huge numbers to escape poverty at home. Exact region by region figures are hard to come by except for the year 1906 when it has been established that around 100,000 Sicilians arrived in the US. Mussolini introduced legislation in 1924 which virtually stopped the flow, although Mussolini was also responsible for the flight of anti-fascists, many of whom found refuge in America. One of these was Giuseppe Antonio Borgese, a native of Polizzi Generosa in the Madonie mountain range as well as novelist, essayist, political activist, and author of works of acute analysis of both Sicilian and American life. In a brief article on Sicilians in America, he wrote these harsh, debatable but thoughtful words:

> If among all the white people in America, the Italians are probably the least adaptable to the Anglo-Saxon standard, perhaps it could also be said that the Sicilians are the most closed and most difficult of Italians in their way of life. This has terrible practical inconveniences but has also certain deep implications.
>
> They, my fellow-countrymen, and above all my fellow Sicilians, have helped me somewhat to explain to myself what I have come to do here in America. The first impulse, the first temptation of any one of us is to take flight, to board the first liner back home. The second state of mind consists in carving out a little niche inside this world, in staying there on our own terms, ignoring it: real emigrants, or more precisely real exiles, long-faced, with a veneer of sadness that cannot find expression but which can be recognized even on people who have been here for thirty years, and who may well have made a success of their business. I do not believe that any other race has preserved this inhibiting character, this silent objection, like ours.

America was not the only destination. In the early stages Sicilians moved inside the Mediterranean basin, particularly to nearby Tunisia. When international travel and migration became easier, Brazil and Argentina were favored destinations, although Australia was also a major draw. There is an area of Buenos Aires called Palermo, and all the major Australian cities have Sicilian societies, but increasingly the US became the destination of choice. Communities of Sicilians were established all over America, and not only in the big conurbations. Fishermen and their families settled on both the Atlantic and the Pacific coasts, and others carried on as farmers in the plains, even if on a larger scale than had been possible at home.

San Diego still has a Sicilian Festival on 20 May, while there is a Little Sicily in Chicago and a Little Palermo in New Orleans. On occasions people from the same village in Sicily moved and settled together, or more commonly followed the "chain migration" process which saw new immigrants congregate in places where relatives and friends had made their homes. Natives of Cinisi, for instance, occupied the area around E 69 Street in New York. These immigrant communities brought their traditions and feast days with them, so the feast of St. Joseph on 19 March, a significant day in the Sicilian calendar, is celebrated in many American towns. Residents of Favara came in numbers to New Orleans, and still celebrate the Feast of Maria Santissima di Favara (Most Holy Mary of Favara), and the Fisherman's Feast is still marked in Boston by people whose ancestors came from Sciacca.

The list of men and women of Sicilian ancestry who made their mark in public life in America is long, ranging from Frank Sinatra and Frankie Laine in show business to Ferdinand Pecora in politics. Pecora chaired the commission which investigated Wall Street in the aftermath of the 1929 Crash and made recommendations for the division of banking into private and entrepreneurial sections. Other well-known figures have included the cartoonist Joseph Barbera, the film director Martin Scorsese, the actor Al Pacino, and the baseball star Joe Di Maggio. There was also a darker side. Italian Americans, not only those of Sicilian descent, complain of the racial stereotyping which has seen them all branded as mobsters. Hollywood was guilty of the attribution of collective guilt long before Mario Puzo, who was of Neapolitan descent, published *The Godfather,* but there can be no doubt that the mafia or Cosa Nostra was a reality, that it was a Sicilian import and that it was irredeemably pernicious.

It has to be added that mainstream American popular culture, notably the movie industry, embraced and mythologized organized crime and was responsible for enveloping the mafia in a sinister romanticism. *Little Caesar,* with its facile glorification of the rise and fall of Rico (Edward G. Robinson) was a representative example. The novel and even more the three parts of *The Godfather* film show both sides of the one bent coin, particularly evident in that abrupt switch from the grim, grey climate outside the restaurant in which Michael clinically kills the police officer and mobster rival, to the sun-drenched orchards and beguiling palaces of Sicily where he finds refuge and a wife. There was nothing romantic about the ways in which mafia power flourished in society. Sam Giancana, who reached national notoriety for alleged involvement in various plots ranging from the attempted assassination of Fidel Castro to the assassination of J. F. Kennedy, had his fiefdom in Chicago while the activities of the "five families" in New York—Genovese, Bonanno, Gambino, Lucchese, and Colombo—were publicized by the egregious Joe Bonanno himself when he was so ill advised as to write his autobiography. *Man of Honor* was a revealing work about mafia affairs, even if also one of the most illiterate books ever penned.

Sicilian-American culture found more positive expression in the works of writers of Sicilian origin, whose goal was to keep alive a tradition, to maintain links, and preserve an identity. Sicily's rich folklore has produced a multiplicity of storytellers, whether grandmothers who gathered the children around them or more recognized tellers of tales who performed

Booker Taliaferro (originally Tagliaferro) Washington (1856-1915), born into a slave family, activist in struggle for rights for Blacks in the US and author of work which exposed conditions in Sicilian sulphur mines

at public and private feasts, and this tradition can still be glimpsed behind some of the diaspora novelists who have emerged. The cultures of Sicily and America have shown themselves to be complementary, not competing, and to be twin poles of a happy dialect where Sicily plays the part of the anarchist id to the more rationalist ego of American culture. The outstanding figure is unquestionably Jerre Mangione, whose *Reunion in Sicily* was much admired on both sides of the Atlantic, but he is not alone.

American travelers have produced arresting accounts of Sicilian life, none more so than the astonishing writer, educationalist, and activist, Booker Taliaferro Washington. He was an Afro-American but his middle name indicates Italian origins. Whatever the truth of his birth, his 1910 book *The Man Furthest Down* contains the most graphic of all exposés and condemnations of the conditions of semi-slavery in which boys were compelled to work in the sulphur mines of southern Sicily.

SICILY IN AMERICAN IMAGINATION

Sicily also exercised an unexpected fascination on two of the greatest modern American playwrights, Arthur Miller and Tennessee Williams, neither of whom had a drop of Sicilian blood. Miller was appalled at working conditions of longshoremen in Brooklyn. Every morning he watched them gather in sullen groups to wait for the foreman to come along and choose the men who would be permitted to work that day. Having made his choice, he would contemptuously toss some work tokens into the crowd, leaving the men to scramble on the ground and fight over them. After visiting Sicily in 1948, Miller believed that such conditions were a reproduction of practices imposed by landlords and their criminal agents in Sicily:

> As I realized after a trip to southern Italy and Sicily, the hiring system on the Brooklyn and Manhattan waterfronts had been imported from the Sicilian countryside. A foreman representing the landowners would appear in the town square on his horse: a crowd of job-seeking peasants would humbly form up around his spurs, and he would deign to point from favored face to favored face with his riding crop and trot away with the wordless self-assurance of a god once he had lifted from hunger that number of labourers he required for that day. In troubled times, one more element was added—the armed *carabinieri*.

At the same time Miller was intrigued by the cultural mindset of the poor Sicilian communities in America. In his political conversations with two activists who were struggling to persuade the men to rebel against their subservience, he was told of a Sicilian docker, perhaps motivated by sexual jealousy, who had committed the cardinal sin of denouncing to the American authorities two illegal immigrants of his own family. The social and individual ramifications of the dramatic masterpiece, *A View from the Bridge,* grew from that action. Miller used as commentator and chorus figure in his play Alfieri, a New York lawyer, who impotently observes the clash of the Mediterranean and the American, of the ancient and modern codes.

> But this is Red Hook, not Sicily. This is the slum that faces the seaward side of Brooklyn Bridge. This is the gullet of New York swallowing the tonnage of the world. And now we are quite civilized, quite American. Now we settle for half, and I like it better. I no longer keep a pistol in my filing cabinet.
>
> …and yet, every few years there is still a case, and as the parties tell me what the trouble is, the flat air in my office suddenly washes in with the green scent of the sea, the dust of this air is blown away and the thought comes that in some Caesar's year, in Calabria perhaps or on a cliff at Syracuse, another lawyer, quite differently dressed, heard the same complaint and sat there as powerless as I and watched it run its bloody course.

Before writing the play, Miller visited Sicily and to his dismay met in the only restaurant operating in a Palermo which was still a long way from recovering from the devastation of war Lucky Luciano, freed from prison in America in gratitude for his help with the Allied invasion of Sicily but an unwilling exile in his homeland. In his autobiography, *Timebends,* Miller provides an acute, memorable portrait of the mafia boss.

> I had a chance now to realize that I had never seen a face so sharply divided down the center. The right side was hooded, the mouth down-turned and the cheek drawn flat. This was the side he killed with. The left, however, had an eye not at all cold but rather interested and intelligent and inquisitive, his social eye, fit for a family dentist. And he wore

rimless middle-aged glasses. Lincoln was the only other man with so divided a face, at least that I could think of …

I now invented: "I'm thinking of writing about Sicily, and I want to take a look around."

"No, no, no come on, we got a car, we drive you," he persisted, and it was clear that we were not to be let out of his sight. At this point, the street door was unlocked by the bowing proprietor; I had not noticed it being locked in the first place.

"Beautiful car," I said, admiring his sporty big green Lancia as we got in, the bodyguard behind the wheel with me beside him, and Vinny in next to Luciano in the backseat.

"Gimme a Chevy anytime," he said. He certainly was homesick.

Tennessee Williams too visited Sicily, but left no record of it apart from the dedication to the play, *The Rose Tattoo,* "To Frank, in return for Sicily." It seems a reasonable exchange. Frank Merlo, who became Williams' lover, was a first-generation Sicilian. Like Miller, Williams employed a Sicilian community for a play which is in the tragic tradition and draws on the dignity, the scale of values, and a sense of precariousness of life which underlies Greek drama and is part of the Greek heritage of Sicily. The setting is precise.

> The locale of the play is a village populated mostly by Sicilians some-where along the Gulf Coast between New Orleans and Mobile. The time is the present.
>
> As the curtain rises we hear a Sicilian folk-singer with a guitar. He is singing. At each major division of the play this song is resumed, and it is completed at the final curtain.

The time is not really the present, since the cast includes archaic characters like the *strega* (witch) and the conflict concerns passions which cannot be confined by laws and transgressions of those laws which will be bring inevitable punishment. Serafina, who was played by the great Anna Magnani in the film version, was an incarnation of female sensuality, left bereft when her man, who had been involved in drug dealing, is killed, leaving her to discover only after his death that he had been unfaithful. He found Sicilians, as he had been taught to view them by his lover, the ideal embodiment of age-old human urges and clashes. Tennessee Williams created his own, American, myth of Sicily.

Chapter Seven

THE LANDING STAGE

MESSINA

At Messina the straits which separate Sicily from Reggio Calabria on the mainland are only five kilometers wide, allowing ferries, ships, and even quite small boats to ply their trade between the two coasts. When the magical forces of the *fata morgana* allow, or when, according to a duller explanation, meteorological conditions are right, the Calabrian city of Reggio and the Sicilian city of Messina seem from a distance to blend into one and make the sea between appear composed of columns and arches. In a fine poetic rapture Vincenzo Consolo regrets that the Strait of Messina does not have a time warp which would permit a glimpse of "infinite vessels, infinite sails of every shape and color, merchants and soldiers of every race: we would read infinite histories, the history that has gone by on those waters."

Since classical times the poetical-mythical significance as well as the strategic importance of Messina and the Strait have been well-known. The confluence of the Ionian and Tyrrhenian seas is nearby and the difficulties in navigating those waters were aggravated by the twin menaces of Scylla and Charybdis, known to both Homer and Virgil. Scylla is positioned near modern Ganzirri and was regarded then as a sea monster but is registered today as a rocky hazard to shipping, while the whirlpool Charybdis has now vanished with changes to currents and tide-movements. Its actual site is much debated, but it is as certain as anything can be in poetry that Odysseus sailed these waters and faced the hazards of the sea off Messina. Other poets have created their own vision of Messina; Shakespeare's *Much Ado about Nothing* is set here. There is no reason to believe that the Bard ever set foot in Messina although local historians have written books and produced documentaries demonstrating that Shakespeare's family originated in these parts, and that his English name is a literal translation of a local name, even if, unhappily, there are divisions of opinion over which local name. *Scuotilancia* or *Crollalanza* are the main contenders.

The city was the site of one of the three mythological underwater pillars on which Sicily was believed to stand, the others being near Trapani and Pachino. Once known as Trinacria (the triangular island), Sicily has as its symbol the same three-legged image as the Isle of Man. One of the most beguiling of post-classical legends concerns Colapesce (Colafish), a male creature which was half-human and half-fish but not related to the mermaids which, as sirens, were once to be seen and heard in abundance in these waters. There are many versions of the Colapesce tale but in all he dives under the sea at the behest of the King of Sicily to examine the pillar supporting Messina. In some versions, he is dismayed to find that the pillar is crumbling because of the activities of Etna and remains underwater to support the island with his own frame, but in others he returns to report that Messina will one day face ruin. And that part of his report has come true in many forms on many occasions.

Messina was the port where in modern times European travelers first disembarked in Sicily and where many armies massed to launch an invasion after making the crossing from Calabria, or before beating a retreat. History and legend merge in the tales associated with the Norman Conquest of Sicily. Count Roger, known as the Great Count, is reported to have stood in 1060 on the shores of Calabria listening across the seas to the strains of music and relishing the fragrances of lemons—an enduring symbol of Sicily used centuries later by Goethe in a poem. He was told that Sicily was under Muslim control, and to reinforce his shaky resolve to return the island to Christian hands, Morgan Le Fay, the sorceress of Arthurian legend incorporated into Sicilian lore, came to meet him and allowed him to see in a vision a path by which Messina could be reached by land. He swore he would liberate Sicily in the name of another lady, the Virgin Mary, and launched his invasion the following year. By sea.

Messina has had to face adversaries even more pernicious than human malice. All Sicilian cities have been caught up in a struggle with nature at its most destructive—earthquake, volcanic eruption, flood—as well as with humankind at its most savage—war, invasion, enslavement, and more recently aerial bombardment. Messina has suffered them all except volcanic eruption, since not even the power of Etna reaches so far. The city has had to be periodically rebuilt, with the result that Messina is both one of the most ancient of Sicilian cities and the most modern.

Modern Messina is a city of straight roads, tree-lined avenues, and nineteenth-twentieth-century buildings where occasional *art nouveau* gems by Ernesto Basile are scattered among the brutalist tower blocks whose functional ugliness is imposed by company accountants. Buildings from other times do survive, and some, notably the cathedral, have been rebuilt in accordance with the same architectural principles as their destroyed predecessors, but Messina's history cannot be traced in stone as is the case with other Sicilian cities, or at least not so completely.

There is, then, no guarantee that the modern traveler is really seeing the same city his or her predecessors saw. "The approach to Messina is the finest that can be imagined," wrote Patrick Brydone, and this is still largely true but it is more doubtful if he would still be of the opinion that "the quay exceeds anything I have ever seen, even in Holland." The modern quay is a bustling, untidy, chaotic port, with queues of cars waiting to be loaded onto ferries and lines of anxious passengers searching for signs to indicate the correct entrance to their ship. It is dominated still by a high column with *The Madonna of the Letter*, the letter in question being supposedly written in 42 AD by the Virgin Mary herself to promise her protection to the city. There has been in history much acrimonious theological dispute over which language is used in the kingdom of heaven, but the

Statue of the Virgin Mary at the entrance to the port of Messina, greeting visitors and blessing the city

actual words inscribed on the plinth are in Latin, which would appear to clinch the argument. *Vos et ipsam civitatem benedicimus* (We Bless You and the City Itself), it reads. The delivery of the letter is celebrated on 3 June, when the *Varetta*, a festive trolley holding a statue of Mary handing over the letter, is pulled around streets by the ecclesiastical confraternities, all bedecked in traditional outfits. This is not to be confused with the celebrations on 15 August when the structure called the *Vara* is similarly paraded around the streets on the feast of the Assumption. The movement of this alarmingly tall, unstable, swaying structure seemingly depicts the flight of Mary's soul into heaven.

The arrival in Messina by train-ferry, which has been operating since 1899, is exhilarating, even for those drugged into torpor after what may have been a draining trip from Rome. The train itself is loaded onto the ferry, a process which can take up to three hours but which allows the traveler to go out onto the deck and savor the first sight of Sicily. To the far right at Capo Peloro, the very tip of the island, stands a lighthouse and to the left behind the city are the Peloritani Mountains, rugged and uneven, capped by inaccessible castles or sanctuaries and only for brief periods in mild seasons covered by temperate green grass. In spite of earthquakes and tidal waves, the harbor retains the sickle-like shape on which ancient writers commented and which gave the city its first name, Zancle. The lines of cars on the roads alongside the port scarcely add to the charm of the sight, but small craft and fishing boats in whatever state of repair scudding over the water cannot fail to create an attractive if not quite picturesque scene. The city is dominated by the Church of Cristo Re (Christ the King), built in 1937 to commemorate soldiers killed in the First World War. The view over Messina from the piazza in front of the church is spectacular.

The experience of first arrival will change if the much debated Bridge over the Strait is finally built. The project was first mooted at least a century ago by Giuseppe Garibaldi in a meeting with the King, and in the post-Second World War era various projects were drawn up, announced with fanfare, celebrated in the press and quietly forgotten. Silvio Berlusconi revealed himself a more strenuous advocate than any previous prime minister, and commissioned architects and engineers to draw up plans. In 2009, he even arrived in the city to lay the first stone, but years later the second stone is still unplaced. During the judicial enquiry into the feasibility of the Bridge (the capital letters are *de rigueur*) satellite technological data were produced to show that Sicily was moving inexorably away from mainland Italy, even if only by a couple of millimeters a year. This fact led some comedians to suggest that the Bridge would have to be made of elastic or rubber. Opinion in Messina is divided over the desirability of the Bridge, but the changes it will make to life in Sicily, not only in Messina, will be deep and lasting. If it is ever built.

A Long History

Messina is accustomed to change. History states that when it was founded, Rome was not even a village. It was populated in prehistoric times, and its first name Zancle can still be seen over several local shops. Greek settlers made it their own, and the early *Messinesi* had the shrewdness to side with Rome in the war against Carthage. In gratitude the Romans raised the status of the city, a move which was of importance in its rivalry with Palermo for primacy in Sicily. In the Byzantine era Calabria became a center for monastic orders and hermits, many of whom gravitated to Messina and the surrounding area. Messina's next moment of real European prominence came with the Crusades. The city was a crucial stopping-off point, and among those who spent time there en route for the Holy Land was the English King Richard the Lion Heart, who did nothing to endear himself to the inhabitants of the city.

In succeeding centuries Messina was an arena in the war of civilizations between Christian and Islamic forces. The Emperor Charles V arrived in 1535 fresh from his victory in the Battle of Tunis to oversee the building of fortifications and castles such as the well preserved fort of San Salvatore (Holy Savior) on the peninsula, which Richard the Lion Heart had attacked. The Gonzaga castle, some seven kilometers to the south-east of the city center, was built in the same period. It has suffered from civic neglect but its star-shaped structure, moat, and tunnels around bastions are in good shape. In 1571 the Christian fleet, led by Don John of Austria, son of Charles V, returned to Messina after victory over the Turks in the Battle of Lepanto. In Piazza Catalani a bronze statue of Don John with his foot firmly planted on the head of the Turkish admiral, Ali Bassa, was erected in 1573 to commemorate the victory. The old gods of Messina, Neptune, and Orion are embedded into the pedestal. Neptune was accorded that honor as lord of the seas, while Orion had the position as defender of peace and honor. Both gods have fountains in their honor elsewhere in the city, Orion's in front of the cathedral and Neptune's in Piazza Unità d'Italia. The statue of Don John, on the other hand, has had ups and downs which reflect Messina's history. It was damaged in the anti-Spanish insurgency of the years 1674-78, was knocked off its pedestal by the earthquake in 1783, and has survived subsequent tremors. There is no plaque to record the fact that Cervantes, author of *Don Quixote*, was taken to recover from injuries sustained at Lepanto to a hospital which used to stand alongside the Church of Santa Maria degli Alemanni (Our Lady of the Germans). In 1943, in the course of the Sicilian campaign, Messina, being the port nearest to the mainland, was bombed relentlessly by the Allies, perhaps more relentlessly than any other Italian city. The devastation was overwhelming. The American historian Carlo D'Este uncovered a report by a fascist officer who arrived in the city to discover

> …the harbour still in flames, the city half destroyed, and the population in a state of terror. No one seemed to have foreseen a disaster of such magnitude… Everyone including the military was in a confused and despairing frame of mind… we witnessed four frightful bombardments of Messina, Villa San Giovanni and Reggio. Messina was destroyed beneath our very eyes… we were surrounded by straggling, ragged bands of soldiers, sailors and airmen (particularly the latter two) making their way by German ferries to the mainland. There were painful sights at the stations of Scilla and Bagnara. Crowds of soldiers and civilians were storming the trains.

The history of man's inhumanity to man, however poignant or tragic it may be, is only one side of the story of Messina. The other is the tussle with natural forces. If all Sicily is, in the bloodless words of scientists, an area of high seismic activity, this is emphatically true of Messina. There are records of earthquakes in ancient times and unquestionable evidence of major quakes in 1169, 1295, 1693, 1783, and 1908. That is not a complete list. The earthquake of 1693 caused devastation over the whole of eastern Sicily. The toll of death and the destruction in 1783 made even pious chroniclers wonder where God was. Goethe visited the city as part of his journey through Sicily in 1786, and recorded

Desolate, abandoned victims of the great earthquake in eastern Sicily in 1908

…a terrifying picture of a devastated city. For a good quarter of an hour we rode on our mules through ruin after ruin till we came to our inn. This was the only house which had been rebuilt, and from its upper floor we looked out over a wasteland of jagged ruins. Outside the premises of this sort of farmstead, there was no sign of man or beast. The silence during the night was uncanny.

The 1908 quake may have been the worst to affect any European town, ever. The epicenter was Messina itself, it occurred at 5.20 a.m. and was followed by a tsunami. The loss of life and destruction of property were on an apocalyptic scale. It is now calculated that perhaps 93 percent of the city's buildings were destroyed or damaged so badly that they had to be demolished, and estimates put the number of people killed at anything between 60,000 and 120,000.

D. H. Lawrence found the city still in a state of shock and devastation when he visited it in 1921 en route for Sardinia.

Oh horrible Messina, earthquake-shattered and renewing your youth like a vast mining settlement, with rows and streets and miles of concrete shanties, squalor and a big street with shops and gaps and broken houses still, just behind the tram-lines, and a dreary-hopeless port in a lovely harbour. People don't forget and don't recover. The people of Messina seem to be today what they were nearly twenty years ago, after the earthquake: people who have had a terrible shock, and for whom life's institutions are really nothing, neither civilisation nor purposes. The meaning of everything all came down with a smash in that shuddering earthquake, and nothing remains but money and the throes of some kind of sensation. Messina between the volcanoes, Etna and Stromboli, having known the death-agony's terror. I always dread coming near the awful place, and yet I have found the people kind, almost feverishly so, as if they knew the awful need of kindness.

Civilization and purpose did return to Messina with the rebuilding programme. The town planning in the aftermath aimed at a dramatic redesign of the city. If the *piano regolatore* is now criticized for being too drastic and disrespectful of the city's heritage, the central aim was to reconstruct in such a way as to ensure that Messina was able to withstand any such catastrophes in the future. Some surviving structures were pulled down, but others of historical value were either preserved or rebuilt.

THE CATHEDRAL AND SURROUNDS

The cathedral on Piazza Duomo has suffered from the recurring natural disasters to which the city is prone. It is believed that a temple to Neptune stood on the site. It was followed by an early Christian church, which was in its turn converted into a mosque by the Muslim authorities. The Norman Count Roger demonstrated his special affection for Messina by ordering in 1078 the construction of a new cathedral, and in spite of later modifications and radical reconstructions, the present building preserves the broad lines of the original Norman architecture. It was consecrated in the presence of Henry IV in 1197, but during the later ceremonials in 1254 accompanying the funeral of Corrado IV the wooden roof caught fire. The cathedral was again damaged in the 1693 earthquake, and suffered yet more damage in 1783 when the bell-tower collapsed. Reconstruction was ordered but received a setback in the tremors of 1894.

In 1908 the cathedral was again razed to the ground. It was decided that the restored building should respect the Norman inspiration. It was consecrated in 1929, only to be destroyed by the Allied bombing. There are heart-breaking photographs of the ruined walls and collapsed roof outside the cathedral, and inside the statue of St. John the Baptist by Antonello Gagini still shows burn marks from the fires caused by the bombing.

The cathedral stands on a lower level than the nearby streets, the result of movements caused by the instability of the area. The magnificent façade which dominates the surrounding area is divided into two tiers, the upper tier of stone and the lower of marble. The centerpiece is an elaborate entrance porch with saints neatly tucked into their niches, and vigorously executed scenes of country life. The reconstruction allows visitors to see why this building was once viewed along with Cefalù and Monreale as part of a chain of great Norman cathedrals, and its preservation even as a faint simulacrum of the original is a testimonial of the determination of the *Messinesi* to maintain a historical continuity. Much of this façade is, incredibly, a survival from the medieval original, but the same cannot be said for the interior, grandiose though it is. The wooden, beehive roof and

The cathedral and bell-tower in Messina, destroyed by the indifferent malice of nature and the premeditated malice of man. Always rebuilt as it had been "before"

the huge Christ Pantocrator over the high altar are reproductions which recall works in similar style carried out by Arab-Norman craftsmen in the Cappella Palatina (Palatine Chapel) in Palermo. Behind the modern organ lies the tomb of Anglo-Norman Archbishop Palmieri, whose name was actually Palmer. He died in 1195, and his tombstone is the oldest surviving craftwork in the cathedral.

The bell tower is a curiosity in its own right. There has been a *campanile* of some sort for centuries, from time to time reduced to rubble and rebuilt, so the present one dates only from 1933. It claims to have the largest astronomical, mechanical clock in the world and crowds gather for the performance it puts on daily at one o'clock. The lion which stands on a level above a cockerel gives a brief roar, the cockerel itself flaps its wings and crows, an angel nods its head, and small figurines process on a platform to the strains of *Ave Maria*. Statues of two local women, Dina and Clarenza, who distinguished themselves in the Sicilian Vespers rebellion in 1282, stand on either side of the cockerel.

The center of the piazza is occupied by the elaborately carved Fountain of Orion, the work of a Tuscan sculptor Giovan Angelo Montorsoli, who was a pupil of Michelangelo. A church once stood on this spot but was demolished on the orders of the senate in 1547 to make way for the fountain, which features substantial, Michelangeloesque male nudes representing four great rivers, Nile, Tiber, Ebro, as well as the Camaro which supplied Messina with water. Orion, looking very pleased with himself, stands atop three levels of smaller statues grouped in inside circular basins. The base is decorated very prettily with masks, angels, and other motifs.

The pillars and vaulted ceiling of what was once Santa Maria del Graffeo (Our Lady of Graffeo, the name of a noble family), a church of some importance in the Middle Ages, stands nearby on Via 1 Settembre. At the Great Schism of 1168, when the Eastern Orthodox Church and the Western Catholic Church separated, the congregation wobbled between the two, finally ending up on the Catholic side. The church was damaged in 1783, rebuilt in 1852, but weakened again in 1908, and so pulled down by the City Council to make the replacement building conform to new anti-seismic standards. In Via Cardines the Church of Santa Annunziata dei Catalani (Our Lady of the Annunciation) has survived successive earthquakes intact. Curiously enough, it is considered to have benefited from the 1908 earthquake in the sense that the basic structure survived and later, discordant modifications were swept away. It was originally a Norman church but was given in the sixteenth century to the Catalan community. The style is not Catalan-Gothic, but an earlier Romanesque, with some overlay of Byzantine and Arab-Norman motifs. It is on a lower level than the surrounding streets and although it is perhaps the most remarkable building in Messina, it can only be admired from the outside since it is rarely open.

The former Church of Santa Maria degli Alemanni (Saint Mary of the Germans), in Via Garibaldi has had a chequered history. The name derives from the fact that it was the chapel of the crusading Teutonic knights, given to them by King Henry VI of Sicily, himself German, when the order was still young. It is one of the few examples of "pure" Gothic, that is, neither Norman nor Catalan, in Sicily. When the order left, it became a parish church but suffered in the 1783 earthquake and was never really rebuilt. During the Napoleonic Wars, British forces in Sicily under Lord Nelson used it as a weapons dump. The British-American bombing raids in 1943 wreaked further havoc, and the church lay abandoned for decades with nothing more than some walls remaining. It was recently restored for use as a conference center or concert hall.

Artworks

The Via Garibaldi has other, more modern, attractions. The Cassa di Risparmio (Savings Bank) is a work in the *art nouveau* style by Ernesto Basile. The Vittorio Emanuele is a mid-nineteenth-century theater built in a period of intense theatrical activity when, following political centralism, every town was driven by a need to emphasize cultural diversity and autonomy. It suffered damage in the 1908 earthquake but its structure remained intact, so it was reconstructed. If it is not remarkable architecturally, it houses a vigorous painting by Renato Guttuso of the dive of Colapesce, his ribs carefully picked out and a small penis protruding almost unobtrusively from his athletic body. His dive is watched by entranced, highly sensual, mermaids with disheveled hair, open mouths, and generous breasts.

An unexpected British contribution to the city is the Villa Sanderson, now rechristened Villa Pace and housing the university's drama and music departments. The palace overlooks the port in the direction of Calabria, and Sanderson had actually sold it before the 1908 earthquake reduced it to rubble. It was rebuilt according to the original design but then briefly abandoned before being acquired by the university. Restoration work is still underway. The gardens cover only a small part of the family's private park, but they are attractively laid out and the shade offers welcome relief from the summer heat. There is an interesting photographic exhibition of family history, illustrating its rise and integration into Sicilian literary, social, and aristocratic life.

The Regional Museum has a rich collection of works of art, many of them originally in buildings destroyed in the 1908 earthquake. Byzantine and Gothic items would fully merit attention for their own merits, but the outstanding works are canvases by the two greatest artists associated with Sicily, Caravaggio, who spent time in Sicily both while fleeing from Rome to Malta to escape trial for murder and later in his flight from Malta to escape the Knights of St. John, and by Antonello da Messina.

Antonello (c1430- 79) is one of the most influential of all Renaissance artists. There are works by him in the great galleries of the western world, but the *Madonna and Child* in Messina demonstrates the artist at his best. Antonello exemplifies the mixture of the cosmopolitan spirit and the fixation with Sicily which Sicilian artists of all ages and all genres display. It was long believed that he had traveled to the Low Countries, but if this is questioned by modern art historians it is beyond doubt that he was fascinated by the new techniques of oil painting pioneered by such Flemish artists as Jan Van Eyck. His residence in Venice in 1475-76 was decisive both for him and for the development of Venetian painting, since he introduced new, Flemish-inspired styles to the Venetians and was recognized by them as an innovator and painter of genius, but as a good Sicilian he was drawn back to Messina and stayed there for the rest of his life. The *pietà* now in the Prado in Madrid has in the background identifiable buildings of the Messina of his day. In many paintings, even in his portraits of saints, he reproduced the translucent light of Sicily and the olive-colored faces of Sicilians. He was a quintessentially spiritual artist, yet was rooted to the land, and glimpses of the sea around Messina, of parts of the city and its churches crop up. The apparent simplicity, almost austerity, of his style still allows for psychological probing, so that if his religious works expose the humanity of his subjects, his human portraits are permeated by a transcendent, almost religious, feel.

Madonna and Child by Antonello, now in Messina but originally executed in Venice. Other works on the theme are now in London and Washington

Chapter Eight

SOUTHWARDS TO ETNA

THE PELORITANI MOUNTAINS

The Province of Messina is among the loveliest and most varied in all Italy. The Nobel Prize-winning poet Salvatore Quasimodo, who was brought up in those parts, referred swaggeringly to the area south of Messina as *la terra impareggiabile*, the incomparable land.

It is worth spending time in the smaller centers as well as in the big cities. Motorways are not to everyone's taste, and anyone who claims to find exhilarating the experience of driving along the stretch of *autostrada* southwards from Messina can expect dismayed or puzzled looks. The exhilaration has nothing to do with macho pleasure in speed but arises from the delight of bowling along an expertly engineered piece of road-work, with the Ionian Sea on one side and some spectacular views of the Peloritani Mountains on the other. To add spice to the journey, the time-starved traveler will catch sight of a series of attractive villages, churches, and castles perched on seemingly inaccessible mountain tops. At the uppermost point of the medieval town of Scaletta Zanclea, Frederick II's castle is an impressive, well preserved fortress which now houses a museum and has the odd name of Rufo Ruffo. The castle of Calatabiano is also eye-catching, especially at night when it is illuminated. Further on, the strong-hold in Sant' Alessio, sited for defensive purposes in the early thirteenth century on a promontory jutting out into the sea would now meet any Hollywood's director's demands for the romantic, picturesque setting. It has been fully restored and is a family residence. To cap it all, Etna in all its mystery will be visible most of the way, and when a corner is turned, quite suddenly the famous town of Taormina, with the village of Castel-mola crouching above it, comes into view.

Those who can permit themselves a more leisurely regime may choose to meander along the coast road which follows the old Roman consular Via Valeria, and while the route and the towns it goes through are unremark-able, the journey will appeal to those with the leisure to dawdle and turn off to enjoy the architectural wealth of palaces and ecclesiastical buildings in the mountain villages. The meandering, however, can only start once off the coastal stretch. It is a banal truism to say that the roads through this line of connected villages were designed for a slower means of transport, long before the invention of the internal combustion engine. The problem is that no one has told the local drivers. In every case, the roads could comfortably accommodate two cars going in opposite directions, but one lane is permanently taken up by a line of parked vehicles. Occasionally No Parking signs have been erected by optimistic councils but these have had no observable effect. Sicilians regard the freedom to park where they choose as a right, so while one line of parked cars is a manageable hazard, double parking creates more problematic situations.

Although this area has been inhabited for millennia, the villages along it are relatively modern, since it was only in the nineteenth century that it was judged safe even for fishermen to live beside the sea. The Mediterranean has always been a dangerous sea, and marauding Corsairs and Turks in search of plunder and slaves meant that those who earned their livelihood on the waters preferred to live with their families at some distance from the shoreline. The Sicilian relationship with the sea has always been a complex one. They were never lovers of it and there is no tradition of jolly sea shanties. In folk songs and in literature the sea is seen as a menace, a bringer of death and danger through storm and shipwreck, or else as a bearer of hostile forces.

The villages on the sea front have little of great historical interest, but the territory inland is a different matter. The mountainous countryside is simply beautiful, the panoramas are stunning, and many of the villages fascinating. The town of Alì is a good example. The coastal town of Alì Terme is an uninteresting spa town even if thermal baths have been there from Roman times, while Alì itself not only provides a breathtaking view of the mountains and sea but is also an intriguing, well preserved center with churches from various epochs and in various styles, not to mention two noble palaces.

The most interesting of the coastal towns is Giardini-Naxos, now a lively holiday resort, but the Naxos part of the town's name refers to the first of the Greek colonies in Sicily. Some historians speculate that the site was chosen because the currents from the Strait of Messina lose their force around that point, and the ships came to a natural stop. Substantial excavations have taken place to reveal a settlement of some size and significance, but Naxos chose to support Athens in its war with Siracusa, which meant that in revenge the Siracusan tyrant Dionysius sacked it. It never recovered. It was also within range of the eruptions of Etna, and the black stones on the beach near the site are pure lava. The museum has a store of well displayed relics of the town.

South of Naxos on a mountain top stands the ruined castle of Calatabiano, with its chapel on the hillside below it. Once the town was situated around the castle on the peak, but it moved to its present site lower down in the seventeenth century, a move that was almost completed by 1693 when the terrible earthquake devastated the east of the island. Although the castle is described as Saracen, excavations reveal that it has been used as a stronghold by every occupier of the island. Town and castle were involved in the great conflicts, such as the war against the Anjou rulers, which tore the island apart. Various battles against the Catalans were fought nearby, and its vicinity to the sea meant the castle was besieged by the Turks in the sixteenth century. There are tales of a gallant defence by 150 Spanish soldiers against a French army in 1677, but the complex ended up in the possession of a Catalan family named Cruyllas, whose coat of arms appears in various parts of the town, including on the Church of San Filippo (St. Philip). The castle can now be accessed by a funicular railway and houses a café and a small concert hall. By day, the view of Etna to one side and Taormina to the other is inspiring, and just to the north are the gorges of the River Alcantara. Beautiful and restful in themselves, the gorges are also an important historical point since invaders from the Ionian Sea proceeded along this pass into the heart of Sicily.

Already in the Middle Ages contacts—military, commercial, and ecclesiastical—between the province of Messina and Calabria on the mainland were easy and frequent. Of these, the religious interchange left the deepest impact. The trackless wastes of Calabria attracted hermits and others called to the more ascetic forms of monastic life, but the region was also home to other religious communities who lived in some splendor in large complexes which included whole farms. The most prominent of these orders was the Basilian, who followed the rule of St. Basil of Caesarea, and whose influence extended to north-east Sicily. Some of the Sicilian monasteries known as Basilian were actually Benedictine, an order which flourished in Sicily after the arrival of the Normans. With the Norman introduction of feudalism, some of the peasants who worked the land near to, or owned by, orders of monks were reduced to the status of vassals. None of the great monastic complexes survives intact, but the churches which were part of them do. Isolated, abandoned, untended, deserted, and unused except for rare special feasts, they present a doleful but moving spectacle. There are three in the one district.

The first is the Norman Church of Santa Maria di Mili (St. Mary of Mili) near the village of Mili San Pietro, now isolated by the roadside on the way to the village from the sea. This was once part of a Basilian Abbey, built in 1082 by order of Count Roger. His illegitimate son Jordanus was buried here ten years later. There is a recognizable carving of the Madonna and Child over the door, but no access to the interior. All traces of the abbey buildings are gone, although there are remnants of once cultivated fields and vineyards on what were clearly abbey lands. There is a delightful scent of wild herbs in the air, but the walls of the farm workings are crumbling and the vines on the pergolas no longer bear fruit. Itala, too, was once home to a flourishing monastery, but all that remains is the eleventh-century church of San Pietro (St. Peter), standing alone in the countryside. It too was built by Count Roger as part of a once important abbey which numbered a bone of St. Stephen and a piece of the true cross among its treasures. The building is in brick, topped by an Arab-style cupola, and according to local traditions, the church and abbey were built on the spot where Count Roger defeated a Saracen army.

The real pearl among these buildings is the monastery church of Santi Pietro e Paolo (Saints Peter and Paul) a couple of kilometers outside the village of Casalvecchio Siculo, near the River Agrò, although it is more than likely that the riverbed will be dry. There are road signs, but sharp eyes are needed not to miss them. The church was first built by the Basilians in 560, destroyed by the Arabs, restored to the order by Roger II but then devastated by an earthquake in 1169. The faith of the monks was plainly of the sort that could move mountains, for they set to the work of rebuilding, this time with an architect who may have been French and who, whatever his nationality, was a visionary genius. He had a keen eye for the contours of the surrounding landscape and a talent for the ideal positioning of his work to ensure its harmony with nature. He employed local stone—limestone, pumice, sandstone, and lava rock—to produce a façade that is subdued and elegant even if multi-colored in red, white, and black.

The glory has departed, but the splendor and the beauty remain. The isolated church of Saints Peter and Paul at Casalvecchio Siculo

The architectural style is predominantly Byzantine with evidence of the intervention of Arab and Norman craftsmen, but the whole blends to perfection. The grand arch over the main entrance offers cover to an inscription in Greek and to a Greek cross enclosed in a roundel. The side walls are embellished by *trompe-l'oeil* arches which are actually embedded into the walls. Originally there were four cupolas, now gone but replaced by an unusual upper layer, narrower than the nave of the church and topped by turrets resembling battlements. Once this was a place of great prestige and the abbot sat as of right in the Sicilian parliament. The monks left in 1794 but the church remains a thing of majesty and beauty and even holiness. It is officially closed, rarely visited, and certainly off the beaten track but there is a house alongside, and if requested the inhabitants may let you see the interior.

There are four traditional burghs or *comuni* in the Peloritani Mountains: Fiumedinisi, Mandanici, Forza d'Agrò, and Savoca. I would bow reverentially to Fiumedinisi in homage to its past but move on. Mandanici is a small but intriguing place. Probably founded by the Saracens, it passed to Norman control after a campaign by Count Roger. The Basilians were here too, and their monastery is still intact but uninhabited. It belongs to the local authority, which is unsure what to do with it and would welcome proposals. In the central piazza the cathedral faces the Palazzo Scuderi, named after the once dominant family. The library boasts a remarkable collection of sixteenth-century books, mainly medical, which were found in a garage in the town, having been presumably thrown out by someone who could see no value in them.

Savoca, founded by Roger II in 1139 at the top of a very high mountain, is a village so pretty that it seems stolen from Wonderland. It was donated by the king to a Basilian monastery in Messina. The visitor is greeted on the approach road by a modern metal sculpture of a horse under a canopy, lying on its back and kicking its legs in the air, a work of uncertain significance by a local sculptor. The village has four quarters, and incredibly the San Rocco district was occupied by fishermen, even though the sea is viewed in the distance and the climb is steep. The town is not on

The Bar Vitelli in Savoca was used as a set for *The Godfather*, frequented in the film by Michael Corleone, as photos on the wall remind visitors

a plateau but sprawls upwards from the lower piazza to a castle at the top of the mountain. The sight of the receding horizons, glimpsed through mountain passes to a point where the sea and clouds meet, is marvelous. If there is some dubiety about the horse sculpture, there is none about another in the piazza depicting a cinema cameraman peering into his machine. Savoca was the village used in 1971 for shooting the Sicilian scenes in *The Godfather*. The Bar Vitelli was where Michael Corleone, who had abandoned his American girlfriend when he fled to Sicily to evade a murder charge, met the Sicilian woman he would marry. The bar has, for obvious reasons, remained as it was when Francis Ford Coppola was a client. The *coppola* (Sicilian beret) and dummy *lupara*, the weapon favored by mafia assassins, will be made available to anyone who wishes to be photographed in the part.

The village terms itself a *città d'arte* and is a work of art in itself. It has a remarkable number of churches, including a Capuchin monastery with catacombs containing the mummified bodies of the town's notables from the seventeenth century onwards. The castle at the top is a romantic ruin, and by its very existence the village as a whole is an act of homage to the versatility, adaptability, and creative force of human beings. Every odd corner, no matter how dangerous, that could be productive has been pressed into agricultural use. Casalvecchio Siculo, with its remarkable church, is further along the road from the village.

Forza d'Agrò—and its inhabitants—were once the possession of the nearby Basilian monastery of Saints Peter and Paul. It has become a fashionable spot for evening visits since the mountain air is fresh and there are several high quality restaurants. The fifteenth-century church of the *Triade*, an unusual name for the Trinity, has a striking façade and is approached through an even more striking Catalan-Gothic archway.

TAORMINA

Perhaps no city has ever been the object of so much unstinting lyrical praise as Taormina. The French short-story writer, Guy de Maupassant visited Sicily in the spring of 1885, and went into raptures over Taormina.

> If a man were to pass only one day in Sicily and asked, "What must I see?" I would unhesitatingly reply, "Taormina."

It may be only a landscape, but a landscape where can be found all that seems made on this earth to seduce the eyes, the mind and the imagination.

The town is attached to a rock in such a way that it seems to have rolled down from the summit, but we will do no more than pass through it, although it does contain some pretty remains from the Past, and we will make for the Greek theatre to see the sun go down.

Speaking of the theatre in Segesta, I said that the Greeks as the incomparable embellishers they were, knew how to choose the one place where a theatre had to be constructed, that spot made for the delight of the artistic sense. The theatre at Taormina is so marvellously positioned that there cannot be any place like it in the whole world.

Ernest Hemingway did not focus so exclusively on the attractions of the Greek theater when he was in Taormina in 1918. He had been working as a stretcher bearer with the Italian army in the battles along the Isonzo river in what is now Slovenia, and had fallen in love with an American nurse with a very German name, Agnes von Kurowsky. At the invitation of an American captain, Jim Gamble, who may have been captivated by Hemingway's handsome appearance as much as by his overwhelming personality, he went to spend some time in Taormina. Gamble paid all the bills and even offered to subsidize Hemingway for an entire year's residence in Italy. Agnes suspected Gamble's motives and made Hemingway decline the offer, although that did not stop her jilting him shortly afterwards. Hemingway later boasted that he had never actually seen Taormina or anything of Sicily except what could be seen from a bedroom window, because en route he had been kidnapped by the female owner of a hotel who had taken all his clothes and kept him captive. It was typically Hemingway braggadocio, and the following year, suffering from nostalgia for Sicily, he wrote to Gamble:

> Every minute of every day I kick myself for not being in Taormina with you. It makes me so damned homesick for Italy and whenever I think that I might be there and with you. Chief, honest I can't write about it. When I think of old Taormina by moonlight and you and me, a little illuminated some times, but always just pleasantly so, strolling through that great old place and the moon path on the sea and Aetna fuming

Mount Etna dominates the landscape—the view from Taormina

away and the black shadows and the moonlight cutting down the stair-way back of the villa. Oh Jim it makes me so damn sick to be there.

The origins of the town are Greek, and theirs is the credit for the majesty of the setting. No doubt later Greek writers, anticipating what would be written today by aesthetes about modern Taormina, complained of the vulgar Romans and what they did to their brilliant planning of both town and theater and, especially in the case of the theater, their complaints were justified. Taormina chose the wrong side in the Roman civil war between Augustus and Pompey which followed the assassination of Julius Caesar, and Augustus made them pay by expelling all the inhabitants. It was briefly capital of eastern Sicily under Byzantine rule, was sacked by the Saracens but taken by the Normans.

It fell into a lengthy period of provincial decline in the Middle Ages, so much so that in the 1770s Patrick Brydone noted that "this once famous city is now reduced to an insignificant burgh." Other travelers, however, proclaimed the magnificence of its classical remains, and from that time the chorus of praise has been loud and—almost—unanimous. John Henry Newman wrote that he had "never known that nature could be so beauti-ful," and even believed that he would be "a better, more religious man if

[he] lived there." The Milanese writer Edmondo De Amicis proclaimed: "I believe in Paradise because I have seen it." Not all visitors were so uplifted to transcendental levels. Gustav Klimt did a painting entitled *The Ancient Theatre in Taormina* for the Burgtheatre in Vienna, and while the work is an act of homage to theater in general, only the seascape visible behind the steamy nudes glimpsed through a keyhole has any real connection with the Greek theater in the town. Residents have included D. H. Lawrence, Guy de Maupassant, Oscar Wilde, the last Kaiser Wilhelm II, King Edward VII, and the list of celebrated visitors is endless. All have with more or less elegant turns of phrase agreed with Goethe.

After its "rediscovery" in the later eighteenth century Taormina became the reserve of the élite of wealth and power, not all of whom aimed to be better or more religious persons. In the late nineteenth century, mainly due to German aristocrats who settled there, it came to notoriety as a gay playground, and postcards from that era featuring naked local youths in "Greek" poses still circulate. Various English people arrived too, and in a very English way at least four of them embellished the town with gardens. The most distinguished of these was Lady Florence Trevelyan Trevelyan (she was a Trevelyan on both sides), who married the mayor of the town and left her garden to the local council. It goes by a variety of names—Giardino Pubblico, Giardino Trevelyan, or Parco Duchi di Cesarò, since questions of inheritance meant that the official donation was made by a duke of that name, but it is Lady Florence who deserves the credit. She planted trees from Australia that were then exotic, but her distinctive contribution was a series of strange pavilions to which she was plainly very attached.

Daphne Phelps, a somewhat formidable English woman, inherited in 1948 a house in Taormina from an uncle, and after overcoming initial misgivings, settled there for the rest of her life. She developed an interest in archaeology, and her many guests included Bertrand Russell and Dylan Thomas, as she recounts in her engaging memoir, *A House in Sicily.* The house itself, the *Casa Cuseni,* has been declared a "place of cultural and historical importance" by the Sicilian Commission for Fine Arts.

D. H. Lawrence with his wife Frieda settled outside the town at Fontana Vecchia in 1920 after leaving Capri. He loved Taormina, but not its English residents, as he made clear in his correspondence:

We have quite a lovely villa on the green slope high above the sea, looking east over the blueness, with the hills and the snowy shallow crest of Calabria on the left across the sea, where the straits begin to close in. The ancient fountain still runs, in a sort of little cave-place down the garden—the Fontana Vecchia—and still supplies us…

The worst of Taormina is that it is a *parterre* of English weeds all cultivating their egos. Imagine nettle overtopping dandelions, the languors and lilies of virtue here very stiff and prickly, the roses and raptures of vice a little weedy and ill developments and ill developed. Save me from my countrymen.

The "weeds" Lawrence complained of are now of a more international variety. Along with Cefalú, Taormina has become the most popular holiday destination in Sicily, and recently misgivings have been voiced by those who consider that a process of irreversible vulgarization is underway. "One can't cavil with paradise," admits the American writer Helen Barolini, awed by the perfect positioning of the site on a mountain top between the Ionian Sea and Mount Etna, but (there is of course a *but*) "Taormina is overrun by tourists and has lost its identity to them." Yes. We would all rather see ourselves as refined travelers and wish ourselves free of bothersome tourists. There is some validity to the complaints, whatever the lofty, patrician tones in which they are made, over the ubiquitous display of general kitsch such as the low-quality ceramics and spurious puppets, or over the crush on the main streets at the height of the season.

Yet the marvelous distinctiveness of Taormina has not been lost. The town, and not only the theater, is still magnificent. The main street runs between the Porta Messina and the Porta Catania, following the lines of the Roman Via Valeria, and if it is now an outdoor shopping mall, it retains evident traces of past splendor. The Piazza Vittorio Emanuele just inside the Porta Messina is the spot where the Roman forum and previously the Greek agora were sited, and is the ideal place to relish the beauty of the surrounding landscape. The Palazzo Corvaia still has some Arab details in the turrets in the central building, but it presents itself now as a unified piece of fifteenth-century architecture. Its inner courtyard with a Catalan staircase and some decorative motifs in the same style is its most striking feature. The Catalans are also mainly responsible for the façades of the town's palaces. There is a small, semi-circular Roman theater near the

Fountain in Piazza Duomo, Taormina, built in 1635, depicting an odd
being, half horse and half woman

Porta Messina, and although it looks fairly complete, part of the space it
occupied is now taken up by the Church of Santa Caterina (St. Catherine).
None of the churches, not even the cathedral, has any special quality, but
the piazza outside the cathedral has a strange fountain with creatures of the
sea and a centaur which is, unusually, half-female. This being has been
raised to the status of town symbol.

Taormina is not a large town, and after walking the length of the
Corso it is good to wander around the back streets with their attractive
little corners and lanes. Alongside the cathedral is a staircase leading down
to what is now a hotel but was once the powerful friary of San Domenico
(St. Dominic). The owners are jealous of the élite quality of their hostelry
and are not keen on allowing entry to non-residents, but it is worth per-
severing or even splashing out on an aperitif. The hotel was bombed by the
Allies in 1943 when it was the headquarters of Marshal Kesselring, but
the cloisters are well preserved. There are austere religious paintings
hanging on the walls over fashionable drinks cabinets and it is incongruous
to see fastidious waiters with trays of canapés float heedlessly about under
plaques with sacred inscriptions in Latin.

The *naumachia* is described by some as one of the most important
Roman remains in all Sicily. Goethe was not moved and wrote that the

remains "demand of the spectator a considerable talent for imaginative reconstruction." If he lacked that quality, what chance is there for the rest of us? But persist. There is no equivalent of the great aqueducts to be found in some Spanish cities, but Roman engineers had a flair for providing water supplies to the cities they ruled. The *naumachia* and its immediate surrounds may have had various uses. It was principally a cistern for collecting water for the town but, as the Greek name suggests, it may have been used for the mock sea battles which Roman crowds enjoyed. Perhaps there was also on the site a nymphaeum, a shrine to the beguiling spirits who lived near springs and fountains. Behind it, the Castello Saraceno (Saracen Castle) can be reached via a staircase and there are spectacular views along the way and from what remains of the castle, which is also the site of the ancient Greek acropolis. Higher up still is Castelmola, a beautifully preserved medieval town which has yet another castle, this time Norman.

Apart from the town's loveliness and unparalleled natural site, the fame of Taormina is linked to the unsurpassed and unsurpassable beauty of the Teatro Greco (Greek Theatre). Faced with this celestial construction, writers either throw in their hand and provide dull statistics of the numbers of tiers of seating dug into the rock, of the size of the stage and orchestra or of the number of columns erected at the portico at the top of the stalls, or else they abandon themselves to flights of poetical whimsy. Goethe expressed the view that the theater represents a "stupendous work of Art and Nature." Vincent Cronin memorably compared the theater to a seagull, "poised halfway between two elements," land and sea. The awesomeness of this unique structure derives from the majestic vision of the original Greek architect in the third century BC, a nameless figure who ranks with Christopher Wren and Palladio in terms of architectural genius. His theater was positioned to emphasize and even enhance what nature had provided at that spot—a panorama of sea, sky, headlands, inlets, mountains and, most of all, of that one mountain that Sicilians still call simply *a muntagna*, Etna itself. The Greek audience could see the volcano behind the on-stage action, and they were heirs to systems of poetics and philosophies which allowed them to relish the clash and the harmony of natural and human drama. The Roman audience expected ruder fare, so in the second century AD they modified the theater to make it an amphitheater or an arena where their drama could be performed but also where gladiators could meet. They built a back stage and arches, so the

The Greek theater in Taormina, with the spectacular view which enhanced the theater but must have distracted spectators

theater as seen today is largely Roman. The Greek genius behind it is muffled, but not concealed.

MOUNT ETNA

The ancients knew what caused the eruptions of Mount Etna. The most ferocious of the Titans was Typhon, even if he had respectable parentage, being the offspring of Zeus, the king of the gods, and Gaia, the earth mother. Fire flashed from his eyes and he was given to spitting out flaming rocks from his mouth. When he went too far by opposing the gods themselves and even rebelling against his father, Zeus decided to deal with this problem of teenage rebelliousness once and for all by throwing Mount Etna on top of him and trapping him under it. The unfortunate demigod Hephaestus, or Vulcan, rejected by his mother Hera on account of his lack of good looks, was appointed as jail-keeper. Conveniently, Vulcan had learned the trade of metal-working, which he was able to ply in the forge which was Etna. The mountain quaked and erupted with Typhon's rage, perhaps because, as some alleged, Vulcan struck Typhon with his tools, or because, as others believed, Typhon writhed or rolled about in impotent rage and agony.

The mountain makes frequent appearance in Greek and Roman mythology. Strangely, although Odysseus sailed nearby, Homer makes no reference to it, perhaps the clinching proof that Homer really was the blind poet. Virgil gave a description of the volcano and of the plight of Typhon, called in Latin Enceladus, who "gasps through each vent his sulphurous breath." The mountain also features in Pindar, who named it "the pillar of heaven," and in a tragedy by Aeschylus, who made reference to the "rivers of fire which with ravenous jaws devoured the smiling Sicily."

Another Greek, the philosopher Empedocles, was the first to attempt a scientific study of volcanoes but, unlike more modest, contemporary vulcanologists, he also aspired to be regarded as a deity and jumped into a crater in the belief that his mysterious disappearance would enhance his claims to godly status. Unfortunately, one of his sandals came loose in the jump and was found by disillusioned disciples, and the sheer banality of the discovery undermined his claims. There is still a Philosopher's Tower near the summit, although this may be connected with the god Vulcan or even have been erected in memory of the ascent made by the Emperor Hadrian rather than by the rash Greek thinker. Ovid believed that the mountain could be compared to a beast with many orifices with no telling which one would emit smoke. Lucretius dedicated a great deal of space to it in his philosophical poem *On the Nature of Things,* believing that Etna was an expression of cosmic maladies, while the philosopher-playwright Seneca in one of his philosophical epistles limited himself to encouraging more research. "This subject is a rich field for all writers," he wrote, sounding like a modern academic.

Legends about Etna continued long after the classical ages. The reputation of saints in the vicinity was made or unmade by their success in preserving the cities under their charge from eruptions. St. Agatha of Catania saved the city from the terrible eruption in 1693 when the clergy and people carried her veil towards the lava flow, and her help continues to be enlisted in emergencies today. Patrick Brydone made the ascent and found that the people of the village of Nicolosi assumed that he was heading for the place where Anne Boleyn was being eternally punished for her part in bringing about the Reformation in England. Brydone also conducted some experiments on the newly discovered phenomenon of electricity on the mountainside. His detailed account of his ascent, with its digressions into philosophy and mythology and his poetical touches, is a masterpiece of the genre of travel writing, and there are some critics who believe that his description of "this marvelous mountain" may have altered the very nature of European sensibilities and paved the way for the introduction of Romanticism, especially in Germany. Here is a typical passage:

> The ascent for some time was not steep; and as the surface of the snow sunk a little, we had tolerable good footing; but as it soon began to grow steeper, we found our labour greatly increased: however, we determined to persevere, calling to mind in the midst of our labour that the emperor Hadrian and the philosopher Plato had undergone the same; and from the same motive too, to see the rising sun from the top of Aetna. After incredible labour and fatigue, but at the same time mixed with a great deal of pleasure, we arrived before dawn at the ruins of an ancient structure, called *Il Torre del Filosofo,* supposed to have been built by the philosopher Empedocles, who took up his habitation here, the better to study the nature of mount Aetna. By others, it is supposed to be the ruins of a temple of Vulcan, whose shop, all the world knows (where he used to make excellent thunderbolts and celestial armour, as well as nets to catch his wife when she went astray) was ever kept on mount Aetna. Here we rested ourselves for some time, and made fresh application to our liquor bottle, which I am persuaded both Vulcan and Empedocles, had they been here, would have greatly approved of after such a march.

Goethe was spurred by his reading of Brydone to visit the volcano himself, although he was dissuaded from climbing up it and was told to make do with the view from the foot of Monte Rosso.

More than a micro-climate, Etna is a world to itself, obeying its own laws and producing conditions which are independent of those in the surrounding island. The peak can be covered in snow even in summer, and indeed the prosperity of the Archbishop of Catania derived in no small measure from the monopoly he enjoyed of the supply of ice to the city. It was brought down, stored in underground cellars, and put on sale in booths around the city. Remarkably, the archbishop was able to send it as far afield as Rome, where the pope was among the beneficiaries.

Regrettably modern technology has made these skills redundant, but in the course of a climb one will leave the intense heat of a Sicilian summer to pass through temperate zones and arrive in a landscape which could be arctic. Clouds, not necessarily volcanic, might swirl around the summit even on clear days, and one of the most awesome sights on earth, especially if seen from the Greek theater in Taormina, is that of the peak of Etna seemingly floating free in the skies, cut off by clouds which have wrenched it away from the rest of the mountain.

Vulcanologists are as incapable of agreeing among themselves as economists, but it has been asserted on good authority that there is reliable historical evidence of 135 major eruptions, with the term "major" impossible to define. Etna changes height and even appearance with each new eruption. The Mount Rosso which Goethe was told gives the best view of Etna was formed only after the eruption of 1669. The most recent measurement of the volcano gives it a height of 3,340 meters. A *bocca nuova*, new mouth, appeared in 1968 to become one of the four craters on the summit, but in 2011 new movements meant that it fused with the central crater to create a longer opening for the ocean of fire that lies inside and occasionally erupts. Another is called the Spanish Woman's Crater, deriving from a belief that an imprudent Spanish woman met her end there. There is also a smaller, hopefully extinct, crater at Rifugio Sapienza, which even the most timid of visitors can walk round with impunity. Those who have been on the mountain during volcanic activity bring back reports of roars, explosions, emissions of gas, and the constant fear that these relatively minor movements may at any moment be transformed into a major eruption. Etna is the most active volcano in Europe, always terrifying and majestic, always demanding respect and arousing awe, and yet in its quiet phases it can portray a gentler side. Each person will choose his own favorite aspect. Goethe heeded the advice given him, but I would recommend the view from Carruba on the north, perhaps from the train. From here, the mountain seems welcoming, almost maternal, its two great slopes stretching wide apart, like arms inviting an embrace. The level plains that break the ascent on either side make the climb seem like an afternoon walk which could be attempted with a walking stick. It cannot.

A railway line, the *Circumetnea*, leaves from Catania and runs round the side of the mountain. First opened in 1895, it runs in a great 113-kilometer loop round the volcano from Riposto to Catania and is one of

Eruptions major and minor from Mount Etna are frequent occurrences

the most fascinating railway journeys anywhere. The line has had to be reconstructed several times after eruptions buried previous tracks, and once near Giarre a lava flow swept away a bridge but helpfully filled in the ravine it crossed, making reconstruction unnecessary. It calls at a number of the little villages and affords an unrivaled view of the changing landscape with its lava fields, citrus groves, vineyards, and hardy plants and trees. Prominent among these are pistachio bushes which flourish in astonishing abundance at certain points. The line also passes aristocratic villas which have used the black lava stone in the building process, as well as the peasant *masserie* and rustic houses on the slopes of the mountain. Although it is still necessary to be fit and to have a guide for the final ascent to the highest crater, it is infinitely easier to make the ascent today than it was for the hardier travelers in the eighteenth century who took a minimum of two days. The north-east approach by car or tourist bus goes as far as Rifugio Sapienza, where there is an incongruous conglomeration of shops and bars in the style of an Alpine village. From there, the funicular continues the ascent, but there is still some way to go on foot after that.

It may come as an initial surprise to see villages sited quite far up the side of the mountain, but local people tend to take a benevolent view of Etna, known in the local dialect as the "giant." When it erupted in 2011, distributing ash and magma all around but without the menace of burning lava, people in Catania and surrounding areas gawked like tourists in wonder at the spectacle. The impression was that it was a local marvel, like the Loch Ness monster, a benevolent gift of nature as much as a threat. Agronomists point to the agricultural advantages of the addition of ash matter to the soil. The fields of solidified lava are known as *sciara* and are barren, but the ashes and even gases have given the land a character no other soil can have.

There is now a thriving *strada del vino*, wine trail, around the volcano, with nineteen producers participating. Some wines, packaged in special, grainy bottles with grinning devils or scenes of erupting flames on the label are on sale only in tourist shops but real, full-bodied wine has been produced on the slopes of Etna since ancient times. The wines have a distinctive flavor, which may be in part the product of the tippler's imagination and expectations but which does seem to owe something to the climatic conditions unique to the mountain. These wines, especially the reds, attack the palate rather than tickle it. There is a growing range.

The wines can be said to have a sulphuric tang, and since no one is likely to have tasted sulphur, those who speak in those terms need fear no contradiction.

Now Etna is the focus of the new science of vulcanology, but its proponents admit that their research cannot produce the one thing everyone would like, a prediction of when the next eruption will occur. Science has its limits. Etna retains its mystery, as the poets and myth- makers always knew. The subject is as rich a field for exploration today as it was in the days of Lucretius.

Chapter Nine
UNLIKELY CONNECTIONS
BRONTE, THE BRONTËS, AND LORD NELSON

Bronte stands in the shadow of Etna, on the less populated, landward side, roughly equidistant from Randazzo and Adrano. All three towns have stations on the Circumetnea railway line.

Randazzo, although constructed of lava stone, seems to have been spared the ravages of volcanic eruptions and retains its austere medieval appearance, but if the inhabitants have lived in harmony with nature, they have had greater difficulty in living in peace with each other. The town has three distinct zones, once home to three communities, Greek, Latin, and Lombard, who spoke different dialects and worshipped in separate churches—Santa Maria (St. Mary), San Nicolò (St. Nicholas), and San Martino (St. Martin)—each of which took it in turn to act as cathedral. The last two were badly damaged by Allied bombing in 1943 when the retreating German-Italian forces made Randazzo their last stronghold. Santa Maria is a magnificent church, with a splendid Catalan-Gothic portal, while from the outside San Nicolò could be mistaken for a fortress, although the interior is more delicately decorated. In front of the church stands the statue of a human figure with an eagle, a lion, and a serpent which seemingly symbolize the three communities, but no one is now sure which is which. All three churches have intriguing and subtly different bell-towers.

Adrano is in the area covered by the Archaeological Park of the Simeto Valley. It too suffered from Allied bombing and from the fierce fighting in the town during the German retreat. Although the area was inhabited from prehistoric times, the original town of Adranon was founded by Dionysius in the fourth century BC as a colony of Siracusa. Its strategic position means that it was fought over in all the wars waged in western Sicily. It was a military and political center for the Normans, as is evidenced by the huge, imposing castle they built there, now the site of the archaeological museum which has exhibits from Greek, Roman, Byzantine, Arab, and

Norman times. Of particular interest is the Norman chapel of the Countess Adelasia which has been reconstructed on the second floor. The town gives the impression of being a self-satisfied, old-style, inward-looking provincial center. The men gather in the Piazza Umberto in the shadow of the castle to chat, debate, gossip, or argue as they have done for centuries, with women discreetly out of sight.

These towns are of greater architectural and probably of greater historical interest than Bronte, but it is Bronte which commands attention. The sign posts at the entrance to the town proclaim it as the capital of the pistachio, and only unimaginative shopkeepers sell the nuts in little bags. Those with greater fantasy have devised cakes, ice-creams, and even a sweet wine with the pistachio flavor. This is all very well, but the interest in Bronte derives from the curious ways in which it has been entwined with British history. Incredible though it may seem, this town gave its name to the most distinguished family of novelists in English literature. When the father of Charlotte, Emily, and Anne Brontë moved from Ireland to take up the parish of Haworth in Yorkshire, he was known as Patrick Brunty. He changed the spelling to the more familiar form, ensuring that the final vowel be pronounced by placing a diaeresis over it, the only example of that usage in English. The Rev. Brunty/Brontë was a somewhat snobbish man, and it seems the change was motivated by a desire to associate his name with the family of Lord Nelson, who had been given the title Duke of Bronte in Sicily in 1799 by Ferdinand IV. The Inghams and the Whitakers, the leading importers of the new Sicilian wine, one brand of which was called Bronte Marsala, were themselves from Yorkshire, which may have made the name Bronte better known in the county than elsewhere. Be that as it may, the outcome is that the authors of *Jane Eyre* and *Wuthering Heights* carry the name of a Sicilian village.

There is a theory that King Ferdinand displayed a wicked sense of humor in giving Nelson that particular title rather than another. In Greek mythology the Cyclops Bronte (the Thunderer) had, like his brothers, only one eye situated in the center of his forehead. As is well known, Nelson lost the sight of his right eye during an engagement in Corsica in 1794, so perhaps the king found the association between the one-eyed Cyclops and the one-eyed admiral amusingly appropriate, although it has to be added that this would endow Ferdinand a wit he never otherwise displayed. Lady

Hamilton, however, savored the connection and referred to Nelson as "My Lord Thunder."

The title and the vast estate were Nelson's reward for protecting the royal family, but also for what even Nelson's most hagiographic biographers regard as the most nefarious act of his life. In his 1999 novel *Losing Nelson,* Barry Unsworth portrays a twentieth-century Nelson-worshipper going insane in Naples as he strives to reconcile Nelson's conduct in that city with his more common image as great, untainted hero. The story is complicated. In 1798, when the French were at the gates of Naples, Nelson organized the flight to Palermo of the royal family, together with that of the British ambassador Sir William Hamilton and his wife, Lady Emma, who was by now Nelson's lover. The French army occupied Naples, but faced the dogged resistance of a loyalist force under Cardinal Ruffo, who eventually forced them out. Nelson arrived back in Naples to find that the cardinal had promised an amnesty and safe conduct to the Jacobins and their leader, Commodore Francesco Caracciolo, whom Nelson had met in Palermo. Nelson appeared to acquiesce in public, but when Caracciolo

A Sicilian palace fit for an English hero

put to sea in a small boat to reach a French man-of-war, Nelson had him arrested and put on trial. The not yet invented term "kangaroo court" would have been an accurate description for a judicial travesty which lasted a mere two hours and where the defendant was not permitted to call witnesses. Caracciolo was hanged on board HMS *Minerva*. The king approved Nelson's action and in August 1799 conferred on him and his successors in perpetuity the title Duke of Bronte, together with an estate which included the historic chapel and Abbey of Maniace, twelve kilometers to the north of Bronte.

Maniace, Nelson's Estate

The estate was some 34,000 acres in size, and produced a large income which had previously gone to a hospital in Palermo. The royal gesture, especially the "in perpetuity" clause, dismayed the inhabitants of Bronte whose views had not been sought. Nelson never visited his estate, but he fantasized about retiring there when the hostilities were over, and making Emma Hamilton his "own little Duchess of Bronte—and a fig for them all!" He used the title in various forms, sometimes signing himself Bronte Nelson or Bronte and Nelson. On his death the estate passed to his brother, William, an Anglican clergyman, and subsequently through marriage it became the property of the Hood family, who were also Viscounts Bridport. It remained with them until 1981 when, much reduced in size, it was finally sold by the Seventh Duke of Bronte to the Sicilian Regional Government, who presented it to the town of Bronte.

The Hoods were detested landlords. In 1920 D. H. Lawrence made the acquaintance of Alec Hood and regarded him with humorous scorn. He wrote to Lady Cynthia Asquith:

> Did you ever hear of a Duca di Bronte—Mr Nelson-Hood—descendant of Lord Nelson (Horatio)—whom the Neapolitans made Duca di Bronte because he hanged a few of them? Well Bronte is just under Etna—and this Mr Nelson-Hood has a place there—his ducal estate. We went to see him—rather wonderful place—*mais mon Dieu, M'le Duc*—Mr Hood I should say. But perhaps you know him
> Tell me where do Dukedoms lie
> Or in the head or in the eye –
> That's wrong.

Tell me where are Dukedoms bred
Or in the eye or in the head.

If I was Duca di Bronte I'd be tyrant of Sicily. High time we had another Hiero. But, of course, money maketh a man: even if he was a monkey to start with.

The local peasants were subjected to a de facto feudal regime, which outlived the official abolition of feudalism in Sicily in 1812 and even the fall of the Bourbons. The fact that some of the best land in the district was in the hands of largely absentee foreign owners was a source of simmering discontent and an injustice which rankled with Sicilians. Carlo Levi, best known as author of *Christ Stopped at Eboli*, visited Bronte in the 1940s to publicize the poverty created by the removal of the land and its proceeds from the local economy. Leonardo Sciascia denounced the royal gift of a possession, land, which was not the king's to give. There were sporadic outbreaks of rioting or rebellion, the first in 1820 and the most serious and notorious in 1860 in the wake of Garibaldi's landing at Marsala. The *Brontesi* rose up in support of Garibaldi, expecting that the liberal revolution heralded by his landing would free them from the yoke they had had to bear. The rising in Bronte was violent, causing murder and mayhem on the streets and leaving sixteen people dead and many more injured. At the behest of the British agents on the estate, Garibaldi dispatched his violent, sadistic lieutenant, Nino Bixio, to restore order, which he did by executing a group of supposed insurgents, including a liberal lawyer, Nicolò Lombardo, who had worked for the Unification of Italy but who was considered, with no proof being offered, the leader of the uprising. Another of the victims was Nunzio Ciraldo Fraiunco, a poor simpleton who had gone around chanting slogans he could not understand. He too faced the firing squad and, being unhurt by the first round of fire, fell on his knees to thank the Madonna for his delivery, but was then shot in the head by Bixio. "The Facts of Bronte," as the incident became known, are commemorated in a grim monument in the town, and have been the subject of many books and films, including the only film, simply entitled *Bronte,* for which Sciascia wrote a script.

Bronte itself is frankly a dull place, not to be numbered among the more memorable of Sicilian towns, but the Nelson estate and the castle (ex-abbey) of Maniace are intriguing, not only on account of its associations with Nelson. The abbey took its name from the Byzantine General George Maniakes, who in 1040 defeated a Saracen army there. The valley and the stream nearby are still known as the Saraceno. The abbey was built over a century later by Queen Margaret of Navarre in commemoration of the battle and has been occupied by various orders of monks. It was badly damaged by the 1693 earthquake and was a ruin when presented to Nelson. The chapel, designed in Norman style, still has the icon of the Virgin Mary said to have been painted by St. Luke the Evangelist and donated by Maniakes himself in thanksgiving for his victory.

At the center of the courtyard stands an implausible Iona Cross, while the ex-abbey has been fully restored and converted into an English-style palace, with Regency furniture and works of art which belonged to the Nelson-Hood family. After the sale of the property the family was banned by the Italian government from removing heirlooms which they claimed as family possessions, so visitors can peer at various framed documents, including the charter by which Nelson was raised by George III to the peerage. Along a narrow, lengthy corridor are charts of sea-battles, copies of cartoons from *Punch*, portraits of generations of Hoods, the decanter and two glasses from HMS *Victory*, medals, and correspondence from British royals.

Just outside the castle is an English cemetery where lie some members of the Hood family and their retainers. This is also the last resting place of William Sharp, a Scottish poet from Paisley who wrote in Gaelic as well as English and who sometimes published his work under a female *nom de plume*, Fiona MacLeod. In his youth he contributed to the *Yellow Book*, and frequented Decadent and Celtic Twilight circles in Edinburgh and London. He was a frequent guest at the castle, and persuaded the Alec Hood whom Lawrence ridiculed to take up writing. Hood produced some volumes of stories and essays on Sicily. Sharp's tombstone has two grandiloquent epitaphs: "Love is more great than we can conceive," and "Death is the keeper of unknown redemptions." These are quotations from his own work and express truths which may be poetically profound but are prosaically unfathomable. But there is something unfathomable and troubling about the history of Bronte and Maniace.

Chapter Ten

THE SECOND CITY

CATANIA

It is a particular misfortune to be labeled "second city." It entails entanglement in niggling, rancorous disputes with the "other place" of a sort no one believes likely to bring any credit to either but which seem unavoidable. Catania is embroiled with Palermo in one of those centuries-old rivalries over status which sets Paris against Marseille, Melbourne against Sydney, or Amsterdam against Rotterdam. To make Catania's dilemma more acute, it is the industrial-commercial capital of Sicily, thus a city viewed as indispensable to economic well-being but lazily written off as a dull, polluted, noisy, hard-working place inhabited by earnest, striving people who follow slavish routines and who are strangers to the ease and grace of living. It is true that Catania has a large, highly unpicturesque dock area used by both tankers and cruise ships, that the twentieth-century suburban sprawl is ugly, and that the coastline outside the city is dominated in part by huge petrochemical and other industrial plants. The city also seems to arouse the most bilious reaction among fellow Sicilians, not only Palermitans, who brand Catania as corrupt, crime-ridden, a den of pickpockets and handbag snatchers.

It is not true. Catania is in fact an intriguing city, with a center of real beauty enriched by Baroque architecture that was influenced by the Roman rather than the Spanish school, which means that it is as sober as the Baroque can be, certainly when compared to the more fanciful styles further south. The level of crime, corruption, or mafia penetration is no higher than elsewhere in Sicily, and there is no basis for believing that the quality of life there is impoverished. Catania has a vivid history dating from Greek times, and has been and remains a lively cultural center which was home in the nineteenth century to composers, novelists, and, above all, to playwrights and actors who transformed the Italian stage and enriched Sicilian culture.

The city center is compact, and overall Catania is remarkably unified

An awesome sight but a rowdy neighbor for Catania

in appearance and architecture, partly because it needed to be planned coherently after normal spontaneous, age-by-age development was choked off by a series of natural disasters. Catania effectively dramatizes the Sicilian tension between the old and the new, or between the longing for some form of continuity with the past and the need to keep restoring, renovating, altering, and adjusting in response to the uncontrollable intrusion of nature. Etna is less than thirty kilometers distant and the city lies in the heart of a zone of threatening seismic activity. Catania sits with every appearance of comfort in the shadow of the volcano and if other cities have more easy-going neighbors, none can savor from the very heart of the city such an awesome, inspiring, overwhelming sight. Etna also imposes itself in positive ways. The fertility of the fields surrounding the city is due to the residue of historic volcanoes, while the black lava has provided in every age the characteristic stone used for the construction of the principal buildings in the city, from the Roman amphitheater to the medieval cathedral and including the great ecclesiastical and aristocratic monasteries and palaces of the Baroque age.

The Greek founders were not ignorant of the threat from the twin natural forces which have menaced Catania down the centuries. The first peoples found their own explanation in myths and turned to goddesses for protection, as a later population put their trust in saints, also mainly female, invoking them to prove their value by combating the threats which overhang Catania when ordinary human action prove inadequate. The city was founded around 729 BC and given the name Katane. Its great assets were its port and the fertile plain which surrounded it, but these were equally attractive to invaders. Catania had troublesome human as well as natural neighbors, notably Siracusa, and tended to make unwise alliances. It was overrun by Siracusa after Catania signed a pact with the invader during Athens' fifth-century BC Sicilian Expedition. It was later conquered by the Romans in 263 in the course of the Second Punic War. Its alliance with Augustus during the Roman civil wars benefited the city, and the Fall of Rome did not represent the end of history for Catania. The date of the martyrdom of St. Agatha, the city's overworked patron saint, is conventionally given as 231, and it seems the city was completely converted to Christianity by the fourth century AD. Thereafter, periods of Arab and Norman domination followed. Palermo was the center of political power, but left to itself the city prospered and trade flourished, for a time. In the Swabian era Catania turned rebellious and Henry VI in 1195 and Frederick II in 1232 overran and sacked the city. The Angevins were better disposed and made Catania capital of the island: some of the Angevin monarchs are buried in the cathedral. The most recent military disaster to befall the city was the sustained bombing campaign unleashed by the Allies in April 1943.

Political and dynastic vicissitudes are only one half of a troubled story. There is evidence of seismic and volcanic activity from early times, but reliable knowledge from the classical age is available only in random ways. Diodorus Siculus records an eruption in 475 BC, the historian Orosius Paulus mentions an earthquake in 123 AD, and there are several accounts of the devastation caused by another tremor in 1169. Etna erupted with a particular violence in 1669, engulfing the city in lava and leaving, according to contemporary accounts, up to 27,000 people homeless and untold numbers dead. Rebuilding was not complete in 1693 when the city was struck by a massive earthquake, caused not by Etna but by shifting tectonic plates. It nullified all the rebuilding work that had been done and left, according to some estimates, up to two-thirds of the population dead. Contemporary chroniclers paint pathetic pictures of the widespread fear of the wrath of God and of injured people searching desperately for lost relatives, of piles of rubble everywhere, of devastation, of the stench of death. These geophysical catastrophes also changed the urban landscape, so that Ursino Castle built by Frederick II in the 1240s as a part of the marine defensive system now stands further back from the sea.

Most people prefer their blessings undisguised, but optimists write of the twin seventeenth-century catastrophes as blessings in disguise, or at least as providing opportunities. Rebuilding took place over decades, but the ecclesiastical authorities were enlightened and energetic, and enlisted the help of talented architects, notably Giovanni Battista Vaccarini. Although rebuilding work was already underway before his appointment as architect in chief in 1730, the present city center largely reflects Vaccarini's vision. He was responsible for the overall urban layout as well as for the design of individual palaces, monasteries, and ministries. The streets are straight, the roads stand at right angles to one another, the piazzas are tastefully laid out, and there are areas of park land in the center. The work was largely complete by the time Patrick Brydone arrived in 1770 to pronounce the city "most noble and beautiful."

Vaccarini had learned from Bernini and Borromini in Rome, and his Baroque, and thus Catania's, is marked by restraint, discipline, and a sense that the overall impact should take precedence over incidental design. There are limits to the compatibility of the terms "Baroque" and "restraint," and the statement is true only where Vaccarini was in charge. Elsewhere, local craftsmen responsible for the balconies which adorn the houses all over the central area were not moved by such considerations and their work shows a different kind of inspiration, combining functionality with extravagance. Why have plain supports and flat ledges on balconies when the opportunity was granted for creating serrated edges, curious geometric shapes, and circular underpinnings, or for using mermaids, sea monsters, grinning dwarves, or grotesque animal figures to embellish the otherwise undistinguished front of a domestic dwelling? It is worth wandering along the Via Vittorio Emanuele II, or round the district known as Civita, once aristocratic but now somewhat in decline, just to enjoy the elaborate wrought-iron balconies and window frames which are characteristic of Catania.

Vaccarini was not wholly immune to the attractions of the grand flourish, as is clear from the façade of the cathedral, which is his work. The finished product is a skilfully blended hybrid, with Roman columns taken from the amphitheater standing harmoniously alongside rose windows. Flamboyantly decorative motifs around the door and statues of saints, with St. Agatha herself in pride of place in the center, round off the work. The first cathedral was Norman, erected in the eleventh century by Count Roger on the ruins of the Achillian baths built by the Romans. There is an entrance to them at the right of the cathedral. The transept and the central apse around the high altar survived the 1693 earthquake and are still Norman, but the body of the church was rebuilt in the Baroque style in the eighteenth century. It has become the burial place of great inhabitants of the city, with many tombs of bishops and cardinals, and the grand tomb of Vincenzo Bellini, whose remains were brought back from Paris in 1876. The fifteenth-century sarcophagi of the Aragonese Kings of Sicily were rediscovered in the 1950s and given greater prominence. There are many stained glass windows and paintings in honor of St. Agatha, with one particularly repulsive depiction of her torture by Filippo Paladino in the left nave. She looks unconcernedly upwards while one torturer applies pincers to her nipples and another bends over to take nasty implements from a basket. It was hoped that the contemplation of such scenes would uplift the spirituality of the faithful.

The feast of the saint, one of the most colorful and elaborate in Sicily, is celebrated annually between 3 and 5 February. Once again, the continuity with the pagan celebrations of the goddess Ceres, once held in mid February, is beyond dispute. A fourteenth-century reliquary containing the head and shoulders of the saint and fashioned from gold, silver, and enamel and inlaid with precious jewels can be seen in the Treasury. In the same part of the cathedral the carriage on which the relics are pulled around the city on the feast day is on display, although the present one is a reconstruction, the mid-fifteenth-century original having been destroyed in the 1943 bombing. The whole city participates in the celebration, and it is still an honor to be allowed to pull the carriage by one of the long ropes used for that purpose. The procession is made up of eleven *candelore*, a word whose connections with "candle" do nothing to give an idea of those finely designed, elaborately decorated, mobile sculptures. There are eleven in all, representing the guilds of gardeners, fish-sellers, butchers, pasta-merchants, etc.

The elephant with the Egyptian obelisk on its back, now symbol of the city of Catania.

In the center of the piazza outside the cathedral stands another of Vaccarini's inventions, the elephant carved out of black lava stone, with an obelisk on its back, the whole mounted on a plinth which has water fonts at the side to symbolize the twin rivers that supply the city with water. This odd combination has become the symbol of Catania. It is suggested that the elephant in some way refers to King Pyrrhus, who employed elephants in his battles with the Romans, and the obelisk to Sicily's position as a mid-Mediterranean power drawing to itself all that is best from the great sea. The monument as a whole is known to *Catanesi* as Liotru, a corruption of the name of the sorcerer Heliodorus, who according to local legend could change men into animals, but who was trapped when one of his spells on himself went awry and he found himself incapable of returning to human form. This tale is very moving and dignifying, but in all probability Vaccarini pinched the image from a similar statue by Bernini placed in front of the Church of Santa Maria sopra Minerva in Rome. As T. S. Eliot said in another context, mediocre poets are influenced, major poets steal. Vaccarini was a major poet-architect. The piazza is the center of ecclesiastical and municipal power, and from the steps of the cathedral can be seen the Municipio (City Chambers), another building Vaccarini worked on, the Archbishop's Palace and the seminary. The nineteenth-century Amenano Fountain, which sprays water into a basin below, is named after a river which is represented by the naked young man standing atop the structure. The grand Porta Uzeda alongside it leads out onto the fish market.

ANTIQUITY AND RECONSTRUCTION

The street running north from Piazza Duomo in the direction of the volcano is Via Etnea, one of the most striking thoroughfares in Europe. The Greeks, who founded this city, knew how to take full aesthetic advantage of all that nature offered, and even if later Sicilians have shown a genius for blocking off their most spectacular sights, no one in Catania wished to disturb the view of the imposing mountain. The monster looks peaceful and tame from the street, and when it gives one of its minor displays of fireworks, the sight is breathtaking. Via Etnea is a bustling, traffic-choked thoroughfare with excellent cafés, street vendors who deal in second-hand books, and the fashionable boutiques that are standard in any big city.

From Piazza Duomo the street runs past several splendid palaces, including the original, grandiose university building which is illuminated

An idyllic view of Via Etnea in a more peaceful age. The road runs through the heart of Catania and affords a view of Etna in the distance

by four giant lamps standing on bronze pedestals, and the fine Palazzo Sangiuliano, which retains something of its Baroque character even if it has undergone several restorations and alterations. The street is in the shade even at midday, so the visitor can plod on in reasonable comfort to the Botanic Gardens, to the Roman amphitheater, to the elegantly laid-out gardens named in honor of Vincenzo Bellini, and to the Church of Sant' Agata al Carcere (St. Agatha at the Prison), where the saint was, according to popular belief, detained, mutilated, and eventually martyred. The form of torture St. Agatha underwent was especially obscene. Gaolers cut off her breasts, an event which has given artists commissioned to produce sacred art the excuse for venturing across the line into holy pornography. It has also given local chefs, whose intention is supposedly to commemorate the saint's suffering, licence to manufacture marzipan sweets suggestive of nipples and soft, sensuous, white flesh.

Catania's most interesting buildings and the ruined remains from successive eras are within walking distance of each other in the city center. There are many archaeological sites and these are now part of what has been designated the Catania Greek-Roman Park, but the park has no

The Roman amphitheater in the center of Catania

boundaries and is an administrative device for managing the various classical ruins. Only part of what was once a huge Greek-Roman theater just off Via Vittorio Emanuele II has been excavated: it is now used as a venue for plays and concerts. This fan-shaped theater is surrounded by housing, a living demonstration of the development and redevelopment of the central area across centuries. Alongside stands an indoor exhibition space which was until recently an inhabited, *art nouveau* style house occupying part of the former theater, but has been transformed into a museum for displays of works found in excavations.

Excavations are continuing under the eighteenth-century Gravina-Cruyllas Palace, where Bellini was born. The Odeon behind it can be seen only from the street. Roman baths were part of the theater complex, and later the Byzantine Church of Santa Maria della Rotonda (St. Mary of the Rotonda) was built over the site. The church and thus the baths are open for visits. The change of ground level caused by seismic activity has meant a continual restructuring of all constructions. An even smaller section of the Roman amphitheater has been excavated but what is visible can be glimpsed only through railings in Piazza Stesicoro. The rest is concealed under houses or has been converted for use as a part of the urban sewers, so it is not clear how excavation work will be able to continue. Other baths (Terme dell'Indirizzo, in the piazza of that name) lie under a car park.

Ursino Castle was constructed in the reign of Frederick II, a monarch who took a personal interest in architecture. There are several similarly designed castles on mainland Italy, but it is impossible to say how much of the design was due to him. Subsequently the Angevin dynasty used the building as their royal palace but it was badly damaged in the seventeenth-century disasters. It was converted for use as a prison in the nineteenth century but was then reworked to restore its original design. Much of the restoration has been criticized as guess-work, but it is an imposing building which now houses a well stocked, interesting museum.

For long periods, dynastic power struggles left a vacuum at local level. In Catania this meant that the real lord was often the abbot of the enormous Benedictine monastery, on Piazza Dante. The monastery itself is now part of the University of Catania, which was founded by the Angevin monarchs and is the oldest in Sicily. The university's ownership of the ex-monastery enables visitors to roam about freely, although there are also some highly professional guided tours. The building was once the second biggest Benedictine monastery in Europe, and in its heyday it greeted all the most famous travelers to Sicily, including Goethe and Brydone. From the basement upwards, literally and metaphorically, all the strata of the city's history are here: Greek walls, Roman mosaics, medieval columns, lava stone, Baroque exteriors, traces of the impact of earthquakes and of rebuilding under the guidance of Vaccarini, as well as more recent work to meet university needs. The façade is more appropriate for a palace than for a house of prayer, but these were very worldly monks whose lifestyle caused Patrick Brydone to wonder if they were "not determined to make sure of a paradise in this world, if not in the next." This particular earthly paradise and its fate after the fall of the Bourbon monarchy is the subject of one of the greatest of Sicilian novels, *The Viceroys* by Federico de Roberto, a nineteenth-century work which covers the same period as *The Leopard*, with a very similar outlook.

The monastery façade is a reminder that what the Catanese Baroque lacks in virtuosity it makes up for in sheer scale, a lesson underlined by the monstrous, adjacent Church of San Nicolò (St. Nicholas), the largest church in Sicily. It is hard to decipher the motivations of the architects and the community with this vast building. Work was started after the eruption of 1669 but suspended after the 1693 earthquake and never completed. From the piazza, it looks like the mad scheme of some deranged dictator whose aim was to issue a super-human challenge against all rivals, earthly or divine. The most prominent features of the façade are gigantic half-columns around the doorway, but the spectacle is sad. Restoration work is still going on, but the intention is now to convert the building into an arts center.

Catanese Baroque

There is no shortage of Baroque buildings nearby to admire. The churches in Via Crociferi should be sufficient to satisfy non-specialist appetites, and since the opening times are unpredictable, a visit to San Francesco Borgia (St. Francis Borgia) will probably suffice. At the top of the same street the Villa Cerami, always open because it is now the seat of another university Faculty, is an intriguing eighteenth-century noble residence, with frescoes from that age. The playful, tantalizing façade of Palazzo Biscari can be savored, but published images of the staircases and the dance hall inside can only whet curiosity since the interior is closed to the public.

Former Benedictine monastery, now building of the University of Catania,
designed by Vaccarini and completed by 1752

The city flourished artistically as well as commercially in the nineteenth century and can be regarded as being at that time the theatrical
capital of Italy. However, since Italian theater was then actor- rather than
author-centered, there are few scripts which allow that theater to be recre-
ated. There were two especially celebrated actors, Angelo Musco, known
principally as a comic actor, and Giovanni Grasso, famed for his tragic
abilities. Both were feted worldwide, and when Grasso brought his troupe
to London the *Daily Mirror* hailed him as "the greatest actor in the world."
Catania was also the city where Giovanni Verga and Federico De Roberto,
the principal Italian novelists in the *verista* mode, were based.

Vincenzo Bellini (1801-35) died at the young age of 33 in Paris, and
was immediately given in the public mind a place in a Romantic Valhalla
as a Don Juan and a lost genius, but this dubious status led to the under-
estimation of those works he had actually composed in his short life. His
friend and first biographer Francesco Florimo must take responsibility for
the creation of this distorted image and thus for the low esteem accorded
his work in the period immediately after his death. Before publishing the

letters Florimo twisted the evidence and even burned many of them lest the deeds discussed or the opinions expressed be harmful to Bellini's reputation. However, his achievements have been reassessed by posterity and Bellini's fame is solidly based on three masterpieces, *Norma*, *I sonnambuli* and *I puritani*. It may be, as some critics aver, that there are echoes of Sicilian folk song in his music, but Bellini was granted a traveling bursary when he was only eighteen and thereafter returned to Sicily only briefly and out of a sense of family obligation. He made his home and his name in Paris. He was first buried in the French capital, but Catania campaigned to have his remains returned, and the French eventually agreed. His body was brought back in 1876, stopping at many railway stations en route for ceremonial concerts and recitals. The city he had never known as an adult greeted him as a heroic son, and he was entombed in the imposing monument in the cathedral. The opera house and the piazza on which it is sited are both named after him, and one of the frescoes in the theater is a worshipful *Apotheosis of Bellini*. Catania also commissioned a statue which sits in the city center and converted his birthplace into a well stocked, well ordered museum which contains many letters and copies of operatic scores.

Catania is in the midst of a process of regeneration, so it is worth taking a look at Le Ciminiere, a complex of sheds near the railway station and port, once a sulphur refinery and now reborn as an arts center. It includes a display of the history of the city and there is also a permanent exhibition of the Allied landing and Sicilian campaign in 1943.

Chapter Eleven
GODDESSES AND MADONNAS
ENNA

Enna has long been defined as the "navel of Sicily," a title it has enjoyed since ancient times, but it was only in the 1990s that the town authorities erected an obelisk near the Church of Maria di Montesalvo to mark the geographical center of Sicily. The town is equidistant from Palermo and Taormina, and nature has ensured that it is endowed with an imposing dignity in keeping with the central role conferred on it. Enna is built on the top of a mountain, some thousand meters above sea level making it virtually impregnable, as successive invaders have found. From a distance on the *autostrada* which cuts across the island it can be seen rising up majestically amid the scorched fields of the central Sicilian plain. Access to the town is via a tortuous, winding, ascending road with a large number of sharp elbow bends.

Such a mountain was destined to be selected either as a military center to command the surrounding territory or as a sacred place to arouse religious awe. Enna has played both parts. The city and the nearby Lake of Pergusa are associated with one of the most elemental and enigmatic of all chthonic myths, the story of Demeter and Persephone, known as Ceres and Proserpina in Latin. Demeter was the goddess of corn or the harvest, and mother of Persephone. The father was Zeus, the king of the gods, who happened also to be Demeter's brother. Persephone is also known as Korè, which means simply daughter, so the close relationship the myth establishes between Demeter and Persephone-Korè has been taken as a symbol not only for mother-daughter relationships but also for the development of women from daughters to mothers.

The myth has other resonances. A Demeter figure is found all over the Mediterranean world, and indeed it seems likely that the Greeks inherited her worship from earlier peoples, perhaps the Sicans. Every culture has to provide an explanation for the cycle of the seasons, the facts of agricultural fertility and of the sustenance provided by the earth. In the

Greek-Latin tradition, Sicily was believed to be, according to the speculations of the ancient historian Diodorus Siculus, the favorite residence of the Demeter. One day, while Persephone was playing near the Lake of Pergusa she was enchanted by a narcissus, but as she bent to pluck it, the earth opened up and Hades, or Pluto, emerged to snatch the girl and carry her off to the underworld in his chariot to make her his wife. The myth of this rape or kidnap deals with profound themes which psychologists such as C. G. Jung have explored, and has fascinated writers of all languages down the ages. Ovid dedicated one of his *Metamorphoses* to it and it is the subject of one of the *Homeric Hymns*, of which Homer was not the author, translated by Lord Tennyson. The French pamphleteer Paul-Louis Courier, an officer in Napoleon's army stranded in Calabria because of the failure of the winds to Sicily, lamented that not reaching Sicily meant that "he would never understand why the devil had taken his bride in that country."

Demeter was devastated by the act, and traveled far and wide in search of her daughter, and even lit two torches from the flames of Etna to allow her to continue the search in the darkness. She found an article of Persephone's clothing, variously described as a girdle or a veil, near the Cyane Fountain outside Siracusa, but this did nothing to bring her daughter back. Her monomania had disastrous effects for humanity. The planet was left in darkness, no plants flourished, and those that had been growing withered. Demeter was informed by Helios, the god of the sun, about what had actually happened, but this still left her powerless and the earth barren. In despair, Zeus dispatched Hermes, the messenger of the gods, to Hades to beg for Persephone's release. An agreement was reached, but the girl's return depended on her not having eaten any food during her stay in the underworld. She had been in a state of anorexic depression since her kidnap and had eaten nothing, but as she was preparing to leave she was offered and accepted a single pomegranate seed. The deal was off, but Ascalaphus, the man who revealed her lapse, was punished for telling tales by being turned into an owl. Further negotiations ended in the compromise that Persephone would spend three months with Pluto in the underworld, but would return to the earth for the other nine months. In other words, in prosaic interpretation, the three barren months of winter would be followed by the three seasons of fertility and growth.

The Sicilians showed their gratitude by annual sacrifices to Demeter, and special ceremonies were arranged around the Cyane Fountain which saw the blood of bulls mixed with the waters. Sicilian agriculture flourished and the island became the "granary of the Roman Empire." Persephone is displayed in some pottery as inhabiting a grand palace in Hades, and in some accounts Sicily was given to Pluto as a dowry by Zeus to mark his marriage to Persephone. Once again, this act is open to conflicting interpretation: Sicily as land of special fertility as guaranteed by the daughter of the goddess, or Sicily as the land given to the devil.

The Rock of Demeter-Ceres is still there in Enna, sited inside the town at the highest point overlooking the countryside below, but access onto the rock is not currently permitted since restoration work is being carried out to prevent it crumbling or perhaps falling into the valley. The huge boulder at whose foot the temple stood was a place of pilgrimage, and religious ceremonies were certainly held here from the earliest times. The exact form of worship is much debated since the cult of Ceres was international and so the rites may have differed from those practised elsewhere in the Greek world. Alongside a more modern staircase, there are still traces of the ancient steps leading to the top where sacrifice may have taken place. We have it on the authority of Cicero that the site was adorned by two beautiful statues of the goddess, one in marble and another in bronze, but they were stolen by the avaricious consul Verres in 76 BC.

The Lake of Pergusa is some twelve kilometers away, and even on a bright day it is a dark, haunting place. There are no visible inlets or outlets, and the mystery of the source of the water is part of the reason why the lake was regarded as having some special association with devilish activities. More modern diabolic practices have been worked in these parts, however. Some decades ago a Formula 3 racing circuit was built round the shores of the lake, with access to the waters impossible. The racing track is fenced off to keep the paying public on race days away from the cars, there is a road alongside the fence, making it possible to walk or drive around the lake. It is a source of disbelief and a matter of deep regret that any entrepreneur could have been given permission to desecrate such a spot with anything so crass. Perhaps there is a modern allegory here.

Enna was a Sicel fortress, later colonized by the Greeks from Gela on the coast. The Romans took possession, but they had to face a particularly troublesome slave revolt led by Eunus, who resisted the Romans for two years and whose deeds are recorded on a plaque outside the castle. The Arabs seized control, but to break the resistance of the defenders they had to crawl one by one through the sewers. They changed the name to Jasr Janni, which was altered to Castrogiovanni, the name by which the town was known until Mussolini re-Latinized it. No occupying force could ignore such a strategically important stronghold, but the Normans found it no easier to take than had the Arabs. Roger took the family of the Emir prisoner and offered to return them safe and sound and even give the Emir safe passage to Puglia, provided he converted to Christianity. Sicilians, born or adoptive, have a tradition of making offers which cannot be refused.

There are mementoes of the presence of these famous men of antiquity. In Via Roma, not far from the cathedral, is a plaque advertising Cicero's dwelling-place when he was governor of Sicily, although on what historical basis it is hard to say. The plaque also says it was placed there as an act of gratitude for Cicero's campaign two thousand years previously against Verres, who had robbed Sicily of statues and works of art, even from the holiest of shrines. Cicero prosecuted Verres in the courts in Rome, and it was his polemical speeches, *Against Verres*, which first alerted the Roman senate and people of the arrival of a new political force. The efforts of Eunus are commemorated on the castle walls.

One of the more unexpected visitors to Enna was John Henry Newman, whose journey to Sicily in 1833, recorded in a pamphlet entitled *My Illness in Sicily*, was the only extended trip he made in the ninety years of his life. He was extremely unwell and arrived in Enna in a feverish state after traveling partly on foot and partly by donkey from Catania. There he took to his bed and was bled, as contemporary medical science dictated, but in spite of that he made a complete recovery. He believed that "God had work for [him] to do," and it was on his way back to England that he wrote the famous hymn *Lead Kindly Light*. In human terms, he put his recovery down to the kindness of his host in Enna and of the servant he had engaged. Newman was free of the Victorian distrust of foreigners and went out of his way to acknowledge "the great honesty of his attendants." In Enna, as his appetite returned, Gennaro his servant gave him "an egg baked in wood ashes and some tea for breakfast & cakes," and no doubt that most English of cuisines aided his healing.

With his austerity of Christian belief, Newman would not have been pleased by the theory that the choice of the Virgin as patron saint under the title St. Mary of the Visitation is a continuation of the cult of

Good Friday procession in Enna

Persephone. The visitation of the Virgin Mary to St. Elizabeth can be seen as a replay of the reunion between Demeter and Persephone. Unusually, this notion is accepted by the local church itself. The exterior walls of the cathedral are highly decorated with nineteenth-century frescoes, and the captions under them draw attention to the fact that devotion to the Madonna was a baptism of the cult of the goddess. The feast of the Visitation is celebrated by processions and festivities on 2 July. To give thanks for that year's successful harvest, the faithful place bundles of hay and flowers before the statue of the Virgin Mary, as had been done on the pagan feast of the *cerealia*. The statue carried through the town is the work of a Venetian sculptor, which came into the hands of Enna in dubious circumstances. The vessel carrying the statue ran aground in the Ionian Sea, but since it was known to have miraculous qualities, the people of Enna, indifferent to any Venetian counter-claims, decided to keep it. The statue was weighty but assistance was given by farm-workers, who turned up in their working clothes. This style of informal dress is commemorated in the name given to those who draw the cart today, the *nudi*, which means naked, although in fact they are merely barefoot. Enna also has elaborate processions in Holy Week, starting from Palm Sunday when the confraternities in the town come out in force and in traditional garb. On Easter Sunday there is a re-enactment of the meeting between the Risen Christ and Madonna. Reunions of parents and their offspring are part of the psychical history of Enna.

The cathedral itself is believed to be built on the site of a temple to Demeter, and experts suggest that the base of the left-hand holy water font comes from the pagan temple. As a church it was founded in 1307 by Queen Eleanor of Anjou, wife of Frederick II of Aragon, in thanksgiving for the birth of their son. It is a remarkable building, of striking beauty and originality both inside and out. Although it has been redesigned on several occasions, the façade and even more the side porches retain distinctive Gothic features. The carved ceiling and choir stalls, the elegantly designed pulpit, and the wooden hanging crucifix are all beautiful works of art.

Those visitors who have been fortunate enough to be able to visit the Alessi Museum speak enthusiastically about it. The museum is owned by the church but the collection is not limited to sacred art. It includes archaeological findings, Greek and Roman coins from the neighborhood, the work of goldsmiths, jewelry, and paintings, and above all a much appreciated Madonna of the Visitation. However, this will need to be taken on trust, because a bizarre stand-off between the cathedral and the town council led to the doors of the museum being closed on 1 January 2006 and not being subsequently reopened.

There are no such problems with the Archaeological Museum, housed in a palace which is worth visiting in its own right. The palace belonged to different noble families before ending up as the residence of the Varisano dynasty who gave it its final, eighteenth-century form. Garibaldi was here, obviously, and it was from one of the windows of the palace that he uttered his rallying cry: "Rome or Death!" He knew a good line when he heard one, so other towns claim he made the cry there. Probably they are all right. For such a small town, Enna has an unusually rich variety of buildings. There is the tower of Frederick II, but for decades there was no agreement over which Frederick II it was, Frederick II the Swabian monarch or Frederick II of Aragon. It has an octagonal structure which was the favored design of Frederick of Swabia, so current opinion assigns the work to him. Lombards arrived in Sicily in the suite of the Normans and the town's Castello di Lombardia is a romantic ruin, spacious and welcoming with excellent views from the ramparts.

CALASCIBETTA

Like Enna, the town of Calascibetta stands atop a mountain, but was never viewed as having the same strategic importance. The twin towns are divided by seven kilometers and by a history of rivalry and enmity. They glower at each other from facing peaks and are now separated by the *autostrada*. These are not friendly Tuscan-style "hill towns" but defensive settlements, built in places where invaders would fear to tread. The mountains are craggy with shoulders of rock protruding from the yellow shrub which it would be optimistic to call grass. Even from close up, it is hard to distinguish the built environment from the natural rock formations, since both feature the same, brown-grey stone.

Calascibetta's mountain has un-Italian name of Xibet. It is 800 meters above sea level and has a population of some five thousand hardy souls. The

Calascibetta, perched on a mountain top to ward off enemies

Mosaic by Roman-African school of young women at play or perhaps engaged in some competitive sport. Female fashions are less transitory than was thought!

name is probably Arab, but its fortifications were built by the Norman Count Roger as a base for his operations against the supposedly impregnable Enna. Some say that the relations between the two cities never recovered. The cathedral, including the Palatine chapel built in 1340 by the Aragonese Peter II, has been restored on several occasions. There is an interesting Byzantine village dating from the sixth century, which consists of layers of caves which seemingly had some civil or religious function. It contains two church buildings, one in a cave the other open to the elements. However, the origins of the town are older than Christianity, and about five kilometers from the town, at Realmese, a necropolis dating from the ninth or tenth century is being excavated. Towards the end of July each year the local people host theatrical work which is part of an adventurous circuit called *Teatri di Pietra,* literally Theatres of Stones. The town is keen to raise its standing, particularly in competition with Enna, and accommodation may be provided in one of the unoccupied residences in the center for anyone with relevant skills who wishes to help in the restoration of the historical center itself.

There are many other towns in the province of Enna which are worth attention. Aidone to the south has been much in the news recently because of the return of the statue of a goddess from the J. Paul Getty Museum in California. The present town has a medieval structure with the lanes and little squares which are typically Arab, but Aidone was originally a Greek colony, and excavations and exhibits on display in the Archaeological Museum reveal that it was probably a wealthy one.

Slightly further on the Villa del Casale in Piazza Armerina has re-opened after an extended period of closure for restorations. The villa, the center of a private estate, is one of the comparatively few Roman remains of any substance in Sicily and one of the best preserved anywhere in the Roman Empire. The exact status of the owner is unclear, but he was undoubtedly a man of wealth and influence as well as of highly developed artistic taste. The baths, the rooms, the wonderful courtyard with its central pool are all of great interest but what raises the place above comparable residences is the beauty of the mosaics. The one which has caught popular attention is the so-called bikini room, depicting young women frolicking with a ball and bedecked in what had only shortly before the rediscovery of the villa been given the name "bikini." If these mosaics had come to light slightly earlier, this outfit might have been called after them, but whether a suggestive lyric about a skimpy *armerina* would have had the same effect is another matter. Other mosaics show hunting scenes, cupids as fishermen, mythological scenes, chariot racing, and provinces of the Roman Empire, and these are the works of master-craftsmen whose achievements rival anything produced centuries later by the Arab-Norman artisans who decorated the great cathedrals.

Chapter Twelve
THE SICILY THE GREEKS LEFT
CLASSICAL REMAINS

Since until the arrival of the Romans, Sicily was part of *Magna Graecia*, Greater Greece, there are ruins of ancient Greek colonies, sub-colonies, settlements, shrines, temples, and fortifications all over the island. The area lying south of Catania and inland from Siracusa is particularly rich in such relics. Access to sites is unreliable but in recent years a number of "archaeological parks" or open-air museums have been established, often bringing together a number of existing sites and generally administered by knowledgeable, enthusiastic managers who are deprived of adequate resources to do their job properly, as they will explain at length.

The systematic researcher will start from Naxos, half way between Messina and Catania. This was the first Greek colony in Sicily and if it is now in a suburb of a thriving town which becomes a resort in summer, the ruins of the ancient settlement occupy a clearly delineated area. From there, anyone on a Greek trail southwards might like to veer round the back of Etna towards Adrano, a sub-colony of Siracusa founded by Dionysius in the fourth century BC and now a well populated center. The town has been incorporated into a vast Simeto Valley Archaeological Park, whose exact limits are yet to be defined but where extensive excavations have taken place. The Simeto is the longest river in Sicily and the proximity to the volcano has created in the valley some striking natural features. Other features to be found there include the Ponte dei Saraceni (Saracen Bridge), the oasis of Ponte Barca, where herons gather and the ancient walls built by Dionysius, now in the middle of an orchard. The Norman castle in Adrano has been converted into an interesting museum of local finds, including a bust of Persephone.

There is no advantage for the dilettante in separating Greek history too rigorously from Greek mythology, and the area around Etna is rich in mythological references. On the coast slightly to the north of Catania there are eight villages whose name begins with *Aci*: Aci Castello, Aci Trezza,

Acireale etc.—a prefix which brings us back into the realm of poetry and of Homeric myth. Ovid recounts that Acis, son of the nymph Simaethis (after whom the River Simeto is named), was a good-living shepherd who aroused the love of the nymph Galatea. Polyphemus, the savage, one-eyed Cyclops who was son of Poseidon and Thoosa, was the villain of the piece, for he too loved the nymph and was driven to such extremes of jealousy that he stoned Acis to death. The gods were moved to pity and converted Acis into a stream which to this day runs from the volcano into the sea, and since Galatea was a sea-nymph, she and her lover were thus reunited. Several Greek figures along this coast ended up in watery form. Polyphemus met his nemesis some time later when Odysseus and his wandering crew landed in Sicily. They went foraging for food and came across the cave of Polyphemus when he was absent, but on his return he blocked the entrance and proceeded over the following days to devour six of the Greeks until Odysseus blinded the giant with a flaming club and tied his men to the underside of sheep to allow them to escape. When he realized he had been duped, the Cyclops went into a rage and hurtled great boulders after the Greek ship in 2010. Recently this myth was reinterpreted by Raffaele Lombardo, then President of the Sicilian Region, who attacked Homer as the first of a line of writers who have humiliated Sicily.

> The first invader of Sicily was not Garibaldi but Odysseus... Polyphemus was a poor Sicilian, a shepherd who tended his flock and sold his cheeses. Odysseus arrived from the sea, overcame the wicked giant, blinded him, left him for dead and passed into history as the good civilizing force. The sack of my island, too rich not to attract looters, dates from there.

Aeschylus and Sophocles rewrote the myths to meet their own tastes and needs, so why not signor Lombardo? The boulders thrown by Polyphemus after the retreating Greeks are now the Faraglioni, also known as the Cyclops Islands, plainly visible off the coast. The best view is from Acitrezza, which is also the village where Verga set his novel *The Malavoglia*. Acicastello has an intriguing castle in lava rock which clings precariously to a protruding rock on the sea.

Those with stamina and determination may wish to stop on the coastal road south at the villages of Thapsos and Megara Iblea, while those

The Faraglioni off the coast below Mount Etna, where they landed after being thrown in rage by the Cyclops at the fleeing Odysseus

without such qualities might abandon the search in exasperation after futile attempts to make sense of the road signs. Megara Iblea is south of the port city of Augusta, and is offputtingly situated in the middle of an industrial area of large petrochemical plants. The town has associations with the mythical figure of Daedalus, who arrived here after his flight from Crete (there are other candidates for his stopping-off point), but in history it was certainly founded shortly after Siracusa, and was named after its mother city, Megara Nisea in mainland Greece. It was destroyed in 483 BC by Siracusa but rebuilt in a style not substantially different from the original, so that the ruins and the outline of the town date from the archaic period. Some of the most remarkable items on display in the Siracusa museum, including a mother breastfeeding twins and the beautifully carved statue of a young man, come from here. Further on, Thapsos is a much older site and is to be found not far from the modern town of Priolo. The road signs will send you circling aimlessly round Priolo, and the correct exit, once located, runs along a seaside road which is very popular in summer. The ruins, at the extremity of a promontory, show that Thapsos was once an important trading center, and the curious, circular habitations are of interest.

The town of Lentini, once the Greek Leontinoi, a sub-colony of Naxos, lies some seven kilometers inland. The modern town merges with Carlentini, which was founded in the sixteenth century to house the population left homeless after an earthquake, but many of the inhabitants preferred to stay in old Lentini. The archaeological park with the remains of the ancient city is situated in the valley of San Mauro and covers two nearby hills, but its opening times are erratic. Leontinoi had its problems with powerful neighbors: Siracusa ousted Naxos to make Leontinoi a satellite city with the same status as its own sub-colonies, Helorus (Eloro), Akrai (Palazzolo Acreide), and Casmenae (Casmene). These settlements were conceived as part of the defensive barrier Siracusa erected for its own safety from invading armies and so never attained full autonomy.

Eloro stands on the sea, and excavations have revealed the street plan of the old city. The Eloro Archaeological Park takes in the Villa del Tellaro, another of the few Roman remains in Sicily. First unearthed some forty years ago, it is similar to the villa at Piazza Armerina and it too was plainly the residence of a powerful, wealthy man, as attested by the quality of the mosaics. The colony was also a sacred place, with a large shrine in honor of the goddess Demeter.

Akrai, the modern Palazzolo Acreide, was the first colony founded as part of the expansionist designs of Siracusa, and its inland site was chosen to guarantee its communications with Selinunte, the most westerly of the Greek colonies. Visitors approaching the town from the Ragusa road may be discouraged by the forbidding phalanx of high-rise apartments which provide a more effective defensive structure than anything constructed in the seventh century BC. The further obstacle is that the site of ancient Akrai is normally shut but may be opened by a guard who will insist on accompanying visitors. The remains indicate that there was a sanctuary, probably to Aphrodite, and there is a magnificent and very well preserved theater cut into the side of a hill. The town had the same kind of stone quarries as Siracusa, and later they served as burial chambers. The most remarkable feature is the rock carving of a goddess surrounded by young men and women, possibly the Great Mother Goddess, Cybele.

About twelve kilometers to the west near Monte Erbesso lies the probable site of ancient Casmenae, although the question is not definitely settled. It was seemingly a place to which recalcitrant malcontents were exiled and it is a suitably desolate spot suitable for such purposes, although the alternative sentence to exile was more unpalatable. Archaeologists have uncovered the site of the acropolis, and most of the excavated items are in Casmene's Antonino Uccello Museum.

Camarina on the south coast was also founded to be part of the Siracusan defence circle, but it turned out to be as troublesome and rebellious as the American colonies towards the British crown. It made common cause with enemies of its Mother City including the Sikels and Carthaginians, and for this disloyalty it was sacked, rebuilt, and re-sacked on more than one occasion before it drifted into the sphere of influence of Gela. The town covered an extensive area, and the remains and the museum with its unique collection of vases were reopened to visitors in 2010 after being closed for eight years. The real problem for the future of the site is human activity and the fear of the land erosion by the encroaching sea. There is a holiday village called Kamarina near the beach, meaning that the places where Greek traders put to sea are now the playgrounds of the gilded youth and slumbering age of Italy and beyond. Perhaps this is a welcome sign of the cohabitation of history and modernity, but there is little evidence of modernity's respect for the values of the past. Many of the recent discoveries of Corinthian helmets or Athenian *amphorae* have been made by underwater divers, who have also brought back photos of columns and shipwrecks. Such random discoveries can be made on land too, since only a small part of the ancient town has been systematically excavated or examined. Cooking items or storage vessels and coins can be picked up by the alert searcher.

One of the great economic activities in the area was the production on an industrial scale of honey. Greek dramatists and philosophers did not spend all their time ruminating on the destiny of humankind or pondering the nature of the ideal state. Some were happy to celebrate the delights of the flesh, so the sweetness of the honey from around here, exported all over the Greek world, was a topic for cheerful lyrics. Incredibly, there once existed what was called a "bee factory," consisting of a cistern where the honey was stored prior to being loaded onto trading ships or carts. There is not much left of the factory apart from some stones which designate the limits of the circular structure, but those with an eye for the curios of history might like to see it, near the village of Maulli, not far from the Irminio river.

Morgantina, roughly seven kilometers from Aidone towards the center of the island, predates the Sicilian-Greek expansion, and was once occupied by the army of Ducetius, the Sikel leader who united his people against the Greek invaders. Siracusa took possession of the town by force of arms and Hellenized it thoroughly, giving it a cleverly designed theater, various shrines as well as an *agora* (central square). The town planning of all these colonies was executed by men with carefully nurtured aesthetic sensibilities and a sense of what was went into the civilized life. Along the carefully laid out central street, the ruins of the House of Ganymede stand out. The name is derived from a mosaic on the floor which illustrates the myth of the beautiful Trojan youth who so delighted Zeus that he changed himself into an eagle to carry him off to Olympus. For the non-specialist who wishes only one taste of the Greek past or whose interest is likely to fade rapidly under the scorching sun, this could be taken as a representative site. It is lonely and picturesque, and in addition to the ruined columns and residences it offers all the picturesque noise and natural movement of the Sicilian countryside, with lizards darting about and cicadas making the grating sound that only bewitched poets can call song.

Siracusa, the Prodigious City

In ancient times Siracusa was a major political player not only in Sicily or in *Magna Graecia* but all over the Mediterranean, enjoying periods of military, imperial, economic and, in consequence, cultural dominance. Going there today is in some senses like visiting Ephesus or Antioch, cities once famous centers of power but bypassed by history. Even during its long decline the reputation of Siracusa lingered on in the European memory. Patrick Brydone was mindful of the "glory, magnificence and illustrious deeds" that were Siracusa for him, but he was disgusted at the derelict, depopulated wreck he found. "This proud city that vied with Rome itself is now reduced to a heap of rubbish," he wrote. A century later, however, Guy de Maupassant found the city "unusual and delightful," and this represents the more common view. Over a span of time that goes from Cicero to the more bureaucratic-minded inspectors of UNESCO, who gave

Siracusa the status of World Heritage Site, the city has aroused admiration, affection and awe.

Modern Siracusa is the capital of a Sicilian province, of some political and economic importance, and a thriving, attractive city. There are reminders everywhere of ancient glories. The palaces, the Baroque and Catalan-Gothic churches, the remains of the temples of the old gods, the sculptures from both Greek and Roman times, the harbors in use since the days of the Greeks, the medieval Jewish baths (Miqwè) in the district still known as the Giudecca, the splendid museums, the paintings executed there by the great Caravaggio, the magnificent piazzas particularly the Piazza Duomo, the island-zone of Ortigia, the dark lanes, the promenade along the seafront where the Athenian vessels once moored, the fountains, and mythological associations make Siracusa one of the glories of European civilization—and all that without mentioning Archimedes.

The Greek days were the days of real splendor, and although some visitors from Cicero onwards have considered the city to be in permanent decline, all have been motivated by an antiquarian yen to uncover and respect its civilization. In his prosecution speech against the infamous Verres, Cicero described Siracusa as "the most splendid of Greek cities", and he spent days in archaeological or cultural pottering like a modern tourist. One of the most celebrated of Siracusans was Archimedes, who devised mirrors capable of setting fire at a distance to Roman vessels attacking the city, and who was killed by a Roman soldier during a siege. Cicero found and restored the tomb he believed was his and whether or not it was the genuine article, it still stands in the grand archaeological park in the Neapoli zone of the city. While the combination of the great Roman orator and the great Greek mathematician might seem likely to interest modern visitors, access is prevented by an iron fence, although people can peep at it from the road which runs alongside. Running up a street naked shouting *Eureka!* in imitation of Archimedes was once a student pastime, but is now frowned on.

What sent Greek poets into lyrical frenzies over Siracusa was not just its temples, palatial architecture, artistic treasures, and magnificent public sculpture, but the fact that all this was combined with a cultured lifestyle and the best cuisine in the Greek world, so much so that life in Siracusa represented for many thinkers the all-round, multifaceted good life which was the real ideal of philosophy. There are claims that comedy was actually invented in Siracusa, with the merit going to Epicharmus, although he may have been only a reformer of an already existing genre. We know from Theocritus, a native of Siracusa in the third century BC, that there was a statue in the city in honor of Epicharmus, and the poet underlines the fact that his comedies were not merely escapist farces. Epigram 18 rendered in a fine translation by Robert Wells reads:

> The voice is Dorian; the man, Comedy's father,
>> Epicharmus, Dorian too.
> Dwellers in Syracuse, the prodigious city,
>> Bacchus, have set up for you
> This Bronze image, their fellow citizen's likeness:
>> Cast features stand for the true.
> It is right that men who took his precepts to heart
>> As boys, should honour the debt.
> He spoke their questions: how to live, what to do;
>> Their thanks are due to him yet.

Aeschylus' tragedy *The Persians* was certainly premiered in the city, and other Greek tragedies including masterpieces by Sophocles and Euripides were also performed in the city's theater. Pindar was virtually court poet to the tyrant Dionysius I, and Simonides was also in residence for a time. But man does not live by poetry alone, as the Greeks were well aware. The Siracusans were said to build as though there was no death and eat as if death would come the following day. The first work which can be called, approximately, a cookbook was written in the fifth century BC by Mithaecus, another Siracusan. Indulgence in such sensual pleasures then as now will delight some but draw equal and opposite disapproval from others. The relation to alcohol was not always healthy and balanced, as suggested in a mock-serious poem by Theocritus in Wells' translation:

> Listen to Orthon. His death proves him right.
> Never go out drunk on a winter's night.
> He did. Now he lies wrapped in foreign earth
> Lost to great Syracuse which gave him birth.

Plato, who made two visits to the city to widen his search for virtue and for those who practiced it, tut-tutted at the over-indulgence of the citizens and frowned on their habit of eating "to repletion twice a day" and then heading for the bedroom for other activities he also disapproved of. Later Diogenes, Europe's model cynic, turned the tables on the philosopher by sniggering that Plato had only gone to Siracusa for the food and drink.

Thucydides states that Siracusa was founded in 734 BC by people of Corinthian origin, and archaeologists by and large accept this date. The site had two excellent harbors, still in use today even if land erosion and rising sea levels have shifted their positions slightly. The first colonists settled on the island of Ortigia (Quail Island), which was joined to the mainland, then as now, by a causeway. Cicero records that the city was divided into four: Tycha, named after the temple of the goddess of Chance or Fortune, Neapolis, which is the site of the modern archaeological park containing the theater and quarries, Achradina, and the island of Ortigia. To this list should be added Epipoli, a couple of kilometers from the center, which contains the magnificent ruins of the defensive castle of Euryalus, designed by Dionysius himself. The city is still divided along those lines, and the division provides a handy way of getting around.

The politics of the city fascinated and horrified other Greeks in equal measure. If it is true that the term "tyrant" can have in Greek a more moderate sense than it has acquired in English, it is equally true that Syracusan tyrants were capable of a cruelty which even Machiavelli found abominable. In *The Prince,* he devotes a chapter to rejecting the idea that mere wickedness can be an acceptable basis for rule, and takes as his case study Agathocles of Siracusa, who in the fourth century BC dominated the whole of Sicily. Long before Rome became a force in Mediterranean affairs, the city had acquired power and prestige on land and sea, and became the leader in the wars with Phoenician and Carthaginian colonies. Plato worried that the cult of sensual pleasures in Siracusa would leave the practitioners unfit for essential, virile political and military pursuits, but empirical experience proved him wrong. Gelon the Tyrant, whose name is commemorated in the main street leading down to the bridge to Ortigia, led the Greek forces in 480 BC in the victorious and decisive battle against the Carthaginians at Himera (Imera). It is said that this battle took place on the very day the Athenians defeated the Persians in the sea-battle at Salamis, leaving the Greeks as the world's only superpower. Siracusa began a period of expansion, still underway a century later when in 397 BC Dionysius sacked the island of Mozia, on the far side of Sicily, selling into slavery those inhabitants he did not slaughter.

Having seen off the Persians and Carthaginians, the Greeks showed they did not require external enemies to wage war. Siracusa was drawn into the Peloponnesian War between Athens and Sparta. It was suspected of pro-Spartan sympathies, but Athens, resentful of Siracusan power, was in any case spoiling for a fight and dispatched its navy, initiating what has become known as the Sicilian Expedition. Few military campaigns have been dissected more tellingly or more incisively than this, for the chronicler was a historian of genius, Thucydides, himself an Athenian but one who deplored internecine warfare between Greeks and considered objectivity a moral imperative for a historian. The armada arrived in the western of Ortigia's two harbors, but the Athenian leadership was incompetent and failed to press home its initial advantage. The expedition lasted three years, from 416 to 413, and ended in the rout of the Athenians. Those who were not killed at sea were rounded up and imprisoned in the huge, deep, uncovered quarries, the *latomie*, which had been hewn from the ground to provide the rock used to build the city.

These *latomie* form deep cavities well below the level of the surrounding land, and are nowadays a central feature of the Neapoli archaeological park. The cliff walls are of limestone, whose use down the centuries gives the city's buildings that lightness of appearance which must have embellished the temples as much as it does the Baroque palaces. The depth of the quarries prevents the soil from being blown away, so carefully tended gardens with labyrinthine pathways and a variety of glorious plants and bushes—laburnum, azaleas, bougainvillea—have been put in place. It is now a garden of earthly delights but was once the place of inhuman suffering. The *latomia* of the rope workers is so called after the trade which was plied there, the latomia di Santa Venera is the most lovely in its layout, while the most famous has the beguiling name of the latomia del paradiso, but even Cicero was obliged to record that its beauty is fragile and deceptive, since these places had once been used to detain prisoners from all over Sicily. The artist Caravaggio came here during his sojourn in Siracusa, and it may have been him who gave the name "the ear of Dionysius" to a curious S-shaped cavern which stretches from ground level to the upper surface

The "ear of Dionysius," a fanciful name seemingly coined by Caravaggio,
but a place of inhuman suffering for the Athenian prisoners

and where legend has it that idiosyncratic acoustics allowed the tyrant to
eavesdrop on the conversation below.

The quarries place in the history of human misery derives from the
fact that it was here that the defeated Athenians were brought. They were
denied food or water, and even the visitor who spends an hour there under
the scorching sun with access to bars or provided with his own bottled
water will understand the nature of the torment involved. Those who were
confined there were the object of scorn and taunts from the fashionable citizenry who came to jeer from a safe distance. Any Athenians who were
still alive after ten weeks were sold into slavery, as was customary at the
time, although Siracusa maintained its reputation for cultured refinement
by releasing those who could recite from memory passages from Euripides.
Athens and Siracusa were two of the most sophisticated cities in human
history, the home of some of the greatest poets and philosophers the
western world has produced, but culture, as the twentieth century rediscovered, is no barrier to savagery.

The words of Thucydides describing the plight of the Athenian
prisoners could in essence apply to later acts of inhumanity:

Those who were in the stone quarries were treated badly by the Siracusans at first. There were many of them, and they were crowded together in a narrow pit, where, since there was no roof over their heads, they suffered first from the heat of the sun and the closeness of the air; and then, in contrast, came on the cold autumnal nights, and the change in temperature brought disease among them. Lack of space made it necessary for them to do everything on the same spot; and besides there were the bodies all heaped together on top of one another of those who had died from their wounds or from the change of temperature or other such causes, so that the smell was insupportable. At the same time, they suffered from hunger and thirst.

This [the Sicilian Expedition] was the greatest action that took place during the war, and in my opinion, the greatest action that we know of in Hellenic history. To the victors the most brilliant of successes, to the vanquished the most calamitous of defeats. For they were utterly and entirely defeated; their sufferings were on an enormous scale; their losses were, as they say, total; army, navy, everything was destroyed, and out of many, only a few returned.

Other classical sites are on the island of Ortigia. The road from the mainland goes past the remains of the temple sacred either to Apollo or Artemis, and while it is not possible to walk around the temple itself, the site is easily visible from the road. Siracusa later became part of the Roman Empire, and was well treated. After the Fall of Rome, the city came under the sway of the various ruling powers in the island: Byzantines, Arabs, Normans, Catalan-Aragonese, Spanish Bourbons. Perhaps the most significant legacy is that of the Spaniards, for Siracusa, which was badly damaged by the 1693 earthquake, is well endowed not only with ancient ruins but with beautiful Baroque buildings.

CHRISTIAN SIRACUSA

The conversion of Siracusa to Christianity was carried out in apostolic times, and the Acts of the Apostles record that St. Paul spent three days in the city, probably around 60 AD. The Church of St. Paul alongside the temple of Apollo is a candidate for the place where the apostle preached during his stay, but the evidence is not strong. The heart of Ortigia is Piazza Duomo, but before entering the cathedral itself it is a rewarding experience simply to sit on the steps outside, between the statues of Saints Peter and Paul, to enjoy the vista of the piazza, surely the most splendid and harmonious of all Sicily, perhaps of all Italy. This square can be regarded as the Parthenon of Siracusa, the civic and religious heart of the city from the days when it rivaled, and finally outdid, Athens. The piazza has been repaved in stone and cars have finally been banned, so there is a very un-Sicilian absence of clutter, chaos, bustle, and noise. Excavations have revealed that this has been a meeting place, and later a holy space, from the earliest times. The city has been periodically devastated by earthquakes, and early historians record a massive one in the sixth century BC. Remains of an Ionian temple built in the aftermath of that cataclysm, and possibly never completed, can be seen in the basement of the Palazzo del Senato (Town Hall) to the right of the cathedral.

To the left of the cathedral stands the Archbishop's Palace and further down the *ipogeo*, underground caves used to provide water to the city. Santa Lucia alla Badia (St. Lucy at the Abbey), a tall but somewhat squashed-looking church built after the 1693 earthquake, is at the foot of the square and is now a shrine to Caravaggio's painting of the *Burial of St. Lucy*. This was the artist's first work in the city after his escape from Malta

Burial of St Lucy by Caravaggio, painted after his arrival in Siracusa in 1608, on the run from the Knights of Malta

and was done in a hurry, although this is scarcely apparent. The focus is on the bishop administering a blessing to the dead saint, but the gaze shifts spontaneously to the muscular grave-diggers in the foreground, intent on the job, and to the throng of onlookers behind the bishop.

Facing the cathedral stands a line of palaces including the Palazzo Borgia and the Palazzo Beneventano del Bosco, once the headquarters of the Knights of Malta, with a somewhat implausible numismatic museum in between. Anthony Blunt was especially impressed by the Palazzo Benevantano, writing admiringly of the grand, sweeping staircase in the inner court which he judged to be "among the finest open staircases in Sicily." It was not the way of the Sicilian aristocracy or architects to bother about designing buildings to blend with one another, but these palaces unite like notes in a symphony. The Baroque balconies and the Palladian columns in the structure of the façades do not ostentatiously call attention to themselves, but seem content to be one part of a gracious whole.

The dominant building in the square is, obviously, the cathedral itself, which can be viewed as a history in miniature of Siracusan architecture over the last two millennia. The basic structure is provided by the Doric temple of Athena, ironically the goddess-protector of Athens, itself raised on the site of a pre-existing place of worship. There are grounds for believing that the Greek temple was built by the tyrant Gelon in thanksgiving for his victory over the Carthaginians at Himera. Cicero, less restrained than Blunt, went into ecstasies in his description of the portal, the inner architecture, and artwork, notably the gold and ivory doors which he believed the finest anywhere. They are long gone, but the original columns of the temple have been incorporated into the cathedral's walls and stand where they did when Dionysius came to pay homage to the goddess. Above them, an inscription on the inner walls of the nave boasts that the cathedral is the "daughter of St. Peter" and the second dedicated to Christ after the church in Antioch. St. Peter did not visit Siracusa in person but he dispatched his disciple Marcian, who was martyred there and gave his name to the crypt inside the catacombs of San Giovanni in the Neapoli district.

The middle of the three naves was the central part of the temple, and the high altar occupies the place where the pagan sacrificial table once stood. The temple dates from the seventh century BC, and with perfect symmetry it became a cathedral in the seventh century AD, but the

Detail of the Baroque façade of the Cathedral in Siracusa

conversion was scarcely a once-and-for-all exercise. In later times the building underwent changes to make it a Gothic church before it became an Arab mosque. When the Normans took control they eliminated all trace of Muslim worship but their church was in turn transmogrified into a Byzantine basilica before being altered in accordance with emerging Renaissance tastes. After the damage caused by the major earthquakes of 1542 and 1693, Baroque features were added. All these styles are visible in different parts of the cathedral. Restoration means that the interior has the bare-brick, austere look of early Christian basilicas, although there are some fine paintings, notably the tableaux of *Christ and the Apostles and Evangelists,* probably executed by the school of Antonello da Messina but possibly even by the *maestro* himself in his younger days. The left nave houses the last of the apses raised in Byzantine times, and the altar has a statue of the *Madonna of the Snows* by Antonello Gagini.

The sternest of architectural critics have complained that the façade, the purest of Baroque built in the first half of the eighteenth century, clashes with the style of the much older interior, and this may be so, but it is in itself a thing of wondrous beauty. Blunt was enthusiastic and considered it to be of its type "without equal in Sicily." Built on two levels with prominent columns on both, endowed with a beautifully sculpted porch and perfectly positioned statues, the façade is decorative and disciplined, not so much a work of theater, as Baroque architecture is reputed to be, as a lyrical composition in stone.

THE DISTRICTS OF SIRACUSA

One of the most amazing survivals from classical times is the Fountain of Arethusa, not far from Piazza Duomo, overlooking the bigger harbor. The legend behind this fountain is one of the sexiest and most beguiling of all Greek myths. The priapic river god Alpheus, whose river was near Olympia in mainland Greece, became enamoured of the beautiful nymph Arethusa, who did not return his affections. One day Alpheus attempted to take her by force but she made off with him in hot pursuit. When he was on the point of seizing her, she implored Artemis to help and the merciful goddess changed the nymph into a stream, which flowed under the Ionian Sea and emerged in Ortigia. Undeterred, Alpheus plunged in after her, reverted to watery form, and their waters, it is recorded, mingled together. There is no need to be a Freudian analyst to prise some intriguing *double entendres* from that union.

The main archaeological park is in the Neapoli zone. Apart from the quarries and the tomb of Archimedes already mentioned, the park contains a huge altar the size of a football pitch built by Hiero II as a place for animal sacrifices to Zeus the Liberator. The park contains two theaters, the Greek theater and the Roman amphitheater, from different ages and serving different purposes. The amphitheater, now closed off but clearly visible from the perimeter walkway, was the site of gladiatorial contests and even of the mock sea battles Roman audiences relished. The theater, the largest in the Greek world, is admirably positioned, with a splendid view onto the sea behind the stage. It was initially reserved purely for drama and for democratic political debate but it was modified by the Romans before they built their own venue. There are still Greek initials carved into the rock at the back where the dignitaries were seated, and a portico at the back where spectators could take refuge when the weather turned unpleasant.

The theater in Siracusa was the largest in Greater Greece. Some historians believe comedy was invented here

This theater was visited by Arthur Miller during his tour round the island chauffeured by a driver assigned to him by the mafia boss, Lucky Luciano. The stop there prompted some telling reflections on the theater and on drama.

> The driver would utter not a word mile after mile, hour after hour. But suddenly in Siracusa, a town still in partial ruin as a result of the war, he stopped the car, shut off the engine, got out and opened the door, and with a gesture behind him said, "*Teatro*".
>
> I got out and indeed there was the steel-fenced ruin of the tremendous Greek theatre. Why had he stopped here?—unless Luciano or the young bandit had had instructed him to, for me, a writer of plays. I made my way down the stone tiers of that vast, vine-grown, sun-blasted amphitheatre chiselled out of the mountain, and at last stood on the rock stage that ended with a sheer drop to the blue sea just behind it and the arch of the sky overhead. I felt something close to shame at how suffocatingly private our theatre had become, how impoverished by a psychology that was no longer involved with the universalities of fate. Was it possible that fourteen thousand people had sat facing the spot on which I stood. Hard to grasp how the tragedies could have been written for such massive crowds when in our time the mass audience all but demanded vulgarization.

The theater in Siracusa now hosts every summer a festival of Greek plays. At least on that site, there is no concession to vulgarization.

Not far from the park stands the modern, circular church dedicated to the cult of the Weeping Madonna, an otherwise unremarkable statue which was one day observed to be in tears at the degradation of contemporary humankind. The shrine has become a place of pilgrimage, not yet quite rivaling Lourdes or even Tindari. During the building many Greek artefacts were unearthed and these are now housed in the hugely impressive Archaeological Museum on the other side of the road. This museum was recently restructured and is a model of its kind, with exhibits from prehistoric times and from all nearby Greek settlements. Since Siracusa was a city of such wealth and poured so much of that wealth into public sculpture and into embellishing its many temples, the beauty of several of the busts and vases is overwhelming. No other work can rival the marvelous, sensual, tactile Venus Anadyomene, naked save for a modest drape which she clutches over her most private parts. Guy de Maupassant wrote poignantly that he had lost his head and heart to the statue, and wondered if the flesh would give way to the touch. It "is the body of a woman expressing all the real poetry of a caress," he enthused. To help the viewer get his breath back after this ethereal loveliness, another room displays a repellent, grimacing, grotesque Gorgon Medusa, commemorating one of the three sisters who made up this menacing, misanthropic figure. She had snakes in her hair and turned men to stone if they looked on her. According to Aeschylus, the three sisters had only one tooth and one eye which they shared between them, but in this representation Medusa has one eye but many teeth, visible behind a protruding tongue.

Those who have not had their fill of nymphs and mythological pools could make their way out the city to the Fonte Ciane, at the mouth of the river of that name. The pool was formed by the tears of the nymph Cyane, distraught when her bosom friend Persephone was kidnapped and taken to the underworld by Pluto. The remains of the grand temple of Jupiter the Olympian stand nearby. The ancient Siracusans were a devout people and certainly did their gods full honor. The really remarkable site outside the city is the castle of Eurialo (Euryalus), some eight kilometers from the present boundaries but once part of the ancient city, a distance which serves to give some idea of the scale of Siracusa in its glory days. Still officially known as the Epipoli quarter, it is in reality a separate village. The need for the defensive structure became clear when the Athenians threatened to attack the city from this point. The walls of the fort ran down to the harbor on Ortigia, closing off the city to the north-west. The choice of the highest point on the plain was obviously dictated by military considerations, and the fact that it afforded a spectacular view, much marveled at by earlier travelers but now partly obscured by high-rise buildings in the vicinity, was a chance by-product.

The sheer scale of what remains of the fortifications, with the labyrinthine tunnels, passages, towers, walls, and walkways, is stunning. The first plans for the fort were drawn up by Dionysius, but it was restructured on several occasions and it may be that Archimedes himself had a hand in later rebuilding. The fort was in use for a comparatively short time, from around 400 until 212 BC, when the castle was meekly surrendered to the Roman General Marcellus. Archaeological research suggests that the Byzantines occupied it and made some modifications, but in conception and grandeur it remains Greek—as does Siracusa.

Chapter Thirteen

THE GLORY OF THE BAROQUE

THE VAL DI NOTO

The division between Greek Sicily and the so-called Baroque "island" in the south-east is not tidily geographical. The two sit cheek by jowl, or indeed on top of the other. Siracusa, for example, is both a Greek and a Baroque city. Sometimes stones from antiquity were recycled for use in the sacred and civic buildings of later times, but while a traveler's physical movement within the geographical area of the Val di Noto may be slight, the intellectual and imaginative movement from millennium to millennium, from religion to religion, from culture to culture, from one cosmic vision of life to another is huge. What is constant in the region is, as Lampedusa expressed it, the hostile force of nature, not just the sun which makes "a Sicilian summer as severe as a Russian winter," but also the overhanging threat of earthquake and destruction. It was the impact of this natural force which necessitated a program of rebuilding and which created in its turn the group of magical, hauntingly beautiful but relatively unsung towns in the south-east corner of Sicily.

Too frequently in Sicily individual palaces or churches which are masterpieces of the Baroque style now stand shiftily and awkwardly alongside modern office blocks, supermarkets, stalls, and rows of double parked cars, preening themselves amid the banal constructions of the post-war housing boom, struggling to maintain their dignity like a dowager duchess fallen on hard times. The glorious exception to this rule is the Val di Noto, the province in the south-east of the island dominated by the Iblaean Hills, where whole towns and villages were constructed, or reconstructed, in their entirety in Baroque styles. The main towns are Noto, Avola, Ragusa, Palazzolo Acreide, Comiso, and Modica, but there are also some enchanting smaller centers like Ispica or Scicli. This Baroque "island," whatever internal variations there are, was created after a natural disaster and is the product of one culture, one spirit, one set of circumstances, and one historical age, so the planning

The Triumphal Arch at Noto, constructed in 1893 as an act of homage
to the Bourbons, but the symbolic entrance to a world inspired by the
Baroque vision.

has a harmony, unity, coherence, uniqueness, and beauty not found anywhere else in Sicily, or indeed anywhere.

At the entrance to the town of Noto stands a grand arch, the Porta Reale (Royal Gate). Erected to mark the visit of King Ferdinand II in the mid-nineteenth century, well after the Baroque period, it is made of the honey-colored stone which was readily available in the region and which seems to glow with different colors according to the strength of the sunlight. It is not unduly ornate if compared to Roman triumphal arches or even to palaces and churches in the town itself, but it is wholly appropriate that there be some border-crossing to mark the entrance not only to Noto itself but to the Val di Noto as a whole. Passing under the arch and viewing the town beyond for the first time gives the visitor an irresistible sense that this is a step into a new dimension, into a uniquely wonderful world, into a territory ruled by aesthetic and moral standards different from those on the other side.

There was one decisive event which determined the status of this territory and it occurred on the days and nights between 9 and 11 January, 1693. Prior to those days the town of Noto was sited on a nearby hill and was subject to the normal vicissitudes of Sicilian history. Before the coming of the Greeks it was inhabited by the Sicels, whose leader was Ducetius and whose campaign of resistance against the Greek colonists is commemorated by the Palazzo Ducezio, currently the town hall. Some believe that the population still has the DNA of the ancient Sicels, although others believe that this tribe was driven out and are the mysterious people who found refuge in nearby Pantalica, where their dead were buried in the caves carved out in the cliffs. The Greeks were followed by the Romans, by the Arabs (who gave the town the name still in use), then by the Normans, the Swabians, and the Aragonese—the normal progression of Sicilian history. Until the earthquake of the ninth to the eleventh January 1693.

Even by Sicilian standards the tremors that shook the Val di Noto over those three days were devastating. Buildings were destroyed as far away as Catania, and the full force was felt from Siracusa down to Pachino and Scicli in the south and to Vittoria in the west. It was believed that some fifty-eight inhabited centers were affected and of them twenty were left totally destroyed. Contemporary reports to the Spanish viceroy put the number of casualties in the whole district at 53,757, but some recent historians claim that the total may have exceeded 100,000. A contemporary chronicler, Filippo Tortora, provided a vivid account of the apocalyptic event as it affected Noto itself.

> In the year 1693, on the 9 January, at the fourth hour of the night, a ferocious tremor was felt which destroyed many buildings with the loss of two hundred or more persons, and on the following day everyone sought refuge in the open spaces inside and around the city, and fear of this dreadful scourge compelled them to remain there for the whole of the Saturday night… on the stroke of the twentieth hour of the Sunday, forty hours having passed, there occurred an earthquake so horrible and terrifying that the ground moved like a wave in the sea, the mountains shook and broke apart, and the entire city collapsed in a single moment with around one thousand people miserably perishing. When this fierce tremor finally ended, the skies darkened, the sun clouded over giving way to rains, hailstones, winds and thunder.

However, for once in Sicilian history, the response to the catastrophe was immediate, generous, far-sighted, and implemented with high expertise and efficiency. The reconstruction program resulted in an area embellished with some of the most beautiful buildings anywhere. Spanish rule has in general been sharply criticized both by contemporaries and later historians, and with good reason, for its inefficiency and its indifference to the plight of the people over whom the rulers held sway, but the rebuilding program in the Val di Noto was an exception. It involved an alliance between the Duke of Uzeda, the then Spanish viceroy, and a highly enlightened coterie of civil officials. Even the Sicilian nobility distinguished themselves. The viceroy nominated Giuseppe Lanza, Duke of Camastra, as vicar general to take charge of the works and he was backed by the local lord, the Prince of Butera. An unusually talented group of architects and planners, some fully deserving the overused description "genius" and almost all Sicilians, were commissioned to produce plans. The contribution of the local craftsmen, the masons, marble workers, builders, sculptors, and carvers who gave a refined finish to the grand overall scheme was no less important in creating the final appearance of these marvelous places.

The first decisions to be taken after a catastrophe concern whether the rebuilt town should have the appearance of the one it will replace and whether rebuilding should be done on the same site as the devastated center. Surprisingly perhaps, the people themselves were invited to take part in this decision-making process, and different decisions were taken in different towns. Avola and Noto moved to new sites, while in Ispica and Comiso the new town arose on and alongside the old. Ragusa reached a compromise of its own. There had long been rivalry between the parishes of San Giorgio (St. George) and San Giovanni Battista (St. John the Baptist), and the decision of the proletarian parishioners of the latter was to move to the new, upper town, while the aristocracy with their clergy stayed in Ragusa Ibla, the older town lower down the hillside. There was new building and new planning for both parts of Ragusa as it emerged from the rubble, but the agreed plan gives Ragusa the distinctive layout which makes it seem to straddle a crevice between two centers.

The decisions taken for Noto gave the town two completely separate sites. The earthquake-devastated town of Noto Antica (Old Noto), which stood on a hill, was abandoned and a completely new town built on the plain about five miles away. Perhaps an ideal journey through Sicily should begin not in Messina or Palermo but in the twin towns of Noto, since few other places emanate such a visible, almost tangible sense of developing history. The ruined town has the integrity of Pompeii. It was a prosperous place, whose wealth derived largely from agriculture in the surrounding fertile plains. The streets are still laid out as they were before the earthquake and there are traces of all the various peoples who made their home here. This was where the settlers of the Bronze Age, whose burial grounds can be seen beyond the city walls, first established themselves until they were expelled by militaristic Greek colonizers. The Arabs used Noto as a military stronghold, while in the Norman Middle Ages it became a flourishing cultural center. The remains of a castle stand beside the main gate, and in the heart of the town the walls of what was once a Jesuit church are visible. Noto Antica is, after years of neglect, now being more systematically excavated, but in the meantime it offers a fascinating if gloomy spectacle of life as it was, *before*.

The rebuilding was done at that ideal period in the evolution of the Baroque when the need for experimentation and uncertainty had passed, and the subsequent phase of staleness and weariness had not yet been reached. The Baroque was already flourishing in Sicily and on mainland Italy, so there were tried-and-tested techniques and standards which could be applied. The Baroque style was chosen by the planners and designers for the rebuilding of Noto without the discussion there would be in Warsaw centuries later over whether the town should be rebuilt in the old or in a more modern style. There were, inevitably, dissenting voices even then. A French diplomat, Denis Denon, lamented that such excellent prime materials had been employed on projects of "such poor taste," resulting in a city "constructed as a genuine offence to art." The most celebrated travelers, Patrick Brydone and Goethe, simply avoided the place, and even today it is routine in some quarters to refer sniffily to all Baroque enterprises.

Anyone of even moderate sensibility coming through the Porta Reale onto Corso Vittorio Emanuele will have the sensation of walking onto an elegantly arranged stage set. This is a world of order created by refined human intellects, even if those intellects recognized their debts to the Divine. There is an additional element of sun-soaked sensuality in the layout of streets and in the façades of palaces and churches fronting onto them. Anthony Blunt draws attention to the "pale yellow-golden colour" of the stone and its contribution to the beauty of the architecture. Hewn in local quarries, its softness of texture and tactile feel enhance the already overwhelming initial visual impact. In the wake of a natural calamity, especially one on this scale, there is always the fear of the collapse of civilization, especially in a culture in which civilization itself is viewed as precarious, but the abiding impression aroused by Noto is that this is the work of a people refusing to be cowed and broken by disaster, a defiant community determined to assert their own worth and their own sense of aesthetic order in the face of a malevolent nature. This is the best of Sicily and of the Sicilian experience. The Greeks believed that civilization represented the victory of cosmos, the fusion of the beautiful and the true, over mere chaos. Noto represents that vision. The thinkers of the time were concerned with the ideal of the city, and when given *carte blanche* in the Val di Noto they took full advantage of it. This town is imbued with humanist ideals, an ideal city made in the measure of man.

The streets are straight and wide, unlike the narrow lanes of a medieval city; the angles are sharp and crisp, and space is created not just for business but for living. Staircases, with their grand sweep and angled corners, lend themselves to the Baroque style, but while such staircases are normally interior, in Noto they give onto the street, a stylistic device dictated by the unevenness of the terrain after the earthquake. The brief stroll along the Corso from the Porta Reale to the central square, where the cathedral sits facing the center of local political power, should be sufficient to convince anyone of the accuracy of the description of the street as "a garden in stone." The Corso is a spectacle of graceful and harmonious planning. The stone of the buildings glimmers in the sunlight and seems to change color from a mild, pale yellow to a rich rose according to the time of day. It is worth braving the pitiless midday sun, when all sane inhabitants seek shelter at home, to savor in solitude the peace of the place and to relish the sheer joyfulness of an architecture which sings gracefully but *fortissimo*. It is rewarding to make return visits, firstly in the early evening when the stones assume a great seriousness and again after dark when the tastefully arranged illumination enhances the spectacle of loveliness which is the whole town.

Time spent seated on the steps of the Palazzo Ducezio, facing the Cathedral of San Nicolò (St. Nicholas), is rewarding. The palace itself was designed in the mid-eighteenth century by Vincenzo Sinatra, one of the masters of the rebuilding program, and has a colonnade round three sides

A balcony on a palace in Noto

and a balcony on the upper level. Regrettably, what one man has created another can undo, and the palace suffered from work in the 1950s which undermined the balance of the original, although not fatally so. The Bishop's Palace is nearby and various convents are clustered around, but the cathedral, reached by a long, wide, straight staircase, was allocated a central point in the town. Its façade has two clearly divided levels, with columns over the entrance, statues arranged at various points, and the frontage bounded on either side by a bell-tower. The interior has three naves, and in a chapel at the foot of the right-hand nave the body of San Corrado, the patron saint of the town, is exposed for veneration.

The church is entirely free of the decorative excesses of other Baroque buildings, but this was not the way it was planned. Alterations made to the structure put greater stress on the roof and the building was further weakened by an earthquake in 1990. The city and church authorities were warned that the building needed urgent attention if disaster were to be averted, but the inevitable ecclesiastical and municipal inaction meant that the promised disaster occurred in 1996 when a large part of the ceiling

The Church of St. Dominic in Noto, rivaling the cathedral in grandeur

and cupola collapsed onto the floor. The community was mobilized, funds were found for restoration, and the cathedral was reopened in 2007. It is interesting to note that on this occasion the guiding principle of the architectural work was that everything should be reconstructed "as it was, where it was." Paintings of the apostles on the walls have been carried out, but so far no frescoes have been painted on the ceiling.

The two palaces alongside the cathedral, the Palazzo Landolina and the Palazzo Nicolaci, are fine example of civic Baroque. The Via Corrado Nicolaci runs from the Corso alongside the side of the Nicolaci Palace where the balconies are supported by carvings of sirens, sea monsters, grinning heads, and other grotesques, and the street is closed off at the top by the curved front of the Chiesa di Montevergine (Church of the Mount of the Virgin). On the third Sunday in May, the feast of the *Primavera Barocca* (Baroque Spring), the street is carpeted with flowers and decorative motifs chosen to illustrate the theme chosen for that year's festivity. This embellishment heightens the sense that the street is an internal corridor of some grand palatial residence rather than an urban thoroughfare.

There are around twenty churches in Noto, some of which are closed and others of which are located inside religious houses, but there are enough for even the most insatiable of architectural researchers. The Church of San Domenico (St. Dominic) stands further along the Corso and competes with the cathedral in grandeur. The work of Rosario Gagliardi, who was an engineer in the town before the earthquake but who developed into an architect of genius, it was completed in 1737. Gagliardi was often more successful with his inventive exteriors than with his interiors, and while here the interior has a warmth he did not always achieve, the almost circular exterior with inset columns is masterly, but then this town is a triumph of human creativity.

ADVENTURES IN THE BAROQUE

Like Noto, Avola was rebuilt on a plain some distance from the original town, Avola Antica (Ancient Avola). The old town is not as desolate or isolated as its equivalent in Noto and new houses were recently built nearby. The shrine of the Madonna delle Grazie (Madonna of the Graces) is now marooned in this incongruous zone. The site for the new town was chosen by a Jesuit-architect, Angelo Italia, and it was he who gave the *centro storico* (historic center) the distinctive, hexagonal form which can still be made out by those whose imagination will permit them to block out the sprawling city around it. The cathedral and the Church of Santa Venera—the name has no equivalent in English and may even be a corruption of "Venus"—are very fine, but the main attraction of the town is the airy spaciousness of the overall urban plan. The city hosts a large number of religious and secular festivals of which the most popularly celebrated is that of Santa Venera herself and lasts a whole week. The most exciting, however, takes place on 19 March, the feast of St. Joseph, carpenter and stepfather of Jesus. Presumably to offer more work to those of his profession, bonfires of wooden objects are lit in various quarters of the city. The most welcome feasts are the celebrations in August of the wines, almonds and other foodstuffs produced in the locality.

Those who would like some respite from the sun or some rest from the demands of history and of relentless sightseeing might like to continue up past Avola Antica towards a gorge known as the Cava Grande del Cassibile. A river runs along the course of this gorge, and there are some delightful pools along its course, but this is not exactly the secret, less traveled spot which travelers dream of finding.

It would be a sad loss not to find some time to spend in Ispica, a jewel of a town, and one rarely on any itinerary. Once again there are two centers. The old town, now part of the Parco Archeologico della Forza, was continuously inhabited from prehistoric times until 1693, and there are catacombs and ruined churches to be seen, as well as the remains of the caves in which much of the population once lived. Following the catastrophe, the town was rebuilt on a hill, and it is worth starting any visit at the Church of Santa Maria Maggiore (St. Mary Major), surrounded by a semi-circular arcade of cubicles, the work of Vincenzo Sinatra, and apparently intended as a reminder of the earlier cave-dwellings. The Church of the Annunziata (Annunciation) is fronted by a long rectangular, tree-lined square, and has a façade of three distinct levels tapering to the top. The ceiling inside has a series of scenes from the Old and New Testament done in delicate stucco work which somehow belies the cruelty of the scenes chosen. Judith displays the head of Holofernes with alarming *sang-froid,* and the head has been severed with astonishing tidiness leaving a neat hole where the neck had been. For such a small town—the population is around 15,000—there are several very grand palaces, although the two most impressive were constructed long after the Baroque age. The Palazzo Bruno del Belmonte, now the headquarters of the local authority, was designed by the *art nouveau* architect Ernesto Basile, and Palazzo Antonino Bruno also dates from the early twentieth century.

A visit to Scicli, whose name may derive from the Sicels, will require a detour and the use of minor roads, but it is a pretty little place, on the sea, with fishing one of the main occupations, as is reflected in the stimulating local cuisine. The town was rebuilt post-1693 at the intersection of three ravines, and it sprawls over all of them. Once again there are more palaces than such a small town would seem able to support, although few of them seem to be lived in now. The builders of Palazzo Beneventano had curious taste for the grotesque, judging by the heads and gargoyles which are on view on the façade. The Church of San Bartolomeo (St. Bartholomew), a saint who was a great local favorite, is not in any way an example of inferior rustic architecture but a building which can stand comparison with anything in Palermo or Catania, or even Rome. The festival in May celebrating liberation from the Saracens is something of a curiosity, for the central figure is the *Madonna delle Milizie* (Madonna of the

Militias), perhaps the only feast anywhere featuring a bellicose and not motherly Virgin Mary. In 1091 she apparently appeared on horseback alongside the Normans in a battle against Muslim forces, an event commemorated in a shrine in nearby Milici. Also nearby are some of the best beaches in Sicily.

Modica was rebuilt, splendidly, on the site it had occupied before the catastrophe, but is divided into Modica Alta (Upper Modica) and Modica Bassa (Lower Modica), joined by the Guerrieri bridge, one of the highest in Europe. It is a charming city with a labyrinth of small streets and lanes and staircases linking the two centers. It was not as comprehensively rebuilt as other towns in the vicinity, and traces of the older Byzantine or Gothic survive in several places such as the entrance to the Church of the Carmine (Carmen). It has been referred to as the "town of one hundred churches," but the masterpiece is the Cathedral of San Giorgio (St. George) in the upper town, built on the ruins of the earthquake-damaged original, probably by Vincenzo Gagliardi. It is reached by climbing up 250 steps, perhaps the longest ecclesiastical climb in the island but it is fully worth the expenditure of energy. The grandiose façade ascends gracefully to the single, crowning, central tower, and the compact harmony of the design is magnificent. Highly skilled *stuccatori* were active in Modica and left evidence of their talents in such churches as San Francesco Saverio (St. Francis Xavier) and the Carmine.

Ragusa is now the capital of the province and vies with Noto for the title of the most spectacular and beautiful town in the region. Anthony Blunt preferred to compare it with Modica, pointing out that the architectural histories of the two towns run parallel, perhaps because they occupy comparable hilly sites. "In both cities the sites, which are steeply sloping, are of crucial importance and must have encouraged local builders to develop the great scenic effects which are the most conspicuous feature of their architecture." There is no doubting the scenic impact. This town too is divided into an upper and lower, Ragusa Superiore and Ragusa Inferiore, the latter also known as Ragusa Ibla. Social relations were apparently unharmonious, and the two parishes were happy to use the earthquake as an opportunity to move apart. The aristocrats in Ragusa Ibla had a high regard for themselves and viewed those in the upper town as upstart *parvenus*.

The two parts are joined by stairs, cunningly hidden at some points behind and between residences. The descent between palaces, churches, and nicely decorated dwellings is a delight, but the delight evaporates during the laborious ascent. Nevertheless, from any point Ragusa as a whole is glorious in its captivating beauty. The starting-point should be the piazza in front of the Cathedral of San Giovanni Battista (St. John the Baptist), the center of the upper town. The area behind is a twentieth-century muddle, but the area below contains the twin reconstructed and redesigned townscapes.

In Italian, the words *duomo* and *cattedrale* are normally interchangeable, both meaning cathedral. Ragusa may be the only city which boasts both, each standing over an open piazza which allows the full vista to be appreciated. The *cattedrale*, with its six inbuilt columns, its perfectly rectangular windows, its niche over the door for the statue of St. John the Baptist, and its beautifully incorporated bell-tower, has a satisfactory completeness, while the equally lovely Church of San Giorgio (St. George) in the lower town gives a slightly smug sense of having knowingly overcome construction difficulties created by its angled position on a slope. The church is best appreciated from the far end of the square, from where its angled façade seems even more oblique. The elaborately wrought if somewhat intrusive iron gates add to the impact, and the long staircase leading to the doorway seems to constitute an extra level to the three tiers of the church, each of which incorporates cleverly inserted rows of columns. In the center of the façade the towering cross sits over, in descending order, a clock, a stained glass window glimmering inside and out in the sunlight, and finally the portals of the doorway. On the left, a sculpture shows St. George dealing firmly with the dragon, while on the right the same saint rides on horseback in triumph.

Ragusa has been inhabited from the earliest times, and excavations underway in the park at the foot of Ragusa Ibla are bringing to the surface a Roman settlement. Round the corner are the remains of the church of St. George in Sicily's *other* dominant architectural style, the Catalan-Gothic. St. George is the patron saint of Catalonia and the fifteenth-century portal is all that remains of the Catalans' place of worship. Over the door the saint is frozen in the act of driving his spear into the dragon, but the semi-circular rows of carvings on the sides are even more impressive. Some foolish bureaucrat ordered that an iron fence be erected over the entrance to keep the people at bay, but it does detract from the effect.

The old town, Ragusa

The charm of Ragusa, like Noto, is not in individual buildings, stupendous though some of them are, but in the wonder of the harmony of the whole built area.

Comiso and Vittoria would be national treasures in any other country in Europe, but in this district they are merely provincial towns. Comiso may be a small, off-the-beaten track town, but it has the appurtenances of a larger city, and its airiness and evident *douceur de vivre* are captivating features in this relaxed town. There are two churches of note, each with wide spaces in front of both. The cathedral has a Baroque façade with a neoclassical dome and is in some ways reminiscent of Christopher Wren's St. Paul's. Santa Maria delle Stelle (Our Lady of the Stars) has three tiers with five statues built into the frontage. Originally the statues were six, but St. Jerome gave way. The noble Naselli family were once the dominant force, and they lived in the imposing Aragonese castle first built in the thirteenth century. Alongside is the communal theater, which still bears the family name. Their local adversaries were the equally blue-blooded

Occhipinti family, who once used the Church of San Giuseppe (St. Joseph) as their private chapel. The central square is built round a fountain with a reclining statue of Diana, goddess of hunting, and although the present work has been restored countless times, some such statue has stood there since Roman times. The ex-fish market is a grand, colonnaded structure which now houses the Gesualdo Bufalino Foundation, established after the death of the writer in 1996.

Vittoria was founded by the Countess of Modica, Vittoria Colonna, daughter of a viceroy, who modestly named the town after herself. She could not have been all bad for she is said to have introduced the Nero d'Avola grape, and thus the celebrated wine, to this district. The Cerasuolo, a lighter, rosier version of the Nero d'Avola, is another native of Vittoria and a splendid aperitif. Like the other towns in the region, Vittoria benefited from masterly post-earthquake planning, and the regular, rectilinear layout provides an atmosphere of ease. The principal church, dedicated to St. John the Baptist, is more sober than other churches in the vicinity, and there are a surprising number of small churches in the town. A neoclassical theater stands alongside the cathedral, and that in itself is a philosophical statement of values.

In the Baroque Age, the Val di Noto as a whole saw a unique explosion of artistic, architectural inventiveness based on a humanistic vision of life. There are many other villages and towns in the Iblaean hills worth visiting and savoring, making this province probably the largest art gallery in the world. And a wonderful place for living and reflecting on living.

Chapter Fourteen

THE GREAT TEMPLES

AGRIGENTO, SEGESTA, AND SELINUNTE

Traveling in Sicily can be like passing through looking-glasses as magical as those which opened out for Alice in Lewis Carroll's fiction, with moves either into the wonderland of myth or into a landscape redolent of an equally astounding history. Along the south coast away from the beauty of the eighteenth-century Baroque towns, the first place of interest is Gela, once an important Greek colony and the place where the great tragedian Aeschylus met his end. A sea bird looking for a rock to break open a shell in its beak mistook the dramatist's bald head for a hard surface and dropped the object from a height, thereby killing him and committing one of the greatest of recorded crimes against theater.

Gela was one of the landing points for the British and American armies in the invasion of Sicily in 1943. The infantry stormed ashore on the beaches, while paratroopers were landed on the plains outside the city. High winds meant that the parachute drop did not go according to plan and the German resistance made these plains one of the bloodiest battle-fields in the Sicilian campaign. An *autostrada* now runs over fields where hundreds of men died. The town itself is a nest of *mafiosi* who have even set up their own breakaway organization called the *Stidda*, the dialect word for star, but the mafia attends to its own business without harming out-siders. Maybe its presence is felt in other ways, for there is something tired and depressed about the town. It was a flourishing place in ancient times, and excavations, especially near the sea in a district called Bosco Littorio, have brought to light ceramic workshops and evidence of trade with other cities in the Mediterranean. The acropolis too has been uncovered, and the archaeological museum is one of the best in Sicily.

Further along, Palma di Montechiaro has no Greek associations and its history is tied up with that of the Sicilian nobility. The "Palm" of the town's name was taken from the tree which figured on the coat-of-arms of the noble De Caro family who dominated it for some centuries, and the Montechiaro part, added in 1863, refers to a nearby castle, but by that time the town had passed into the family of Tomasi di Lampedusa, ancestors of the novelist. The town owes such renown as it has to its association with him, although in *The Leopard* the town is given the fictional name Donnafugata. Confusingly, there is a town of that name near Ragusa, and the hot, sweaty journey from Palermo to the Ducal Palace depicted in the novel owes more to the author's recollections of journeys in summer to another of the family's properties in Santa Maria di Belice. This is legitimate poetic licence, however confusing for admiring pilgrims. Moreover, for his film director Luchino Visconti shot the Donnafugata scenes in Palma. The palace, the cathedral, and the convent can all be seen side by side from the coastal road. The palace is now part of the Lampedusa literary park, and houses a library relating to the writer. The cathedral has twin bell-towers and a grand stairway, while the nuns in the convent still make the sweetmeats that Lampedusa speaks of appreciatively. As is mentioned in the novel, the convent also contains the remains of the Blessed Corbera, one of the many members of the Tomasi family who went into religious life. All but devotees of everything associated with the writer will be content with the view from the road below.

AGRIGENTO

The road itself proceeds past Licata to Agrigento. Nobody in recent centuries has had a good word to say about the modern town of Agrigento. Even in the eighteenth century Patrick Brydone did not mince his words: "The city of Agrigentum, now called Girgenti, is irregular and ugly. On our arrival, we found a great falling-off indeed; the houses are mean, the streets dirty, crooked and narrow. It still contains near twenty thousand people; a sad reduction from its ancient grandeur." On the other hand, Goethe wrote that he had never in his life "enjoyed such a vision of spring" as he did at sunrise on the morning of his visit, but the impression is that he focused on the light to avoid talking about the town. The quality of the light everywhere in Sicily is bound to dazzle a traveler from the north, and the light and changing colors of sunrise and sunset in the south of Sicily, whether reflected on the waves of the sea or illuminating the hills and fields, are unusually pure, in all seasons. In Agrigento it makes the stones of the temples glow.

Temple F, the erroneously named Temple of Concord, the best preserved of the ruins in the Valley of the Temples, Agrigento

Goethe spent his first day looking down longingly from the heights of the modern city at the temples below, chafing with impatience at the insistence of their guide that they tour contemporary Agrigento before venturing down to examine the ruins of the ancient city. He was here to see the temples, and most people still make their way to Agrigento for the same reason. The town has been on its present site overlooking where the ancient city stood since the Byzantine period in the sixth century. There is some doubt over why the decision was made to move uphill, away from the Valley of the Temples. It was not, as elsewhere, the consequence of earthquake or natural disaster, but was possibly dictated by a desire to find safer territory away from the depredations of pirates from North Africa.

Since the days of Brydone and Goethe the town has suffered further from badly planned, or completely unplanned, expansion. The unlovely post-war additions to the built-up area, including a bizarre, baffling network of flyovers on the approach road from the Palermo side, suggest that the city authorities had little interest in creating a pleasing urban environment. They are not responsible for some high-rise apartment blocks or whole areas which were thrown up with no regard for law or regulations, a phenomenon known in Italian as *abusivismo*, lawlessness rather than abuse. The city has the misfortune to lie within the "mafia triangle," and the stranglehold of organized crime on the city and the mafia's ability to have contracts awarded to companies under its control may go a long way to explaining why some sections are an eyesore.

However, it would be a pity to ignore modern Agrigento entirely, since it has been an important place for centuries and is today the capital of one of Sicily's provinces. The historical center is still reasonably well delineated, and there are some interesting buildings. The main thoroughfare, Via Atenea, is lined with chic boutiques and little cafés, but it is also the core of the medieval labyrinth of lanes and narrow streets and is reminiscent of towns in North Africa. The Arab influence has been strong. After the Greek glory had faded, Agrigento remained too important to be wholly ignored so there are traces, sometimes in the same building, of all the cultures which have swept through Sicily. The thirteenth-century Church of Santo Spirito (Holy Spirit) with the adjoining Cistercian Abbey, also called the Badia Grande (Great Abbey), lies off the Via Atenea and is an example of a patchwork of historical styles. The church has a Catalan-Gothic portal and a Baroque façade, but its most remarkable features are the Arab-Norman wooden ceiling and the stucco sculptures by Giacomo Serpotta. The Abbey was once the home to a congregation of nuns but is now a museum. It is still possible to purchase locally made cakes and sweetmeats made from almond and pistachio which were once manufactured by the sisters. The products come in a variety of zoological or botanical forms, all more chaste than comparable delicacies retailed in Palermo or Catania on the feast days of the patron saints. There is an "almond in bloom" festival in February.

The cathedral, badly damaged by bombing during the war but comprehensively restored, stands at the end of an alleyway at the top of the town, possibly on the site of the acropolis of the Greek city. From its steps there is an excellent view over the countryside, onto the temples, and down to the sea. The church was given its Christian form in the eleventh century by Bishop Gerlando, now patron saint of Agrigento. The name is common in these parts, and has more than once been called out in court when some *mafioso* was finally arraigned. Entrance to the interior and to St. Gerlando's chapel is through a Gothic doorway but the bronze statue of the saint is a copy since the original was stolen, no doubt by devotees who wished to keep the sacred artwork close at hand. The polite word to describe the cathedral's style is eclectic. Elements of the Arab-Norman stand alongside Catalan-Gothic and Baroque. Purists may demur, but the overall impact is pleasing. The cathedral once contained a sarcophagus with carvings of the myth of Phaedra and her incestuous love for her stepson Hippolytus which Goethe judged to be "an example of Greek art from its most graceful period," but it is now housed in the adjacent Diocesan Museum.

Even in the town there is no escaping the Greeks. Santa Maria dei Greci (Our Lady of the Greeks), a thirteenth-century church not far from the cathedral, is built on the site of a temple to Athena which can be accessed from an entrance off the left nave. The archaeological museum on the way out of the town is tastefully laid out with items taken from the nearby valley. Of special interest is the recumbent *telamon*, a gigantic figure, one of three which were intended as supports for the temple of Zeus, and a naked statue of a young boy reassembled from parts which were found at the bottom of a well. Alongside the museum is the Church of San Nicola (St. Nicholas), built from stone borrowed from the temples at different times to produce a beguiling riot of styles. The garden alongside was once the site of a *comitium*, the meeting place for citizens of the city.

The giant *telamon* lying alongside the Temple of Zeus Olympios

When these sights have been seen, even the most conscientious traveler can consider that he or she has done their duty by today's Agrigento, and can proceed to visit the ancient city. The Greeks called it Akragas, the Romans named it Agrigentum, the Arabs altered that to Kerkent, which was then Italianized to Girgenti, the name by which the town was known until 1927 when Mussolini decreed that the classical name be restored. Akragas was founded in the late sixth century BC by people from Gela together with groups from the island of Rhodes. It was and is an ideal site, protected by hills and cliffs to the rear and close to an excellent port. It was an agricultural center, surrounded by vines and olive groves as well as by fertile fields and all this clarified for Goethe why Sicily had been known as the granary of the Roman Empire. The city prospered and became one of the greatest in the Greek world, both in military and cultural terms. For the poet Pindar, Akragas was "the most beautiful city of mortal men, a city that lives upon the hill of lovely dwellings above the bank where sheep graze beside the river." The city gained a reputation for its sybaritic lifestyle, and there is a story that one of the tyrants hewed a cavity out of the rock to create a huge cellar for his private stores of wine. The historian Diodorus Siculus reported that "no country produced finer or more extensive vineyards." Pindar composed odes in honor of victors at the Olympic Games, and the festivities celebrating victors on their return, involving regiments of charioteers and cavalry men, awed the rest of Greece.

Agrigento's great philosopher-poet, the pre-Socratic thinker Empedocles, much admired by Bertrand Russell, believed that human life was ruled by twin forces which he named Love and Strife, and the strife was more in evidence than love in Agrigento's history. Periods of democratic government were interspersed with rule by tyrants, the most notorious of whom was Phalaris, in power in the sixth century BC. A blacksmith in the city invented an ingeniously sadistic execution device in the form of a bull. The condemned man would be locked inside, a fire lit underneath, and the screams of the victim would sound like the roars of a bull. Phalaris declared himself impressed but sceptical, and ordered that the inventor be roasted in his own invention to prove its worth. Phalaris was responsible for reinforcing Agrigento's defensive walls and for constructing the shrine to the chthonic divinities (the lords of the underworld) in the southern part of the temple area. Theron, who became tyrant around a century later, was a leader in the war against the Carthaginians which culminated in the Battle of Himera and established what can be regarded as an Agrigentan empire stretching from southern Sicily to the Tyrrhenian Sea. It was once believed that he was buried in what the signs still call the Tomb of Theron at the extreme southern end of the Valley of the Temples, but this is now believed to be a later Roman funerary monument. Remains of Roman houses, some with traces of mosaics, can be seen in the Hellenistic-Roman quarter near the archaeological museum, but that apart there is little visible evidence of the Roman occupation.

The site known as the Valley of the Temples covers a large, open area, enclosed by two rivers now called San Biagio and Drago, but unbelievably cut in two by a modern road. The temple area is illuminated at night, electricity enhancing the effect of the moon and stars, and when it is seen outlined against the sea from the town above, the effect is overwhelming. Even the most prosaic souls will find their minds filled with reflections on the flight of time as well as of feelings of wonder at this perfectly achieved harmony between nature and human creativity. How powerful were those old gods? What was the force of belief in those Greeks? How great was the vision of the temple designers, how miserable the life of the slaves who gave effect to that vision?

Until fairly recently it was possible to climb up the external stairs and examine the interior area of the temples one by one, but this is no longer permitted. The state of preservation of the temples varies, and if in some cases the removal of the stones for use in the churches was clearly damaging, in other cases, such as with the Temple of Concord, the adaptation of the temple to make it suitable for Christian worship guaranteed its survival. The space between the columns was filled in by the early Christians and remained so until the late eighteenth century when an enthusiastic dilettante, the Prince of Torremuzza, was given permission to restore the place to its ancient form. Other keen amateurs were responsible for giving names to the temples, but it has been established that their attribution of individual temples to specific gods and goddesses was unreliable, so the more dutiful archaeologists of today prefer to use a series of letters rather than sacred names to refer to them. The principal letters and corresponding names are:

A: once known as the Temple of Herakles (or Hercules in Latin)

B: the huge Temple of Olympian Zeus (Jupiter), never completed and no more than a jumble of stones

C: Temple of Demeter

D: Temple of Hera (or Juno) Lacinia

F: the massive Temple of Concord

G: Temple of Vulcan

H: Temple of Aesculapius

I: Temple of Castor and Pollux

There is no more to Temple I than a reconstructed corner standing alongside the circular shrine with central *bothroi,* carefully shaped cavities for offerings to the chthonic divinities. Only the massive Temple B to Zeus can be identified with certainty. In diabolic symmetry it was built to celebrate the victory over the Carthaginians at Himera, but construction work was abandoned when the Carthaginians sacked the city in 405 BC. It would have been perhaps the biggest temple in the Greek world, and such was its intended bulk that the architects planned to use, in addition to columns, colossal statues or *telamones* to provide support for the roof. There is the one such lying alongside the temple, perhaps never erected, perhaps overthrown by the Carthaginians, perhaps displaced by an earthquake.

The Temple of Hera bears more definite marks of the Carthaginian invasion. They burned the temple, and there are red and black fire marks on some columns, but this was not a sign of disrespect for Hera since the temple was not in fact dedicated to her. The Romans rebuilt it, but their work was undone by an earthquake and later by Christians searching for ready-made building material. The temple is roofless, has a commanding position at the top of an incline, and now consists of steps and of twenty-five of the original thirty-four columns, all surrounded by rocks, pieces of wall and *bothroi.*

The most magnificent of the temples, and the one most easily seen from a distance, is Temple F, Concord, a name which is erroneous and was taken from an inscription found nearby. Its style is Doric, like all the temples in Sicily, and rather curiously it stands on a platform, seemingly a solution to the problem of raising such a huge building on a site which was not altogether appropriate. There are four steps leading up to it and it is surrounded by a colonnade of thirteen lateral and six frontal columns. Its use as a Christian church did involve certain architectural changes, but here the construction of walls between the columns minimized damage from the elements and may explain why even the *cella,* the interior, has survived. This is one of the best preserved of Greek temples anywhere, and one can only guess at the original effect when the structure was covered with stucco and painted over.

SELINUNTE

There is no modern city of Selinunte to distract attention from the ancient site. The traveler Swinburne, father of the poet, stopped off and declared that he had never seen "such an extraordinary assemblage of ruins in Europe: they lie in several stupendous heaps with many columns still erect, and at a distance resemble a large town with a crowd of steeples."

Selinunte (Selinus to the ancients) once controlled a large territory in the south-west of Sicily and even established its own colony on the sea at Eraclea Minoa. The town takes its name from the wild celery which grows abundantly in those parts, and indeed the abundant fertility of the

Temple of Hera at Selinunte

207

surrounding fields may explain why this spot was chosen. However, prosperity founded on agriculture requires not only natural fertility and human labor but also conditions of peace, and these were harder to find. The city was founded around 650 BC as a sub-colony of Megara Iblea and was the most westerly of all Greek settlements. As such it was somewhat isolated and had to come to some form of accommodation with the Elymians and Sicels, as well as with nearby Segesta and, above all, with Carthage. Diplomatic and other agreements such as a treaty permitting inter-marriage between inhabitants of Segesta and Selinunte fostered exchanges of varying kinds, and these interactions may explain the complexity of multicultural artworks which emanated from Selinunte and which can be seen in museums around the island.

Diplomacy frequently failed and the city was often embroiled in warfare. It remained neutral in the conflict between Carthage and the Greek colonies which culminated in the battle of Himera, and managed to stay out of the war engendered by the Athenian Expedition against Siracusa, but its growing prosperity aroused the enmity of Carthage which in 409 BC turned on Selinunte and sacked the city. Even by the standards of the time, the slaughter was terrible. Contemporary chronicles talk of 16,000 people massacred and 5,000 sold into slavery. Some of the luckier members of the population found refuge in Agrigento, allowing Selinunte to be partially repopulated later, but it remained under the thumb of Carthage. During the First Punic War Carthage seems to have decided that Selinunte was indefensible and around 250 BC it moved the population *en masse* to Lilybaeum (modern day Marsala). The city was never again inhabited in classical times although there are traces of habitation by Byzantine hermits and by an Arab community. Some of the great temples were reduced to rubble by earthquakes.

Selinunte is the largest archaeological park anywhere in the Mediterranean basin, and few other spots will make such an appeal to those who are sensitive to the romance of ruins. It might be useful for the purposes of a visit to divide the park into four unequal sections: the eastern hill near the entrance, where temples E, F, and G are sited; a walk downhill through light woodland and over a now silted-up port to the acropolis, which has been substantially but not wholly excavated; the area to the north on the Manuzza hill where the inhabited area of the ancient town was; and finally for the real enthusiast, the two sanctuaries on the far side of a river once called Selinon but known in modern Italian as the Modione.

One measurement of the prestige of a Greek city was the number and quality of its public buildings, and the tyrants of Selinunte were anxious to ensure that the city was embellished with architectural projects of the highest order. There are the remains of what were probably eight temples. The doubt over the exact number arises from the fact that in some cases only foundations remain. Modern archaeologists tend to look askance at earlier counterparts who attempted to reconstruct ruins, as did Sir Arthur Evans at Knossos, but Temple C has been partially, and Temple E more ambitiously, rebuilt. Temple E's external columns are still standing, but the two temples on either side are piles of stones with an occasional broken column to emphasize the devastation. Temple E owes its better state of preservation not to superior building techniques but to the fact that it was, surprisingly, reconstructed as late as the 1950s. Temple G, one of the largest temples of antiquity, was dedicated either to Apollo or Zeus, and its construction predates work on the adjoining temples but it was never completed. Work began in the middle of the sixth century BC but was stopped some time in the following century as a result of conflict with the Carthaginians. Experts differ over which war caused the termination of work, and the uncompleted building was later brought down by earthquake in the seventh century AD. The stones in Temple F mark the outline of the temple, which may have been dedicated to Athena.

The hill on which the acropolis stood was leveled to allow building to take place, and in the south-east there is evidence of efforts to extend the area. Town planning was at a sophisticated stage, and the philosopher Empedocles of Agrigento, who was also a skilled engineer, was employed to help drain nearby marshes. He came to regard himself as a minor god and attracted a cult-following of the sort occasionally familiar today. One of the temples in this area, Temple B, may have been dedicated to him. Within the precincts are the foundations of five temples, while the area is protected by a system of walls and towers. The southern extremity overlooks the sea, and the Northern Gate at the end of the north-south axis running through the district was part of an extensive defensive network.

The main inhabited area lay slightly further to the north, but the Carthaginians did a thorough job of destruction. The sanctuary to the goddess Malophoros is to the west, on the far side of the river. She is a pre-Greek goddess, later identified with Demeter, and was the bearer of apples. Votive offerings were found inside but these are now in Palermo. Alongside is a sanctuary to Zeus. Some eight miles away, near Campobello di Mazara, are the fascinating Cusa quarries where columns cut and prepared for transportation to the temple sites are clearly visible. The assumption has to be that the work was abandoned suddenly, probably when the Carthaginians arrived in the vicinity.

Many of the best moveable artworks were taken to the archaeological museum in Palermo. The most striking are from Temple E, which was possibly dedicated to Hera, and include friezes of the marriage of Zeus and Hera, of Actaeon being savaged by his own hounds while Artemis looks casually on, and a fractured but haunting marble head of a woman. Other works are now in the museum in Castelvetrano, the nearby town which has jurisdiction over Selinunte. Of special interest are a delicate bronze statue of an *ephebe*, a young man, unearthed by a local farmer ploughing his fields, and a fifth-century BC parchment with the inscription of a sacred law. This document was sold to the J. Paul Getty Museum in California but was handed back in 1992.

Castelvetrano is an attractive and lively center, with some striking palaces, piazzas, and Arab-Norman churches. The town's name is a corruption of *Castrum Veteranorum*, the camp of the veterans, and that explains an unexpected entry it made into the history of psychoanalysis. In 1910 *en route* for Selinunte, Sigmund Freud and his traveling companion Sandor Ferenczi spent a night there. The following year, according to the account Freud gives in his *Psychopathology of Everyday Life*, both men found themselves unable to recall the town's name. For any other human being this would have been a simple act of forgetfulness, but it caused Freud deep anxiety and led to the development of a theory explaining why certain facts are retained and others not. While searching their memories, the two men came up with various suggestions—Caltanissetta, which Freud thought sounded like a pet name for a young woman, and then Castrogiovanni (modern Enna), which was sufficiently similar to *giovane* (young) to trigger the recollection of the opposite—old, or veteran, in other words, Castelvetrano. Freud concluded that in this case he had preferred to forget the town's name because of his fear of his own ageing, but he had to admit that this notion could not explain the amnesia of the younger man. Castelvetrano enriched psychoanalysis by a theory of mnemonics, convincing or not.

For those who need some relaxation, the resort of Triscina di Selinunte immediately under the acropolis area has some four miles of sandy beach. Having paid their dues to research, tourists can take their ease on the very spot where the trading ships came into and out of the ancient city.

SEGESTA

The road which runs up the center of Sicily towards Palermo leads to the town of Calatafimi, which now prefers to designate itself Calatafimi-Segesta. Newman stayed here, but shuddered at the recollection of the place: "Calatafimi, where we slept! I dare not mention facts." The town entered history in May 1860 when Garibaldi fought his first battle on Sicilian soil against the Bourbon forces. One of his Redshirts, Giuseppe Cesare Abba, kept a diary of the invasion and recorded his dismay at seeing Sicilians gather on a hillside to watch the conflict rather than flocking to join Garibaldi's liberating army, as had been expected. There is a monument to the battle on the hill of Pianto Romano outside the town. The 1968 earthquake caused immense damage in this area, not least to the nearby Aragonese castle.

Abba also records that after the battle in an astonishing display of *sang-froid* many of Garibaldi's soldiers went off to do a bit of sightseeing, visiting the Greek temple of Segesta, which could be seen from the battlefield. For Newman some decades earlier, the visit to Segesta seems to have been the central experience of his trip to Sicily and in a letter home he describes his reactions rather than the sight itself. He enthused:

> Oh wonderful sight and full of the most strange pleasure, from the wonderful position of the town, its awful desolateness, the strange beauty of the scenery, rich even in winter and its historical recollections… Such was the genius of Greek worship, grand in the midst of error; simple and unadorned in its architecture, it chose some isolated spot, and fixed its faith as a solitary witness on heights where it could not be hid.

Only a Victorian churchman could choose to focus on the theological errors of Greek religion in the presence of such a sight as Segesta.

Nothing has happened to lessen the wonder of the site or the excitement of the first glimpse, whether from the modern road which circles alongside or from closer up. The temple stands utterly alone on the level

The temple in Segesta, Greek in design but built for the gods of the Elymian people. The temple was never completed, and its solitary grandeur is unmatched

plain on a small hill surrounded by fields of grass and trees and near to high cliffs. Goethe was impressed by the "melancholy fertility of the country-side," but most visitors are more likely to be moved by the sheer improbability of this isolated, splendid survivor.

Segesta was not a Greek but an Elymian settlement, often in conflict with Selinunte, and had to survive by displaying Machiavellian duplicity in nimbly switching alliances between Greeks and Carthaginians. It was a long-time ally of Athens and even can be held ultimately responsible for the disastrous Athenian Expedition to Sicily. In response to an appeal for help from Segesta, Athens dispatched ambassadors to assess the situation. The Segestans, afraid of seeming too poor to merit assistance, begged nearby Elymian towns for a loan of their gold and silver cups, which were then moved from house to house one step ahead of the Athenian delegation conducting the survey. Some authorities suggest that work on the temple, which was never completed and never had a roof or fully designed and furnished interior, was initiated at this time as part of the trickery. The Athenian envoys were bamboozled, and reported back that a fleet should be sent to attack Siracusa in aid of their deserving allies in Segesta. As has already been recounted, Athens was totally crushed in the war which followed. Segesta, meantime, revived its alliance with Carthage and later participated in the sack of Selinunte. In its turn Segesta was occupied by Agathocles of Siracusa, a psychopath who tortured and slaughtered freely, apparently even firing captives into the air from giant catapults. Segesta was repopulated and made a partial recovery. It received highly favorable treatment during Roman rule due to a stroke of good fortune. The Elymians were believed to be descended from the Trojans, like the Romans themselves, making the populations of the two cities cousins. Segesta prospered until it finally disappeared from the map after the Vandal invasion.

What remains is the magnificent temple, which stood outside the ancient town, and a theater cut into the hillside. The temple is unquestionably Greek in inspiration and Doric in structure, for by the time of its construction Segestan culture was thoroughly Hellenized. Adopting Greek culture meant that a theater was an indispensable accouterment to civil living. It is a venue for the performance of Greek tragedies in the summer months. Nothing besides remains.

Chapter Fifteen

PHOENICIANS, SARACENS, AND YORKSHIREMEN

THE SOUTH-WEST CORNER

MAZARA DEL VALLO

The River Mazara flows through the town and the point where it flows into the sea has created a wide, natural harbor which has since Phoenician days provided a safe haven for mariners and access to the inland towns. The still flourishing port is one of the busiest in the Mediterranean and home to one of the biggest fishing fleets in Italy.

In 827 an armed fleet made the short crossing from Tunisia to Mazara del Vallo to begin the military campaign which led to the 260 years of Arab rule in Sicily. From Mazara the Arabs spread over the whole island, making Sicily a Muslim emirate. If Siracusa and surrounds can be viewed as Sicily's leading "Greek" area, the south-west of the island can be seen as the redoubt of the Arab presence, even though there are no architectural reminders of past histories to compare with those left by the Greeks. Mazara is, at least metaphorically, custodian of the Saracen past, as is appropriate for a town which was the capital of one of the three administrative areas into which Arab rulers divided Sicily. The words "del Vallo" were added to the town name only in the nineteenth century to recall its past. The term itself, as we have seen, derives from the Arabic for region and has nothing to with "valley."

The town has expanded recklessly inland in recent decades, but the old town down by the port in the self-enclosed square delineated by the sea, the river, and two streets, Corso Umberto and Corso Vittorio Veneto, is captivating and has retained its Arab layout and even something of an Arab character. Modern architecture has not been allowed to intrude but far from being a well preserved museum, the center is lively and well provided with the bars and restaurants which have taken over traditional buildings. In certain areas, for instance in the labyrinth of courtyards, alleyways and narrow streets around Piazza Chinea or off Cortile Picu, peopled as they are with merchants, fishermen, and sailors from all over the Mediterranean, it is possible to imagine the town as it was in its Arab days or to see resemblances to a contemporary North African *kasbah*. This has become easier in recent decades since Tunisian immigrants have settled in this quarter, meaning that shops and restaurants offer North African fare and Arabic can again be heard in the streets. Relations between Sicily and Tunisia were always close, with traffic going in both directions and many Sicilians settling in Tunis.

The square known as Piazzetta Bagno (Bath) stands on the spot where the Islamic baths were once sited. The continuity and change of name which maintains a memory of the original function is interesting. None of the streets has kept Arab names or names of Arabic origin nor have any of the mosques or Arab palaces and dwellings survived. The Churches of Sant' Egidio, of the Carmine, and of San Nicolò Lo Regale (St. Nicholas the Regal) are surmounted by oriental-style domes, but all were built after the period of Arab rule and none is a converted mosque. San Nicolò is the most arresting and the clearest product of that unique style to which both Arab and Norman craftsmen contributed. The dome on top is of Arabic inspiration but the quasi-military upper turrets and the layered arches around the windows are more clearly Norman. The Baglio Sulana, a grand farm complex situated in the countryside near the town and once home to several families, is believed to be of Arab origin, but the most enduring influence of the Arabs is not to be found in an architectural legacy but in the innovations they introduced into fishing and agricultural methods. Under them, sugar cane was planted, salt flats were developed, silk farms were established, and at sea the tuna was hunted more aggressively.

The Arab domination was only one phase in the developing history of Mazara. Earlier, the town was frontier land in disputes between Greeks and Carthaginians, then enjoyed a period of prosperity under Roman rule before falling into decline until the Saracen invasion. The city was the last to fall to the Normans, who held the first Sicilian parliament there, and it remains rich in Norman architecture. Only the walls in the Jolanda Garden remain of what was once a Norman castle, and the Norman cathedral was transformed in the late seventeenth century in accordance with early Baroque canons. The complex of sculptures by Antonello Gagini over the high altar depicting the Transfiguration seems to be part of stage scenery.

Christ and the apostles give the impression of coming into view as drapes are drawn apart by very naked and naughty little *putti*. One side of the cathedral sits along the elongated Piazza della Repubblica, whose name is modern but which has enjoyed a central position since the days of the Arabs, and possibly since the Romans. The *loggia* along another side with its arches and columns makes the square as much a salon as Venice's Piazza San Marco.

The town has a delightful theater designed in a style common to grander Italian theaters, with rows of seats in the stalls and tiers of private boxes rising from ground-level to where balconies or upper circles would be in theaters elsewhere in Europe. These boxes were intended for the upper or at least the moneyed classes. This theater predates most in Sicily since it was founded in 1848 as a venue for comedy with the name Teatro del Popolo (The People's Theatre), but after Garibaldi landed at nearby Marsala his name was given to the building. A recent addition to the treasures of the town is the museum containing the Dancing Satyr pulled from the sea by fishermen in 1998. There are debates over how he actually got there, with some suggestions that he may have been on the prow of a ship

Bronze statue given the name Dancing Satyr, found in the sea off Mazara. Perhaps the work of the great Greek sculptor, Praxiteles. Is he in a trance, in pain, or even in his death throes?

217

and others that he was a saleable item in the international art trade which flourished in classical times. One leg is missing, but his flowing hair and the sideways turning pose give the statue not merely a sense of movement but of frenzy, as though the dance were wild and corybantic.

MARSALA

If in Mazara the imagination should people the alleyways with the guttural accents of the Middle East, in Marsala it would be appropriate to overhear in imagination voices from Yorkshire. Englishmen could scarcely claim to have founded or discovered Marsala, whose history goes back to the Phoenicians and Carthaginians, but the present prosperity of the town and its thriving wine industry are largely due to the foresight and entrepreneurial skills of men and women from the North of England. They would still recognize the well preserved, pretty, central complex of streets and squares from which cars are largely excluded. Once again, on arrival access to this area is through an unlovely sprawl of modern suburbs, but the historical center lies in a well-defined square with the cathedral and Piazza Repubblica at its heart.

Marsala began life as a Carthaginian outpost, which grew in importance when the Greeks slaughtered the Carthaginian inhabitants of the nearby island of Mozia. Those who survived took refuge in Marsala, then known as Lilybaeum, but the town fell under the control of the Romans following the Punic Wars. The decisive event was the defeat of Carthage in the naval battle fought in the seas around the nearby Egadi Islands. One of the town's museums, the Baglio Anselmi, houses a Carthaginian warship which was sunk in the battle and lay at the bottom of the sea until 1969. It was raised two years later thanks to the initiative of an English archaeologist, Honor Frost. There were fears that the ship would disintegrate when taken from the seabed, so it was kept under water for some time and eventually treated with wax. It was found to be built of various woods from different parts of the Mediterranean, and incredibly archaeologists were assisted in their efforts to reconstruct it by deciphering letters from the Phoenician alphabet which indicated where the various planks should be inserted, rather like a modern flat pack from a DIY store.

Under Roman rule the town was a center of the cult of the Sibyl, the fortune-teller of ancient times, and the site of her cult was converted into a Christian baptistery which is now incorporated into the Church of San

Giovanni Battista (St. John the Baptist). With the decline of Rome the town was subjected to the depredations of Vandals on land and pirates on sea, but its fortunes revived with the arrival of the Arabs, who gave the town its present name, the port (*marsa*) of Allah. Later the Normans constructed a castle which is still standing but permission to visit is unlikely to be granted since it is in use as the local jail. In following centuries the town was somewhat neglected and unprotected and in 1575 the council took the decision to fill in the port as the most effective means of defense from attacks by corsairs in search of booty and slaves.

The revival of Marsala began with the chance arrival in 1773 of John Woodhouse, discussed in the section on the British presence in Sicily. Woodhouse was a visionary and a man of action, and has a fair claim to have invented modern Marsala wine. It was certainly he who opened the present port, built roads, encouraged local vine growers, and developed trade. He was followed by other entrepreneurs from Yorkshire, Benjamin Ingham and his nephews the Whitakers, as well as by Joseph Hopps and Vincenzo Florio, Sicily's most successful nineteenth-century businessman. There were other British people who were less known, but who arrived and prospered. A luxury hotel on the outskirts of the town now called the New Palace was originally the residence of one Charles Gordon, who worked for the Florios. His drawing-room is now the hotel's *salone* and is still decorated with portraits of British officers and their ladies. By 1927 the Florios had bought out the British winemakers, but in their turn ceded control to the Cinzano concern from Turin. Marsala Florio is now owned by the Illva Saronno company, which specializes in liqueurs.

The English names have been retained on the bottle labels and their original *bagli*, now in a state of disrepair, can be seen on the outskirts of the town. The word *baglio* is a Sicilian term which literally means "court-yard" but which locally has taken on the sense of winery. (The standard Italian is *cantina*, which is also used.) There is an excellent wine trail (*strada del vino*) around the town, and the Florio and the Pellegrino *bagli*, which are open to visitors, offer fascinating historical insights into the wine trade as well as the opportunity to taste and purchase the wines. There is no snob like a wine snob, but there is an entire subculture relating to Marsala wine which might baffle even genuine connoisseurs. There were, of course, wines grown in the region before Woodhouse turned up, and the three main grapes are *grillo, inzolia,* and *cataratto,* and any or all of these can be used in the production of Marsala, which is a fortified wine. Classification of Marsala is by color, ageing, and degree of sweetness. The three colors are *ambra* (amber), *oro* (gold), and *rubino* (ruby). In order of ageing, the classifications are *fine, superiore, superiore riserva, vergine*, which may have the name *soleras*, attached, and finally *stravecchio* (very old). Some distinguished names have lent their names to the marketing of these wines. Admiral Lord Nelson allowed John Woodhouse to call a brand *Bronte Marsala* after the Sicilian estate granted to him by the King of Naples, and Garibaldi agreed that his name appear on the labels of a Florio variation of the wine. No modern celebrity deal could carry such weight.

Garibaldi is the other great name associated with the town of Marsala, for it was here that he and his Thousand landed in 1860 at the beginning of the campaign to overthrow the Neapolitan Bourbon dynasty and to incorporate Sicily into the emerging Kingdom of Italy. There were two British warships in the harbor when Garibaldi's mini-fleet of three ships arrived. The third fleet present that day, the Neapolitan, was under the overall command of Captain William Acton, a member of a family originally from England but which had served the Bourbons for generations. It was the last to arrive, but its freedom of maneuver was restricted by the presence of the ships of the Royal Navy. The real objective of the British task force has been subject to debate ever since. Officially they were in the Marsala waters to ensure that the British interests came to no harm, but the consensus of historical opinion is that they were there to offer at least tacit support to Garibaldi, and certainly Garibaldi stated as much in his memoirs. In theory Britain was neutral but both public and government opinion sided with the Unification cause. The Neapolitan ships were warned by the British captains not to fire on the town in case the British *bagli* suffered damage, and this may explain the vacillation of the captains of the Bourbon vessels when Garibaldi's men rowing ashore in little boats presented an easy target. It seems that there was also some confusion between the red shirts which Garibaldi's men famously wore and the uniforms of British sailors who were in the town relaxing when the landing was underway. The Neapolitans did not dare risk firing on the wrong men, or damaging British ships or property

Garibaldi was able to land his men without casualties, and the Porta Garibaldi (Garibaldi Gate) through which he entered the town is now one of many monuments to him in and around Marsala. From there he proceeded towards Calatafimi, where he fought a victorious battle, and then to Palermo and ultimately to Naples. There is an excellent and highly informative museum dedicated to the landing in the ex-monastery of San Pietro (St. Peter), a grand sixteenth-century building which is itself of considerable interest. It once housed a community of Benedictine nuns who remained there until the dissolution of the religious orders in 1866. It was saved from demolition in 1998 and, in addition to the Garibaldi section, has rooms dedicated to archaeology and folklore as well as a complex of meeting rooms.

As it happens, there is another point of English interest. The cathedral is dedicated to St. Thomas à Becket. The original construction was Norman, and the story goes that a ship carrying columns for Canterbury was shipwrecked off Marsala. It is no loss what a friend gets, so the town showed its friendship for Canterbury by keeping the columns, giving them a place of honor in their own cathedral and choosing a saint associated with Canterbury as their patron. However, veneration of St. Thomas spread rapidly throughout Europe after his martyrdom, so the real explanation for the choice of saint to be venerated may be more banal. The cathedral was entirely reworked in accordance with Baroque concepts in the seventeenth century, but work continued over many years and the façade was completed only in the 1950s.

MOZIA

The Arabs showed no interest in the island of Mozia, which was originally a Phoenician colony, but the English have a role here too.

Carthage had three principal bases in Sicily—Palermo, Solunto, and the island which was originally called Motya, became San Pantaleo in the Middle Ages but is now identified on the map as Mozia. The road from the center of Marsala to the port goes past the saltpans and windmills needed for the production of sea-salt, now a highly prized luxury but once the commonplace. The tiny island, with a circumference of no more than one and a quarter miles, lies not far offshore and was once joined to the mainland by a causeway to Birgi, not the nearest point to the island but presumably the route where the water was at its shallowest. The causeway was dismantled by the residents of Mozia during a siege, and was only partially rebuilt by the attackers. It is still there, now permanently underwater but reportedly negotiable by people with strong nerves and high sided vehicles, but frequent ferries ply their trade for intending visitors gifted with a more normal dose of common sense.

While archaeologists, who have not completed even a fraction of the excavation work to be done on Mozia, operate on scientific premises, other visitors will be moved by the unique, uncanny, haunting spell cast by this place of phantoms and forgotten histories, the site of a civilization which was crushed in the most savage way. Gaia Servadio, author of an excellent book on the island, wonders why she found Mozia "so special, so mysterious."

> Motya is unique in having been destroyed suddenly, leaving its inhabitants just enough time to hide their treasures. Its ground therefore still conceals what individuals buried as their best objects... This for me is one of Motya's main attractions: the slow unveiling of a mystery, of a way of life which had been erased by time and defeat, but civilized enough to leave many clues.
>
> I knew that under my feet lay the secrets of an entire civilization which hitherto had been described only by hostile pens... I knew that every time one scratched the earth of Motya, something of interest would inevitably emerge. The Punics had been hidden; but their stones talked. They had first talked to Schliemann, the father of contemporary archaeology, the man who had discovered Troy and "Priam's treasure", and who paid a visit to Motya. Then they called to Joseph Whitaker, an English gentleman living in Sicily, dilettante turned passionate archaeologist and scholar... In my imagination I went on seeing ghosts, armies, crowds of citizens, women carrying water.

The systematic work of discovery is still underway, but as Dr. Johnson said on arriving on Iona, "that man is little to be envied" whose emotions are not deeply affected and whose imagination is not stirred on coming ashore here. Here a great civilization was built, here great forces clashed, here horrible creeds demanded horrible sacrifices, and here dreadful crimes, including what would now be named genocide, were committed. And here one Englishman followed a non-scientific hunch over what he believed had been concealed for centuries and then probed meticulously, even pig-headedly, until his instincts were proven to be well-founded.

The presiding deities in Mozia are the Carthaginian gods Baal and

Astarte in antiquity and Joseph Whitaker in modernity. Although small in size, the island once housed the city of Motya, which historians tell us included towers, fortresses, staircases (at least one of which is extant and in good condition) all enclosed within defensive walls with large gates. It is not clear why the Phoenicians preferred offshore islands rather than mainland settlements for their trading posts, but they set up a colony here, probably in the eighth century BC. Seemingly such colonies did not establish a standing army of their own and were happy to entrust their defense to the superior power of Carthage. The city would appear to have been more multiracial than was common in those times of rivalry and enmity, and there is indisputable evidence of a Greek community on the island. Motya was a thriving port and trading center, but in 397 BC Dionysius, tyrant of Siracusa, sacked the city after a lengthy siege. The Greek residents were crucified for treachery, and those inhabitants taken alive were either slaughtered or sold into slavery. The city was never again repopulated, and even its name disappeared. A community of Basilian monks arrived and gave it the name San Pantaleo.

Motya had vanished as completely as Troy, although there were unimpeachable accounts of its existence in the ancient historians. In the nineteenth century when Joseph (Pip) Whitaker announced his belief that San Pantaleo was the site of the lost Phoenician settlement, he was subjected to the same derision as was heaped on Heinrich Schliemann over his excavations in Troy. A member of the Ingham-Whitaker winemaking dynasty, Pip had little head for business but had the wealth to cultivate his own leisured interests, much to the annoyance of his wife, who feared the dissipation of the family fortune on nonsensical projects. He was a keen ornithologist, author of *The Birds of Tunisia,* and tenacious in his convictions about San Pantaleo, or Motya, or Mozia. He bought out the farmers on the island and used his own funds to undertake systematic excavations. Of course he was proved right. When he died, he left the island to the Whitaker Foundation, based in Palermo, which still manages the site.

A walk round the island should take no more than an hour, but there are many sites to pause over. These vary from objects which elsewhere would be unremarkable, such as ceramic ovens which still bear the marks of cooking in ancient times, or the staircase which was wide enough for daily use but narrow enough to act as an ambush point against invaders,

The Kouros of Mozia, dug from the ground where it had been carefully buried centuries before. The enigmatic expression is only one of the mysteries associated with him

to more substantial archaeological sites, many of which were unearthed by Pip Whitaker himself. Near the North Gate lies the area known as Capiddazzu, which means something like "ugly hat," a name presumably inspired by the layout of the terrain. There is a fresh-water well nearby, which explains why the Basilian monks chose to site their monastery there. The cemetery with several tombstones lies facing the Egadi Islands, but the really chilling site is the *tophet*, believed to be a Phoenician place of sacrifice. The victims were children and small animals, and their ashes then placed in urns, many of which have been recovered. All that is known about the Phoenicians comes from enemy sources, and there is an alternative but minority view that the stories of child sacrifice were malevolent slanders and that the children whose remains have been found died naturally and that only animals were used as sacrificial offerings. The *cothon*, an artificial dock, can be found near the South Gate. Its exact function is uncertain, but it may have been either a canal giving entrance to the city, a dock for unloading goods, or even a repair center.

The central point is the refurbished Whitaker Museum, which contains items excavated by Pip Whitaker and his successors, principally the extraordinary statue to which the name the *Giovane* or *Kouros di Mozia*

(Youth of Mozia) has been given. This is the work of a master sculptor and is undoubtedly Greek, further proof of the cohabitation of cultures on the island. It was dug from the ground as part of routine archaeological work near Cappiddazzu in 1979. How exactly it got there is, like much else about it, a mystery, for it seems that rather than being concealed by the movement of the earth over centuries it was placed there deliberately, perhaps to keep it safe from enemy forces. The head had been broken off but was found nearby. The arms were never recovered. The lower body is covered with a flowing, pleated skirt so gracefully and delicately carved that the material seems more like silk than marble. Who is he? A god, perhaps even Apollo himself? A victor at the Olympic Games returning home in triumph? What was a Greek doing in a Phoenician town? Was he an indication that the citizenry had decided to imitate Greek standards of public urban embellishment? Was he the property of some private collector, Phoenician or Greek? Was the statue war booty? The expression speaks of haughty self-mastery and the statue is as marvelous as anything even the Greeks ever produced.

ERICE

The mountain on which Erice stands is one of those places whose rugged, majestic, overpowering appearance will spontaneously arouse awe in human beings of any culture and creed, and which will generation after generation be revered as a residence of the gods or shrine of the saints. There are many such around Europe, Montserrat in Catalonia being an obvious example. Erice has been both a landmark for mariners and a shrine venerated by successive peoples, the Elymians, the Sicels, the Phoenicians, the Greeks, the Romans, and the early Christians. The origins of the city belong in the realm of myth, since it was believed that the founders were refugees from Troy. Aeneas himself built a temple there to Venus, who was his mother, and the cult of Venus Erycina took off. After losing his son Icarus on the flight from the tyranny of Minos in Crete, Daedalus came to the temple to pay homage and make the goddess the gift of a golden honeycomb. Seventeen Sicilian cities paid their dues towards the upkeep of the temple and at its height a thousand priestesses, the *hierodules*, served the goddess. The service was not of a sort normally viewed as divine, and "priestess" is, to our eyes, something of a euphemism since the women were practitioners of the sacred prostitution practiced in the environs of the

View from Erice

temple. The *hierodules* were like a harem, not at the service of one sultan but of devotees arriving to pay homage to Venus. Whether drawn by the aura of sacredness or by the offer of free sex, assorted libertines, sailors, pilgrims, and curious travelers flocked to Erice. The volume of fragments of amphorae has led some writers to wonder if these contained offerings by pilgrims, or if they were wine-jars brought by bucolic sex-tourists determined to sample the joys of wine, women, and song. Later the site became a shrine to the Virgin Mary and the mountain was renamed Monte San Giuliano (Mount Saint Julian) by Count Roger who had been visited in a dream by the saint just as his siege of the city was stalling. The Normans built a fortress, still known as the Castle of Venus, on the site where the Greek and Roman temples once stood. Little remains of the temples although the Well of Venus and parts of the ancient wall are still there.

Over the centuries the village has enjoyed moments of prestige and periods of near abandonment. It was occupied by the Arabs but really flourished under the Normans and retains its essentially medieval appearance and plan. The cobbled streets, the carefully tended courtyards often decorated by flowers and plants, the narrow alleyways, the tightly designed piazzas, the rounded arches, the incongruous but delightfully carved Baroque balconies, the sudden vistas onto the plain and sea below, the bare grey stone of the palaces and houses, the swirling mist and cloud which can cut the village off from the rest of the island all contribute to the enchantment, charm, and beauty of this wonderful place. It is an ideal destination for anyone seeking peace, since the permanent population is as low as three hundred, although this rises considerably in the peak tourist season. The altitude means that it will be cool in summer and downright chilly in autumn and winter. There are two main festive days—Good Friday when platforms with scenes from the Passion of Christ normally kept in the church of San Giuliano are carried around the village, and the feast of the Madonna di Custonaci which starts on the last Monday of August and reaches its climax on the following Wednesday. On this occasion a procession led by a man on horseback winds its way round the streets followed by ten couples in medieval dress. Mayors from nearby towns join in, and the central act is the handing over of the keys of Erice to the statue of the Virgin. Biblical scenes taken as referring to the Madonna are acted out on carts as they move round the village.

The number of monasteries, convents, and churches in the village is out of proportion to an inhabited area of this size, and indeed many are now abandoned and crumbling. The cathedral and the adjoining bell-tower retain their magnificence, although it is a pity that the original builders despoiled the temple once standing on the site for the construction of the church. The work was carried out under Aragonese rule, but several styles are evident in the architecture. The entrance porch is late Gothic and shows signs of Catalan influence, while the patterned ceiling unembellished with any painting was plainly done by craftsmen imbued with Arab-Norman notions of style. There are many paintings in the naves and a splendid rose window over the main door. The Monastery of San Salvatore (the Holy Savior) was occupied by Benedictine nuns who received the complex as a gift from the powerful Duke Enrico di Chiaramonte, a member of the most powerful of the Sicilian aristocratic families. The sisters were no doubt more chaste than the votaries of Venus, but the convent was the residence of many highly reluctant nuns who had no sense of a religious vocation. It became the dumping ground of the younger

Church of St. Julian, Erice. Its construction was ordered by Count Roger to express his gratitude to the saint for his help in taking the town from the Saracens

daughters of the Sicilian nobility, who were either unable or unwilling to provide dowries for their daughters' marriage. Plainly magnificent in its day, it has been abandoned for over a century following the suppression of religious orders in 1866, but the former chapel has been reopened.

The Church of San Giuliano was built on orders of Count Roger in thanksgiving to the saint for his help in the siege, and has been restructured many times since. It even suffered a partial collapse in 1926, after which it lay closed for over eighty years. A seventeenth-century wooden statue of St. Julian stands in a side chapel, and the entrance hall holds a more idiosyncratic collection of artworks specific to Erice. These are examples of wax modeling, a minor art which apparently dates back to Roman times, but which now features religious scenes fashioned out of a starch paste by Carmelite nuns. The style is described as realistic and dramatic, but to an outsider looks naïve and prettified. However, there is no denying the skill needed to produce tableaux of the baby Jesus surrounded by floral arches, or of the Last Supper or Nativity. The Church of Sant'Alberto (St. Albert) dates back to the early fourteenth century, and was managed by the

Company of the Whites, a noble, lay order which was strong all over Sicily and whose main function was to assist prisoners condemned to death in their last days.

TRAPANI

Trapani was reputed to stand over one of the three underwater pillars which supported Sicily. All the various rulers of Sicily have made use of the port, which is conveniently situated for both Africa and Spain. Aeneas must have landed here on his way to bury his father in Erice, and Samuel Butler, the British author best known for such works as *The Way of all Flesh*, became a local celebrity when he arrived in the town in 1892 to find proof for his belief that the *Odyssey* was written by a woman from Trapani and that ancient Ithaca was actually one of the Egadi Islands. His views were given final form in the 1897 book *The Authoress of the Odyssey*. The epic voyages described in the *Odyssey* were, in this view, actually made in the sea off Trapani, or were, in Butler's words, "a little tour from Trapani to Trapani." Butler was a pioneering photographer who took many fine photographs of sites he believed corresponded to places described by Homer, but which, whatever they do for his theory, certainly provide an interesting record of life in Trapani in the late nineteenth century. One features a Sicilian farmhouse which be asserted had been the palace of Odysseus himself, and another a hut in a vineyard he believed to be the villa of Laertes.

Today, the tedious approach to Trapani through the ugly buildings thrown up in the post-war era to replace districts bombed by the Allies is off-putting, but the old town, situated on a pointed promontory that has the shape of a scythe stretching out into the sea, still shows its celebrated charms. The network of streets, with churches and palaces from various ages, retains its medieval pattern and demonstrates yet again the planning skills of Arab overlords. The city flourished under the Arabs, and many local crafts such as coral artefacts, or industries such as salt extraction date from that period. Some remarkable examples of delicate coral work can be seen in the Pepoli Museum, a curious and random collection of works which reflect largely the enthusiasms of Count Pepoli himself. There was also a large Jewish community who lived in the area around a street still called Via Giudecca. The Palazzo della Giudecca was not Jewish-owned but is a striking building in the Catalan style.

There are many interesting churches packed into the small area of the town center. Unusually, the cathedral, rebuilt in 1635 in the Baroque style to replace a prior medieval building, has no open space in front of it but gives onto the main thoroughfare, the Corso Vittorio Emanuele. The Santuario dell'Annunziata (Shrine of the Annunciation) was once out of town but is now in a suburb. It has long been a place of pilgrimage and houses a series of individual, brightly decorated chapels including the Chapel of the Fishermen and the Chapel of the Sailors. The most famous is the chapel in which the statue of Our Lady of Trapani, sculpted by Nino Pisano, stands over the altar. It was intended for a church in Pisa, but the ship carrying it back from the Holy Land had to put in at Trapani during a storm. Stories of this sort are common in Sicily, with only minor variations. In the local folklore, the statue was—obviously—discovered to have miraculous powers, which made the Trapanesi keen to keep it and the Pisans equally keen to recover it. An agreement was reached whereby the decision was left to a donkey. The statue was loaded on a donkey cart and the donkey's decision to move towards the port and Pisa or else towards the city center was to be taken as final. The donkey was no fool and made the safer choice, for Trapani.

The breezes from the sea surrounding the old town ensure that air is fresh and (reasonably) cool in most seasons. Most people will find it rewarding to take an evening walk along the Corso Italia, past the old ghetto, under the arch, and out alongside the Palazzo Senatorio, now an art gallery, and then down the Corso Vittorio Emanuele in the direction of the harbor to the newly reopened Torre Ligny. The tower itself is an eighteenth-century construction built to provide warning of attacks from the sea at a time when Algerian corsairs were especially menacing. It has a small museum of Phoenician and Roman naval objects and from the roof there is a splendid view over the city and the sea.

Chapter Sixteen
THE CAPITAL CITY
PALERMO

PALERMO FELIX

Palermo today is not an easy city to love, as those enthusiasts who do love it will openly admit. The novelist Dacia Maraini once said that her idea of hell was a Palermo without the cake-shops. Love at first sight for Palermo as it is now is as rare as any other variation of the same passion, and those who claim to have experienced it are likely to prove unbalanced or mendacious. All the inhabitants of the city are in agreement that once it was different, once it was more ordered, once it was better, even if there is some dispute over the opening and closing of the imprecisely remembered golden period. In the late eighteenth century it was common to talk of *Palermo felix* (Happy Palermo), and Goethe wrote lyrically about the beauty of the bay and the surrounding chain of mountains. Augustus Hare, that most refined of travelers in Italy, took up the refrain in 1905.

> As the traveller approaches Palermo, he finds Monte Pellegrino with its stupendous limestone cliffs towering above the palest of blue skies on his right, and perhaps dove-coloured clouds pouring over from it over towards the calm sea, throwing patches of it into shadow, so that the beautiful grey and orange tones of it scarcely show. This is *Hertke* which Pyrrhus stormed, driving out its Carthaginian garrison. After this, Palermo and the magnificent *conca d'oro,* with its theatre of lofty mountains comes full into view, with possibly snow silvering the remotest ridges. All the valley breathes the lemon-blossom and gives the impression of being a paradise, a land at any rate flowing with milk and honey. No wonder Palermo became called *felix.*

The air breathed today carries less mellifluous scents, and the milk and honey are in shorter supply. Palermo had its own *belle époque* at the turn of the nineteenth-twentieth century when Hare arrived, and there are graceful *art nouveau* residences in the area around Via Libertà and in Palermo's resort town, Mondello, but today it is not a city which caresses, seduces, or beckons invitingly to the visitor. There are cities which are delicate, coy, or seductive such as Paris and Prague, or Ragusa and Marsala in Sicily itself, and other more muscular places which are initially forbidding or alienating and which reveal a more alluring side only to suitors who persevere. Affection for Palermo must be allowed to germinate and blossom after careful cultivation, but once the plant has flowered, it will prove to be an evergreen. Today at first sight Palermo can seem like a city of endless, unregulated chaos and a slightly fearsome place, or even a collection of sorry sights and stages of decay, but there are buildings, piazzas, streets, and corners of the city which are beguiling and of fetching beauty. And the city itself is ultimately enthralling.

Palermo is a port city, but although some promenades along the sea front near Porta Felice have been opened up, much of the coastline is still in use as docks, and in other stretches the sea water is polluted in a way which makes the thought of bathing impossible, so Palermitans have to go outside the city to Mondello to enjoy the pleasures of sea and sand. Elsewhere, there are areas even in the center which have not yet been rebuilt after Allied bombing in the Second World War. There have been many recent "Palermo springs," but never a Palermo summer. Perhaps more than any other city in Europe, Palermo has experienced age after age demolition, devastation, reconstruction, re-planning, reimagining, and restoration, sometimes by conquerors anxious to remake the capital in their own image and likeness, sometimes by well-intentioned improvers, and sometimes by corrupt politicians in complicity with criminal societies. The best and the worst, the most cowardly and the most heroic, the most altruistic and the most venal of men have ruled in Palermo, sometimes embellishing, sometimes brutalizing, sometimes respecting the work of their predecessors, sometimes eliminating all trace of their existence.

It is hard to know which approach to Palermo will offer the most favorable first view to the visitor. Arrival by sea has many advantages and permits a view of the city cradled by the chain of mountains which cut it off from the inland areas. If the approach is accurately timed at sunrise or sunset, the view from on board of the rays of the sun will give all the explanation needed of why the plain and the gulf where the city stands were named the *conca d'oro*, the golden shell. The disembarkation area in the docks is, however, unwelcoming. Arrival by rail is unlikely to be quite so stimulating. Exit from the station onto the grandly named but overpowering Piazza Giulio Cesare (Julius Caesar Square) might be too abrupt for sensitive souls since it will not allow for any gradual initiation into Palermo's chaotic traffic conditions, noise, and endless, unordered movement. Arrival by car will involve being swept onto the ring road, the Viale della Regione Siciliana, which was supposed to keep traffic out of the city center but which has only added to the congestion. The traffic lights are an occasion for women and children to dart forward offering to clean the windscreen, to sell lighters, paper handkerchiefs, or dish towels.

Those who arrive by air may be troubled by the imposing mountain, Monte Pellegrino, which stands alarmingly close to the runways, and indeed has caused crashes in the past. The mountain is part of the city's history and assuming the pilot has negotiated the landing successfully, it is at some stage worth taking a trip up the mountain which Goethe considered "the most beautiful promontory in the world." Halfway up stands the Castello Utveggio, which is no castle but a late nineteenth-century villa now housing municipal offices, but you will be welcome to take a coffee and savor the panoramic view of the city. The shrine of Santa Rosalia, patron saint of Palermo, is further up. Here the saint lived in solitude until her death in 1166. Her bones were providentially rediscovered in 1624 when the city was being devastated by the plague and were brought down and processed round the city, causing the scourge of the plague to be lifted. The grateful citizens ousted the previous patron saint and proclaimed Rosalia their protector, a status she has maintained. Her shrine is bedecked by votive offerings, as well as crutches and prosthetic aids rendered unnecessary by miraculous cures, offered by those whose prayers were answered. Her body is still paraded around the city every year on 15 July, one of the greatest feasts in the Sicilian calendar.

Palermo is both the capital of Sicily and a typical Mediterranean city. It is a city of historical strata, some of which have been recently rendered invisible or irrecoverable by inexpert archaeology or, more probably, by unscrupulous building programs, or even in earlier times by determined efforts to remove unwelcome reminders of prior rule. It has no genuinely Arab buildings but some quarters have an Arab feel which long predates the recent arrival of immigrants from North Africa. It is embellished by magnificent ecclesiastical and secular architecture dating from Norman and Spanish times, and has two of the most massive, overwhelming, over-powering, ponderous theaters of any city in Europe, theaters which arrogantly draw attention to themselves, asking not to be loved but to be respected. It has other buildings which express a more delicate spirit, some intricate Baroque church interiors or some graceful works designed by Ernesto Basile, such as the little kiosks on Piazza Verdi, which proclaim themselves as belonging to the *art nouveau* moment. It has at the same time many buildings, many piazzas, many streets and churches which can only be classified as sorry sights, buildings which may have been magnificent in their day but which are now decaying, ignored, unloved.

The observant visitor will be struck by the lack of architecture of any note or pretension to style from the post-war age. Recent decades have seen at best neglect of the urban cityscape and at worst the criminal manipulation of civic power in authorizing the demolition of historic buildings to make way for the profit-making brutalities in fashion at that moment. It can be stated straightforwardly that nothing built from the 1940s onwards graces the city, and that unchecked expansion and unscrupulous demolition, a process known as the "Sack of Palermo" and executed by compliant or corrupt municipal power in complicity with the mafia, has destroyed much of the beauty that once enchanted visitors. And yet, and yet … there are still wonders in Palermo. With its mixture of cultures of East and West, of Christianity and Islam, of Europe, Asia, and Africa, Palermo boasts a historical and cultural heritage which few cities can rival.

Urban History

In antiquity Palermo was a Phoenician, not a Greek, settlement, so came within the Carthaginian area of influence. In due course the Romans conquered it but did not make it a center of any importance, and there are no Roman or Greek ruins within the city boundaries. The Vandals and the Byzantines came and went, the former creating a dark age but the latter leaving a legacy in art and craftsmanship which would bloom later. Palermo's emergence as cultural center and political capital came with the Arabs who arrived in 831. Islamic chroniclers in the ninth and tenth centuries sing of the glories of this city with its three hundred mosques, its pleasure palaces, its myriad fountains, its cosmopolitan population, its tolerant style of life, and its cultural vivacity. This has to be taken on trust, for little remains visible of that civilization, if one excepts the labyrinth of back streets and alleyways, and the atmosphere of such areas as the Cassaro or the Kalsa. What does remain are the writings of the Arab poets, many of whom produced nostalgic work after the expulsion of their people, and who look back longingly at what was lost. The cubic domes on such churches as San Giovanni degli Eremiti (St. John of the Hermits), the beehive ceilings in the Cappella Palatina (Palatine Chapel), or even the oriental structure of such oriental palaces of royal delight as La Zisa are misleading. The inspiration is Arab, but these works were constructed by the Normans, who seized Palermo from the Arabs in 1071, and who had the discriminating sense to recognize the splendor of the culture and civilization they had ousted and to keep the craftsmen, architects, designers, poets, and even the courtiers to add gilt to their rule. When the Norman sun set, too quickly, the Swabians took over, and another period of glory was ushered in by Frederick II, *stupor mundi*. Frederick was King of Sicily, King of Jerusalem, Holy Roman Emperor, and a great builder of castles and fortresses, but little of that building was done in Palermo. His tomb is in the cathedral.

The Angevin French maintained Palermo as their capital, but it was there that in 1282 the anti-French uprising known to history as the Sicilian Vespers originated. The Church of Santo Spirito (Holy Spirit), where a French soldier's offensive behavior to a Sicilian woman provided the spark for the rebellion, still stands in the cemetery of Sant'Orsola (St.Ursula) to the east of the city. A lengthy period of instability and anarchy followed, and this power vacuum allowed certain noble families, notably the Chiaramonte and Sclafani houses, to assert control. Two great palaces, the Chiaramonte Palace in Piazza Marina which is now the administrative center of the university, and the Sclafani Palace in Piazza Vittoria which is now the HQ of the *carabinieri*, date from this time.

The Aragonese-Catalan royal family were the next to assume control, but even if they had a palace in Palermo, Catania was their capital. Integration into the kingdom of Castilian Spain (1412-1713) meant rule in Sicily by a succession of viceroys who transformed the face of the city. The central Via Cassaro was given the new name Via Toledo, now Corso Vittorio Emanuele, and was extended down to the harbor area, while another street, Via Maqueda, was named after a viceroy and retains the Spanish pronunciation. Maqueda was responsible for the construction in

1600 of the Quattro Canti (Four Corners), the elaborately tiered and sculptured edifice at the intersection of the main streets. The grandiose Porta Nuova (New Gate) near the cathedral was built in 1583 to commemorate the visit of the great King-Emperor Charles V, the only Spanish king to set foot in Sicily.

Power passed to the Neapolitan Bourbons in 1735 and that year Charles III became the last king to be crowned in Palermo Cathedral. Power was exercised by nominated viceroys. King Ferdinand IV and Queen Carolina of the Kingdom of the Two Sicilies took refuge in 1806 from Napoleon's French army in Palermo, where they were wholly reliant on protection by the British fleet. The British presence is best, if inadequately, remembered for the love affair between Lord Nelson and Lady Hamilton, who resided together with her compliant husband, Sir William, in Palazzo Palagonia in the Kalsa district. Garibaldi and his invading force made for Palermo after landing at Marsala, and fought a decisive battle at the Ponte dell'Ammiraglio (Admiral's Bridge) on the outskirts of the city. The bridge, built in 1113 by George of Antioch, an admiral at the court of Roger II, spanned the Oreto river, but the river has dried up, leaving the bridge to cut a strangely pathetic and landlocked sight in the middle of a park.

The success of Garibaldi's mission saw Palermo become an Italian city, but the strength of the Sicilian sense of identity and the city's conceit of itself prevented that from being the whole truth. Little was done to preserve the architectural past or to enhance the urban environment. The main exception is the work of the *art nouveau* architect Ernesto Basile, who on a grand scale designed the Teatro Massimo, and on a more modest scale was the genius behind many houses and shops around the city. There are many other works by him including the Villa Igiea, once the property of the entrepreneur Ignazio Florio but now the most luxurious hotel in the city with a marvelous view of Monte Pellegrino on one side and of the bay on the other. There is a scattering of those muscular, supposedly overawing buildings, the Post Office being the most obvious example, which fascism felt best expressed its world view, but few will regard them with affection. The Allied bombing campaign in 1943 caused devastation and destruction on a scale not even this city had previously experienced, leaving churches, palaces, and whole districts leveled, but the post-war was perhaps even more ruinous. Decades of civic vandalism wreaked their own damage, and the rage of contemporary critics against what was perpetrated then cannot repair the havoc.

There are many ways of getting to know Palermo. A zonal approach has much to commend it, since buildings of different epochs stand one close to the other, but we will proceed by historical period, starting with the contribution made by the Arabs whose architecture comes filtered through Norman power.

ARABS AND NORMANS

As elsewhere in Sicily, there are no surviving, purely Arab monuments, but there is an abundance of Norman architecture, and the union between the two produced a style known as Arab-Norman, a combination which could emerge only in Sicily. However hackneyed the term has become through usage, it should cause any sensitive observer to pause and wonder, since the phenomenon is *a priori* as improbable as finding in Corsica a style of domestic architecture identified as, say, Nepalese-Greek. The two peoples came from different continents, were of religions which had been at war with each other for centuries, held to differing concepts of theological aesthetics, were rivals for the possession of Sicily, and yet their architects, masons, and craftsmen cooperated in the production of unsurpassed works of art. In only a couple of decades King Roger and the two Williams completed an ambitious building program of palaces and churches and of the conversion of mosques which made Palermo the capital of the Mediterranean and raised its European status in the eyes of royalty and of the papacy. Under the Normans, Palermo was no provincial backwater, and there are many works which attest to its own sense of its status.

The magnificent cathedral in Palermo is Norman, although it has been subject to many alterations in style over the course of the centuries. Archaeological evidence suggests that there always was a religious building on the site, and it is certain that there was a Christian church there in the fourth century. This building was destroyed by the Vandals, but reconsecrated in 604 and traces of the newer church remain in the crypt. The Saracens converted it into a mosque, only for the Normans to change it back. The guiding spirit behind the new construction work was the Anglo-Norman Bishop Walter of the Mill, who was sent from London by Henry II as tutor to the Sicilian dauphin. There is a statue of him outside the

The southern entrance to the cathedral, constructed in 1430 and a splendid example of Catalan-style Gothic architecture

cathedral entrance under his Sicilian name, Offamilio, and his tomb is in the crypt. Although he was virulently anti-Islam, he employed Arab workers, as can be seen from decorations on the exterior. The column on the left at the entrance has an inscription from the Koran, which implies that the porch was recycled from the mosque and, probably, that the Christian masters of work were ignorant of the source of the words. The cathedral was consecrated in 1185, but subsequent ecclesiastical authorities could not leave it alone. The southern entrance was added in 1453 and includes some splendid engraved wood decorations from the Catalan period. The old belfry collapsed in an earthquake in 1726, but the replacement has, strangely, an Arab appearance, however anachronistic. The cathedral had a thorough going-over between 1782 and 1801 when the current Latin cross shape, with the uninspiring Baroque cupola at the point of intersection, was imposed.

One of the oddities of the church is that there is no long view of the main entrance. It fronts onto a road separating it from the Episcopal Palace, to which it is joined by a raised walkway, a necessity in an often riotous city. The entrance portico is underneath, between two towers. The scenes from the New and Old Testament which decorate it are modern, but the Madonna above the door is fourteenth-century. The angle at which the cathedral is sited means that people coming from the city center along the Corso Vittorio Emanuele will see first not the façade but the south-facing side. This, however, is magnificent. It is hard to be equally enthusiastic about the impact of the successive restorations on the interior, and it has become a cliché to say that the ideal Norman cathedral would consist of the exterior of Palermo and the interior of Monreale. The tombs of the Norman monarchs are clustered together in the chapel to which they were moved during the eighteenth-century restoration. The sculpting of the delicate porphyry of the tombs was the work of Arab artisans, but they were not responsible for the odd fact that one tomb contains Frederick II, who died in 1250, and the Aragonese Peter II, who died in 1342. Was this a merely money-saving device?

Close to the center of ecclesiastical power stands the Palazzo dei Normanni, once an Arab stronghold, restructured as the royal palace in Norman times and now the seat of the Sicilian Regional Assembly. It too has suffered from the hands of "improvers" so that the so-called Pisan tower is the main visible, external remnant of the Normans days. Other imposing palaces surround the piazza in front of the Palace. On the right is the Palazzo Sclafani, a massive palace built in response to a snigger from one of the Chiaramonte family that no Sclafani could build anything as grand as his family residences, particularly their palace on Piazza Marina. Matteo Sclafani outdid his rivals and deserved to win the bet. There are Norman motifs visible on the outside, but access is restricted because the building is now used by the *carabinieri*. The royal apartments and the Palatine Chapel are at the back of the Norman Palace, which means there is no option but to run the risk of walking through the narrow Porta Nuova, where there is no pavement and scarcely room for both cars and pedestrians. The grand gate, with its eight huge statues of Moors, is striking in itself but belongs to a later, Spanish epoch.

The Palatine Chapel is a masterpiece in any terms and the greatest of the collaborative Byzantine-Arab-Norman works. The chapel was built in the 1130s by Roger II as the place of royal worship, and in its entirety it is one of the most magnificent works of devotional art in all Europe. The mosaics in the vestibule are modern, but of great interest is one of the columns in the gallery which has inscriptions in Latin, Byzantine (Greek), and Arabic, the constituent artistic elements in the design of the chapel. Although small in scale the chapel has the three-nave structure of a basilica, with the royal thrones at the back of the central nave. There are such riches inside that it is hard to know where to look first, but the eye is inevitably drawn to the central Byzantine mosaic of Christ Pantocrator (Christ the Almighty) above the depiction of the Madonna flanked by angels and saints. The marble is from Egypt, and the holy-water font is decorated with the zigzag lines used by Muslim craftsmen to denote liquid. Some of the columns are Roman, presumably taken from nearby villas, but the shorter columns around the altar are Arab. Not even St. Mark's in Venice has mosaics to compare with those which top the columns, bedeck the walls, and are inlaid on the floor. The wall mosaics depict scenes from the Old and New Testament. The ceiling is an extraordinary work of Arab craftsmanship. The wood may be made of the Biblical cedars of Lebanon, but the astonishing beehive, stalactite effect has parallels only in palaces in North Africa. In some corners of the ceiling are remaining traces of worldly scenes of Arab dancers, singers, or hunters, some somewhat scantily clad. These may have been the work of some Islamic workman having fun at the expense of his Christian masters, but the images were for the most part baptized by later rulers who added clothes and even haloes. The Christian masters got their own back in a scene at the bottom of the Pasqual candle showing animals with their paws on Arab heads. That apart, the decorations on the stem of the candle, for example of the king's head bent humbly before the Trinity, express orthodox theological notions. In other places of worship the Hauteville monarchs express a less modest view of their relations with God.

There are other Arab-Norman structures to be seen in the vicinity. The Church of San Giovanni degli Eremiti with its red domes looks like a converted mosque and it may be, but there is no consensus on this. It is safer to describe it as a Norman church which incorporates Arab motifs. The garden at the center of the cloister of the former monastery affords the welcome coolness of the small, green parks flowing with water outside ex-mosques in Andalucía.

Arab-Norman architecture was not exclusively religious. The Normans brought a great deal to Sicily but they were happy to learn and acquire Arab ways of leisure and pleasure. King William I was particularly open to

Mosaic of Christ Pantocrator (Christ the Almighty) with the angels. It dominates the cupola over the altar in the Palatine Chapel, Norman Palace, Palermo

the sensuous delights of the oriental lifestyle and had constructed for his own enjoyment a large park with woods and lakes, known as Genoard (earthly paradise), now in the area around the modern Corso Calatafimi. There are three buildings from the estate still standing at some distance apart, but in varying states of repair. La Cubula comes into the category of Palermo's sorry sights. A small rectangular structure, topped by a dome, it conforms perfectly to the architectural theories and culture of the Fatimid Arabs, which remained in vogue even after the arrival of the Normans. It was once a pavilion in the royal estate but is now completely marooned and abandoned in an overgrown, untended field in the middle of a housing scheme. Nearby are remains of a similar construction, the Cubula Soprana (Upper Cubula), integrated into the eighteenth-century Villa Bonanno, itself a ruin. The third, La Cuba, now in the grounds of the Tukory barracks off Corso Calatafimi, stood at the center of the royal park. It too is of Fatimid inspiration, was built in the reign of William II (the Good) and once stood on the banks of an artificial lake. The king's name and the date of the opening of the building have been inscribed in Arabic on the ceiling. The fame of La Cuba was such that one of the tales from the Fifth Day of Boccaccio's *Decameron* is set there.

However, the queen of the civic buildings in the Arab-Norman style is undoubtedly La Zisa, now beautifully restored after a long period of closure. The name comes from the Arab Al-Aziz, which means splendid, and in its heyday when William I retired there, it surpassed in splendor even the nearby Royal Palace. The work was completed by William II, who was even more open to the culture of Islam and the Orient than his father, so La Zisa, with its lake, fountains, and fish-ponds, must have resembled the residence of a sultan. Here the Christian king kept his own harem, with the choice of his favorites not determined by race or religion. The Normans were men of culture, and these rooms were the venue for learned debates on scientific issues between Arab and Greek savants, for the reading of poetry, performances of music, dances, and chess tournaments. The Sala della Fontana (Room of the Fountain) is purely oriental in taste and carries an inscription in Arabic praising the beauty of the palace. Other rooms have stalactite ceilings in the same style as the Palatine Chapel, little channels of water which provided air conditioning and mosaics depicting scenes of hunting and court life as well as some mildly erotic episodes. It was subjected to the inevitable alteration in 1635 to

The skilfully and tastefully restored La Zisa, a pleasure palace for Norman kings. Once the center of a royal park outside the city, it now stands in a housing estate

make it conform to Baroque tastes, but remains the work of highly skilled Fatimid Arabs employed by appreciative Norman masters.

There are many other buildings in the same style and from the same age elsewhere in Palermo, one of the most remarkable being the Castle of Favara, or Maredolce, on the outskirts of the city near the slopes of Monte Grifone. Arab and Norman cooperation could not go further since this was originally an Arab pleasance built by the Emir Ja'far in the late tenth century and rebuilt by King Roger. The mosque on the site was converted to the Church of Santi Filippo e Giacomo (Saints Philip and James). The palace was surrounded by a lake of fresh water (Maredolce) with an island in the center, and it was in these surrounds that the King-Emperor Frederick II was brought up. The palace is now a romantic ruin. In the same vicinity stands the magnificent Church of San Giovanni dei Lebbrosi (St.John of the Lepers), its elaborately designed interior and square entrance tower topped by a single red, Arab-style dome. It is one of the oldest Norman churches in Palermo and, as the name suggests, was also used in a later period as a leper colony. Not far off is the Ponte dell'Ammiraglio, already mentioned as the site of Garibaldi's first battle in Palermo. It was built in Norman times and its survival testifies to the quality of Norman engineering. The Church of Santo Spirito (Holy Spirit), where the rebellion known as the Sicilian Vespers originated, stands in a cemetery in the same district.

Admiral George of Antioch, commander of the Roger II's navy, built, in addition to the bridge, the church of Santa Maria dell'Ammiraglio (Our Lady of the Admiral), also known as the Martorana. The church is a demonstration of Norman power as much as a place of worship. In one mosaic the admiral is shown at the feet of the Virgin Mary and in another King Roger is crowned by Christ himself. The divine right of kings has never had any clearer affirmation. The involvement of Arab craftsmen is proven by the beautiful door in the right-hand nave, while the figure of the Pantocrator in the dome and the mosaic work reveal the Byzantine presence. Ibn Giubayr, a twelfth-century Arab traveler, described this church as "the most beautiful monument in the world," but once again it has suffered at the hands of restorers and improvers.

San Cataldo, on the opposite side of the piazza, is also Norman and was also built at the behest of an admiral, Maione da Bari, who was given by William I the title "admirals of admirals." In the seventeenth century the Archbishop of Monreale ordered "restoration and embellishment" of the church, words which always carry a dire warning, and it declined so far that in the early nineteenth century it was used as a postal sorting office. It returned to something close to its original form after restoration work in the 1880s and passed in 1937 into the possession of the Order of the Knights of the Holy Sepulchre, whose emblem can be seen on the window above the altar. An adjoining building was damaged by bombing in 1943 and demolished, meaning that San Cataldo became free-standing for the first time in its history. The interior is undecorated except for the mosaics on the floor, but the fine rectangular building with the long, mullioned windows and the three red domes has no need of additional artwork to make an impact.

MONREALE, THE ROYAL MOUNT

The Norman cathedral in nearby Monreale is another magnificent expression of Arab-Norman cooperation. There was always an element of competition between the city and the town, and William the Good commissioned Monreale's cathedral in the 1170s to outdo Archbishop Offamilio in Palermo, whose cathedral was completed slightly later. Monreale translates as Royal Mountain and there were plans to build a royal palace alongside the cathedral, but nothing more than the façade, still visible to the north of the cathedral, was actually completed. The complex then and now includes a monastery and cloisters. The cathedral was constructed in a commanding position at the extremity of a royal park which has long gone, but it still overlooks a panorama of orchards, mountains, and plains stretching down to the city and on towards the sea. However, if the sight is majestic from afar, from close up the first glimpse of the façade, seemingly crushed into inadequate space, is likely to be disappointing. The exterior gives no hint of the marvels inside.

Arab-Norman is the conventional description, but the artistic collaboration was altogether wider and deeper. The Normans were responsible for commissioning the work, Arabs for the architecture and for the stalactite ceiling, Byzantines for the mosaics, Pisans for the bronze doors, Provençal craftsmen for columns in the cloisters, Venetians for later mosaic work, and all of whatever faith or culture contributed to the expression of a twin vision expressing Christian spirituality on the one hand and the glory of the Norman conquering dynasty in Sicily on the other. It could be added that some of the columns in the nave are from ancient Roman temples and carry motifs from the cult of Ceres and Demeter. Apart from incidentals like the eighteenth-century porch, the cathedral has remained largely as it was conceived and constructed by these anonymous geniuses and talents clustered together in the cosmopolitan climate of medieval Sicily. Kings William I and II are buried there, and it is right to pay homage to their (for the most part) humane, tolerant vision which made this building possible.

The mosaics gleam with the gold used in their creation, but in their totality they correspond to a medieval ideal of religious art as *libri idiotarum*, the books of the illiterate. The inescapable, dominant figure high over the altar is the Christ Pantocrator, depicted in the act of giving a blessing, a gesture which makes for a more benevolent, less forbidding figure than similar icons elsewhere. The Virgin and Child are seated below on a throne with angels fluttering around and saints lined up beneath. One of the saints is Thomas à Becket, who had been martyred only shortly before the image was drawn. The church has a central nave with twin aisles and while the designs on the porphyry floor are abstract and figurative reflecting a Muslim view of religious art, the cycles of the mosaics express the Catholic version of the Judaeo-Christian vision in its most self-confident, even triumphalist mood. Scenes from the Old Testament such as the Creation and the Flood are portrayed in the nave, while the mosaics in the aisle depict episodes from the New Testament. Other mosaics in the right aisle are devoted to the life of St. Peter and those on the left to St. Paul. One mosaic above the two thrones, royal and episcopal side by side, shows King William being crowned by Christ himself, another reminder that the Hauteville dynasty had divine approbation, while an accompanying mosaic shows the same king presenting the cathedral to the Virgin Mary. The ceiling had to be replaced after a fire in 1811 but remains faithful to the original Islamic craftsmanship.

The cloisters alongside, built at the end of the twelfth century and the beginning of the thirteenth, are a place of cool repose. The 228 twin columns form a perfect square and each merits individual attention for their carved decorations, their delicate inlaid marble work, and the pretty scenes—flowers, beasts, men drinking, hunters in pursuit of prey—on some of them. There is no greater peace in Sicily than on a seat alongside the fountain in the colonnaded enclosure at a corner of the square, surely Arab art at its purest. Guy de Maupassant rises to heights of poetic rapture in his description:

> The wonderful cloisters of Monreale suggest to the mind a sensation of such grace that one would like to stay there indefinitely. They are immense, perfectly square and of gracious, delicate elegance. No one who has not seen them can have any idea of the harmony of this colonnade. The exquisite proportions, the incredible, slender shape of all those light, twinned columns standing side by side, each distinctive, some bedecked with mosaics, others unadorned; some covered with carvings of incomparable *finesse*, others decorated with a simple stone design which winds around them, twisting like a climbing plant—these are things which are a marvel to the eye, which fascinate it, which enchant it and give rise to that artistic joy which things of absolute taste transmit through the eye to the soul.

Sicily is the homeland of colonnades. All the internal courtyards of old palaces and houses contain some stupendous examples which would be famous anywhere else but in this island which is so rich in monuments.

SPANISH AND BAROQUE PALERMO

Intelligent embellishment of public space was part of the Baroque vision and if attempts at realizing this concept in Palermo under Spanish rule were at best intermittent and restricted to certain quarters, these elements come together in the Quattro Canti, literally the Four Corners, the intersection of Palermo's two main roads, an excellent spot to begin considering Baroque Palermo, or perhaps Palermo as a whole. This crossroad was regarded by the viceroys as the center of the city since it is the meeting point of the main streets, Via Maqueda and Corso Vittorio Emanuele (once Via Toledo), and for that reason they marked it by four highly ornate, curved structures set into each corner. At the foot of each is a fountain, which nowadays has no running water, with statues of the four seasons. The four statues on the next level are Kings of Spain, and those on the upper level Saints Cristina, Ninfa, Oliva, and Agata, the protectors of the four quarters of the city. Remaining space is taken up with coats of arms and symbols of royalty. Staring at the monument can induce dizziness, and since the pavement is narrow here and the traffic intense it is better not to stare up too long.

The imposing, circular, sumptuously ornate central fountain surrounded by naked goddesses of antiquity in Piazza Pretoria, only a few steps away, is the only real Renaissance artefact in Palermo. It was in fact commissioned for a Florentine villa and was purchased in 1574 by the Palermo City Council. The Palazzo delle Aquile (Palace of the Eagles), the City Chambers, its walls covered with plaques commemorating celebrated visitors from Garibaldi to Pope John Paul II, occupies one side of the piazza. The Church of Santa Caterina (St. Catherine), an excellent example of the Palermitan Baroque, is on another side and its uncluttered façade with inbuilt columns is no preparation for the gorgeously decorated, or over-decorated, interior. The imagination and creative energy of the designers is overwhelming, for the Palermitan Baroque required that not an inch of ceiling, wall, or column be left unembellished or untouched. Restraint was no virtue and a vacuum an offense. The preference of the

One of the Quattro Canti (Four Corners), a Spanish Baroque extravaganza which stands at the main cross roads in Palermo

artists was for the flourish and ostentation of the whole combined with the florid extravagance of the small detail, so the church provokes a cascade of varying sensations. Individual *putti*, flocks of angels, brooding saints of the Dominican order, medallions, allegorical figures, and little infants signifying nothing other than *joie de vivre* abound. Artists with the traditional paint brush are responsible for the creation of the frescoes on the ceiling, but local artisans' mastery of the craft of inlaid marble gave this and other Baroque churches in Palermo their unique appearance. In Santa Caterina this craft was employed in the creation of Old Testament scenes, with the scene of Jonah being swallowed by a singularly ferocious whale especially striking. The verisimilitude is heightened by the use of actual wire for the rigging of the ship, another Sicilian device.

The marble work in the Jesuit Church of the Gesù (Jesus), also known as the Casa Professa, is even more spectacular. For some critics, but not for Anthony Blunt, this is the supreme example of the Baroque in all Sicily. The cupola was struck by a bomb in the 1943 air-raid, so what is on view, especially in the ceiling frescoes, is the result of meticulous and scrupulously careful reconstruction and restoration. The street outside is occupied by the Ballarò market, with all the shouting and activity typical of such places, so the church is a refuge. To step over the entrance is to be offered immediately a powerful religious experience in a sanctuary made sacred even for unbelievers by the totality of the vision thrust in front of the eyes of the viewer. The term *belcomposto* indicates the fusion and harmony of architecture, sculpture, marble work, and painting designed to produce the one all-enveloping effect, the Counter-Reformation demand for obeisance, and here the elements fuse admirably. The apse, with its paintings of the *Adoration of the Shepherds* and *Adoration of the Magi,* is awe-inspiring, and the fluttering angels and *putti* a delight.

Those who are not sated with the ecclesiastical Baroque will have many other churches to visit such as Santa Maria in Valverde (Our Lady in Valverde) or San Mamiliano (also called the church of Santa Cita), both of which also suffered from the bombing. The artists in the latter had a taste for the grotesque, as is clear from some of the bizarre animals on the walls. The decorative devices are somewhat odd, with crowns, shells, and faces as well as little tables half way up the walls. This church also has the tombs of the Lanza Trabia family, including that of the Countess of Carini who was celebrated in an epic poem for a passionately adulterous love affair, for which she was beheaded by her own father. San Domenico (St. Dominic) is in the view of many critics the finest and certainly the grandest church in Palermo. This has become the pantheon of the city, where many of its most famous citizens are buried.

The real treasure of Baroque Palermo is to be found in the oratories in the streets behind San Domenico which contain the exquisite stucco sculpture of Giacomo Serpotta (1656–1732). This remarkable man deserves to be numbered among the greatest of Italian artists, but perhaps because he worked in Sicily and in *stucco*, regarded as a minor *genre*, his fame has not traveled. The opportunity to discover, see, and revel in the delightful, joyous, and life-enhancing work by this most delicate of artists is of itself a justification of a visit to Sicily. Stucco is made from marble dust mixed with a binder, meaning that it is more fragile than marble but glistens with its own light. Serpotta's mastery of the skills of sculptor, designer, architectural planner, and visionary allowed him to imbue his creations with a sense of happiness and optimism which is the equivalent of Beethoven's Ninth Symphony. The central religious subject was dictated by the commissioning body, normally a guild or monastic order, but in the surrounding framework he created a space where his own imaginative

Beautiful *putti* by Gioacchino Vitaliano in the Church of the Gesù, but no more than a marginal decorative sideline in a larger sculptural group

exuberance was set free and where he created unruly, mischievous little beings to whom he gave the shape of angels or *putti* but who acted in joyful disregard of any theological narrative. These are little playful creatures who can never be disciplined, never fully taught doctrine, never fully incorporated into a serious vision, but who revel in their own anarchy.

His work can be seen in many other places in Palermo and all over the island, but he never surpassed the work he did in the oratories of San Lorenzo (St. Lawrence), San Domenico, Santa Zita, and Santa Caterina. The oratory of Santa Zita (or Cita), which is attached to the church of San Mamiliano mentioned above, belonged the Dominican order, who introduced the rosary into Catholic worship. The walls of the oratory are decorated with little theatrical scenes depicting the Joyful and Sorrowful mysteries of the rosary, while the Glorious mysteries are on either side of the massive work celebrating the victory of the Christian fleets over the Turks at the Battle of Lepanto. Perhaps no military victory has ever been so comprehensively celebrated in painting or sculpture, and this is one of the finest. The techniques Serpotta adopted for this work allowed the fullest expression of his talents. His approach is essentially theatrical. Rippling stage curtains surround the central scene of galleons clashing on the seas while the Virgin Mary looks down from the clouds. This is a conventional victory scene treated with due piety, but what lifts the work onto another imaginative dimension are the two boys seated at the front, legs dangling outside the frame, wholly occupied with their own thoughts whatever they are. This is the quintessence of Serpotta—universal drama played out in all its ferocity with a balancing glimpse of a more carefree, human scale.

The Oratory of San Domenico contains allegorical statues of Justice, Wisdom, and Purity as well as Fortitude, and on the last Serpotta permits himself a typically harlequinesque visual joke. Fortitude leans languidly against a pillar on which a lizard-like creature is climbing up towards her. This is the artist's visiting card. The Sicilian form of his name would be *Serpuzza*, which can also mean a small snake, and he introduces such a creature into various works of his. The oratory, which was the venue for meetings by a well-heeled association, also boasts a painting above the altar by Van Dyck. One of the cycles in the nearby Oratory of San Lorenzo portrays the life of St. Francis, beginning with the saint naked as sign of renunciation but subject to temptation by a wicked woman, while the *putti* look on in real or feigned horror. Other *putti* here are unusually playful, blowing bubbles, kissing, playing about, and consulting a map. The central drama does not hold their attention. This oratory had a Nativity by Caravaggio, but it was stolen in 1969 and never recovered. Such outrages against Serpotta himself were easier to perpetrate, and his work has been impoverished by systematic theft of individual figurines from his carefully conceived scenes. Curators have placed photographs under the actual work to display the original conception before some of the statues were stolen. A crime, but Serpotta is still supreme.

PALACES, THEATERS, AND SORRY SIGHTS

No one admired the Sicilian aristocracy, even if they gave themselves a posthumous good press with *The Leopard*. Machiavelli himself had words of contempt for them. They increased and multiplied and according to one calculation at the end of the eighteenth century the island was home to 142 princes, 788 marquises, and around 1500 dukes and barons. Such numbers indicate a high demand for sumptuous residences and plainly a true, blue-blooded family required more than one palace. The main

A back street in Palermo. Some parts of the city have never recovered from the Allied bombing campaign in the Second World War

residence in Palermo had to be on a grand scale, but many of these palaces have been abandoned and left to rot, and now come into the category of Palermo's sorry sights. A walk around the city will provide glimpses of grand, aristocratic façades emblazoned with heraldic devices behind which there is nothing but a litter-strewn courtyard, or of decaying mansions now in ruins, palaces which are slum dwellings inhabited by the latest wave of immigrants or by Sicily's most deprived citizens. There are jewels to be uncovered, but today's sorry sights were often yesterday's jewels.

Some palaces, like that of Tomasi di Lampedusa, were destroyed by bombs, others simply declined as the family fortunes declined. Piazza San Nicola all'Albergheria was once dominated by what is now a lonely façade with nothing behind. The palace itself was bombed, evacuated, and never rebuilt. The stone is still of a gentle rose color, a coat of arms of crossed flags is perched above several of the windows while a smiling face was sculpted into the stonework by a mason of some talent. The Piazza Quaranta Martiri al Casellotto has a plaque commemorating the forty martyrs executed there by the Bourbon forces in 1822, and who give the square its name. The plaque was once on a church which is a ruin, and the lane leading to the piazza from Via Ruggero Settimo goes past a wall-shrine erected in 1902 where the faithful can receive an indulgence of one hundred days for reciting an *Ave Maria*, which is better value than the nearby 1780 wall-painting of St. Joseph with the Child Jesus which gives a mere forty days' indulgence. The square once contained the Palazzo Marchese. It is now deserted, although the bell-tower is still standing, but very precariously. There were six storys but in late 2011 the top one fell off. The fencing around the palace offers very inadequate protection. When confronted with such sights, unwary intellectuals may find themselves prey to melancholy sentiments of the *sic transit gloria mundi* sort which they may mistake for wisdom or profundity.

This area bounded by Via Cavour, Via Roma, and Corso Vittorio Emanuele, suffered badly from the 1943 bombing and will provide further sorry sights of damaged and abandoned palaces. Piazza San Giacomo la Marina with the Church of Santa Maria la Nova (St. Mary the New), a sixteenth-century Catalan-Gothic building, is one instance. The frescoes on the walls are a testimony to what the church was, but even if it is still in use, it is now dilapidated. A once grand palace stands on another side of the square. The ground floor is occupied by a workshop and on the three floors above are once grand balconies concealed by washing lines. Neither the church nor the piazza are overwhelmingly squalid, and there are no signs of grinding poverty, but the place is run down and inhabited by people careless of the environment in which they live. Sicilians care about their own private space, but the public dimension rarely engages them.

Other palaces in the city are in a better state but some are open to the public only with difficulty. The most wonderful of these is the eighteenth-century Palazzo Gangi, with its gorgeous ceilings, staircases, hall of mirrors, and ballroom, but this is most easily seen as the set for the swirling dresses and elegant evening suits of the dancers at the opulent ball which is the climax scene in Visconti's cinematic adaptation of *The Leopard*. The palace was the townhouse first of the Princes Valguarnera and then of the Gangi family, and if the Baroque style with which it is decorated throughout was going out of fashion by the time it was completed, so much the worse for fashion. The palace occupies one side of Piazza dei Vespri (step softly on the cobbles, for it is believed that up to two hundred French people, victims of the Sicilian Vespers uprising, are buried here). On the other side stands the Gallery of Modern Art, housed in a complex which started life in the fifteenth century as the family home of a Catalan merchant and later converted into a Jesuit house. The Sicilian Regional Art Gallery is also housed in a converted palace, the Catalan-Gothic Palazzo Abatellis. Designed in the fifteenth century as an aristocratic residence, it was later converted into a monastery and remained such until it was damaged by bombing in 1943. It was reconstructed as the home of Sicilian art, including the dramatic, enigmatic, troubling *Triumph of Death*, the greatest expression of a quintessentially Sicilian vision of life and death. The unknown artist who worked in the mid-fifteenth century portrays Death astride a skeletal horse firing arrows at the insolent rich and powerful, some of whom have already fallen, but sparing the poor, the lame, and the blind. The latter group seemingly includes a self-portrait of the artist, probably the figure standing alongside another man, perhaps his assistant, as they observe the scene. The piece is defiantly didactic and the canvas may have consoled the occupants of the poor house where it initially hung, or perhaps not for the underlying meaning is not easy to decipher. Is death only for those who make life unjust? Is this physical death or death of the soul? In any case, no other work so powerfully illustrates a Sicilian culture of death or so illuminates a dark corner of the Sicilian psyche. However, it is a happy chance that the same museum also houses Antonello da Messina's stupendously graceful painting of the *Annunciation* with its delicate tones of light surrounding the Virgin Mary at the moment of the apparition of the Archangel. It is good to be delighted by this life-enhancing, joyful vision after the fearsome portrayal of the Death force.

Of the palaces open to the public, the Palazzo Mirto in Via Merlo is not the most striking from an architectural point of view, but it has retained intact its original decorative style with furnishings, tapestries, and extravagant ornaments that together give a glimpse of eighteenth-century Palermitan aristocratic life. The Palazzo Alliata di Villafranca on Piazza Bologni was the city residence of one of the leading noble families and every stone conveys a sense of family *hauteur*. There is a plaque proclaiming that Garibaldi slept there, but the proliferation of such plaques in Sicily suggests that the great hero spent most of his time in his bed. The piazza was until recently a car park and general dumping ground, but has been tidied up, giving greater prominence to the statue of Charles V in the center—although in this representation the king on whose empire the sun never set appears unusually emaciated.

The Alliata family, who claim descent from the *gens Allia* in ancient Rome, were originally Pisan bankers who came to Sicily in the Renaissance, married above themselves and started accumulating titles. They bagged twenty-eight *signorie* (lordships), thirteen baronies, one marquisate, three duchies, and eight principalities. Giuseppe Alliata became in 1710 a Prince of the Holy Roman Empire and Courier Major of the Kingdom of Naples. The family also included two saints as well as numerous generals, protonotaries apostolic, and various ambassadors. Those with a taste for heraldry will be able to detect indications of the family's rise and rise in the coat of arms, with its Pisan lilies and Imperial eagles topped by a Crown of Gold. Construction of the palace was begun in 1567, suffered setbacks with earthquakes, notably the one in 1751, reached its peak of glory in the last decade of the eighteenth century before declining to the extent that it was given to the church as a seminary in the 1980s. It did not remain long in ecclesiastical hands, and restoration has brought it back to its pristine state. The stucco work by disciples of Serpotta, the gilded doors, the vainglorious paintings as well as the elegant ballrooms and state apartments leave no doubt as to the status of the family. Portraits of the male lineage make it clear that these were men with a fine conceit of themselves.

For entertainment and cultural activities Sicily has within a hundred yards of each other two of the most magnificently imposing theaters in all Europe. Cinema has made the Teatro Massimo, the opera house, recognizable internationally, for the grand staircase was the scene of the shootout which brought *The Godfather* trilogy to its tragic climax. The theater itself has been the site of very Sicilian scandals, and in the last century it was closed for decades while millions were spent on a supposed work of restoration without any visible improvement being evident. The building is nineteenth-century, the architects were Basile father and son, the style is neoclassical, the shape is circular, and the impact is produced by the sheer extravagance of scale. Nothing in Paris or London can outdo it. Its only rival in grandeur is the Politeama, along the same road. It faces onto two piazzas, the larger of which is the Piazza Castelnuovo. Like the Massimo, it was designed in the style of nineteenth-century neoclassicism, inspired by the architecture of Pompeii, and is topped by a chariot pulled by four horses. This area with its many cafés and outdoor restaurants has been called Palermo's salon and throbs with life after dark, especially in summer when Palermitans venture out after the stifling heat of the day.

QUIRKY CORNERS

Palermo is a delight for adventurous strollers who enjoy nosing about in the less frequented corners, and they are at no greater risk here than in any other large European city. There may be a certain macabre interest in noting the number of plaques on walls. Some record the habitation of celebrated travelers like Goethe, but a distressing number mark spots where brave men were gunned down by mafia killers. These have been incorporated into the city's mental topography, so visitors may be surprised to be told casually to rendezvous near, for instance, "the plaque at the place where they shot Gaetano Costa" on Via Cavour. Costa was a fearless and honest magistrate whose investigations of financial dealings led to the conviction of several mafia criminals. Other anti-mafia heroes like Emanuele Basile or Carlo Alberto dalla Chiesa are similarly commemorated.

There is nothing in Palermo more curious than the church of the Cappuccini (Capuchins), situated not far from La Zisa and La Cuba. The church was built in 1621, but the main interest is in the adjoining catacombs. The Capuchins are a breakaway order of Franciscans, and for some reason all over Europe this order made available facilities for the collection

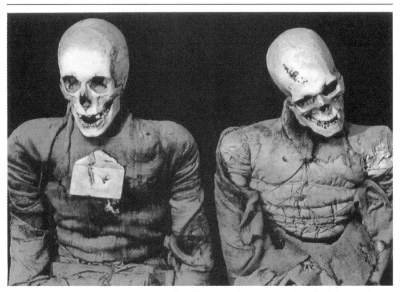

Memento mori, or bourgeois immortality. Skeletons of the great and good of nineteenth-century Palermo, now on show in the Cappuccini catacombs

and display of corpses. The church on Via Veneto in Rome has elaborate, circular designs made out of knee bones of the illustrious dead. The catacombs in Palermo have underground corridors with rooms off which are the last resting place of the well-to-do of Palermo society of other days, grouped according to their profession—lawyers, clergymen, accountants, soldiers etc. Some are encased in coffins, while others are decaying skeletons propped against or attached to the walls, dressed in once fine clothes now reduced to rags. This form of public display ended in 1881, but those who had gained prior entry are still on display. Death has no dignity, but the culture of death again sanctions this odd exhibition. The last room contains the perfectly preserved body of a pretty little girl who could have been no more than five. She is known as "Sleeping Beauty" and the story is that the scientist who mummified her body perfected his techniques with her, but was killed in an accident the following day.

For the living, the markets are thriving centers. The Ballarò is now the city's largest market but it does not occupy the same place in the city's mythology as the Vucciria, whose name is a corruption of the French *boucherie*. Its fame expanded after Renato Guttuso made a lyrical painting,

The statue known as the "Genius of Palermo." The niches on either side are empty
and there is no agreement on what the intriguing sculpture signifies

which seemed to cry out for a musical accompaniment, of the colorful fruit and vegetables on sale as well as of the vivacious dealers and shoppers going about their business. The painting is now in the Steri Palace in Piazza Marina. There are some good and economical eating places near the Vucciria on the streets leading to the Piazzetta del Garraffo, a name derived from the Arabic *gharraf*, "of plentiful waters." Palermo's history, it cannot be too often repeated, is cosmopolitan and multilingual. Inserted into a wall of the *piazzetta* is the statue known as the Genius of Palermo, a much discussed work featuring a male figure with a young man's body but an old man's features. He wears a crown and holds in his hand a snake which is biting into his chest. The origins of this sculpture are obscure, and while all are agreed that it should be taken as a symbol of the city there is no agreement on the interpretation of the symbol. Sometimes he stands with St. Rosalia as the protector of Palermo, but at other times he is taken to represent the self-destructive urge of the city and its inhabitants.

The Piazza Marina on the other side of Corso Vittorio Emanuele has always been a central point of Palermitan history. Its present layout dates from the nineteenth century and the central Garibaldi Gardens with their magnificent trees were designed at that time, but the area has been a center for displays of power and festivities at least since the Middle Ages. "Heretics" and others condemned by the Inquisition were burned at the stake in this piazza after a grotesquely solemn procession around the city for which the grandees of Church and state bedecked themselves in their official finery. These events often ended with a squabble for the best seats in specially erected pavilions overlooking the place where the bonfire was erected. The Inquisition was abolished in the eighteenth century, and later that century Patrick Brydone records how the festivities in honor of St. Rosalia ended with a coach ride to the piazza, and how the darkness allowed the ladies to slip off on their own. In 1909 Joe Petrosino, an Italo-American cop who came to Palermo to investigate the new phenomenon of the mafia, or "black hand" as it was known, was murdered in this square on the day of his arrival. The mafia boss, Don Vito Cascio Ferro, boasted that he had left a cocktail party to kill Petrosino and then returned to finish his drink. It was a lie, but he did dispatch the murderers.

The square is lined with important buildings, starting with the Steri at the eastern corner. Work began on it in 1307 to make it the principal residence of the Chiaramonte family, and although it has been restored and reworked many times the façade still has something of the severe lines of the early style. It became the seat of the Aragonese kings during their residence in Palermo, then of the viceroys and later of the Inquisition. The cells where the wretched victims were held were in this building, and pathetic graffiti and religious artwork of astonishing quality scratched on the walls by prisoners were discovered in the basement. The palace is now the headquarters of the Rectorate of the university, and so it is possible to wander around parts of the building. The courtyard is used occasionally for concerts. Perhaps no other building has seen such a radical change of use.

Santa Caterina della Catena (St. Catherine of the Chain), a striking Gothic-Catalan church on the same side of the piazza, takes its name from the fact that it kept the chain which was nightly pulled across the harbor. In Palermo's *belle époque* the Hotel de France stood alongside the Steri, and here the cream of European society including crowned heads and such figures as Oscar Wilde and Sigmund Freud were guests. There is a city rampart nearby named *delle cattive*, a name which has aroused etymological debate. In modern Italian the translation would be "wicked women," suggesting the spot was the haunt of prostitutes, but a more Latinate reading would give the meaning "captive women," implying that this was a place frequented by widows who were made captive by restrictive social mores.

The hotel in Palermo with the most distinguished history is unquestionably the Grand Hotel et Des Palmes on Via Roma, once Via Ingham. The hotel began life in 1856 as the city residence of the English wine-merchant, Benjamin Ingham. The Anglican church facing it was the private family chapel, and the lands stretching down to the sea and all around the building were the private estate of the Ingham-Whitaker family. Guests included Richard Wagner, who composed *Parsifal* here, as well as the French poet Raymond Roussel, who committed suicide on the premises. After his expulsion from the United States Lucky Luciano was a resident, and here he convoked the 1956 mafia summit which brought together men of honor from both sides of the Atlantic. Nowadays it is a luxury hotel with waiters who will delight in retelling stories of its past and even pointing to the corner where Luciano listened to cases brought to him.

The Ingham-Whitakers had other residences in Palermo. The residence of the prefect is still called the Villa Whitaker, even though no Sicilian can pronounce the name. The Villa Malfitano is the headquarters of the Whitaker Foundation and is almost eerily English in design and atmosphere. The gardens are green in defiance of the climate and the villa itself speaks of a splendor which was once opulent if now faded. The carpets are somewhat bare, the wallpaper several shades duller than when originally attached, but all is authentic. The paintings are a mixture of delicate Victorian oil paintings of the young women of the family and of salacious nude treatments of mythological goddesses. Lying around casually on tables are photographs of British and Italian royalty, and the centerpiece of the main room is a fireplace which was probably never used.

All nations have found themselves at home in the city, and most learned to love Palermo.

Chapter Seventeen
OUT OF PALERMO
CORLEONE, BAGHERIA, AND CEFALÙ

MAFIA HEARTLANDS

Gavin Maxwell is chiefly remembered for his charming books on otters, so few people will associate him with Sicily, but he spent some years there in the 1950s and wrote two books on his experiences. One was *The Ten Pains of Death* (1959), a somber title for a serious attempt to write about Sicilian culture from the inside. By his own admission Maxwell had become "horrified and fascinated by Western Sicily," the horror aroused by the desperate poverty he witnessed, and the fascination by "an intensely individual people." The livelihood of some communities depended on the annual tuna-fishing expedition, a highly ritualized if brutal hunt which reached its climax when boats surrounded a pack of tuna fish and clubbed them to death, turning the sea red with blood. Theresa Maggio's book *Mattanza* sets out the history of tuna fishing as well as the tale of her own affair with one fisherman. The activity had a vocabulary of its own: the headsman was known by the Arabic name *rais*, and the expedition as a *mattanza*, a Spanish word for slaughter. To acquire a deeper knowledge of Sicily and its popular culture Maxwell took up residence in a *tonnara*, the tuna fishermen's seasonal residence, and recorded their talk on their experiences and their vision of life. The tuna is no longer hunted in this way and the *tonnare* around Sicily are now abandoned. There are two in Palermo, both now fashionable restaurant-bars. Maxwell chose to live in Scopello, an isolated village on a promontory to the west of the city beyond the coastal town of Castellamare. The Scopello *tonnara* is on the beach, and many of the implements of the hunt and the subsequent butchering of the tuna are lying around where they were abandoned. The workshop in the village above is now an excellent restaurant.

Maxwell's first book was a biography—*God Protect Me from my Friends* (1956)—of the bandit Salvatore Giuliano (1922-50), a native of Montelepre where he is buried. Giuliano had inscribed on his belt the slogan

I Attend to My Enemies, but God Protect Me from my Friends, and the second part gave Maxwell his title. Giuliano's distrust was justified, for he was killed by his cousin and best friend Gaspare Pisciotta, who himself later died in prison after drinking a cup of poisoned espresso. The tombs of Giuliano and Pisciotta are a couple of yards from each other in the town's cemetery.

In their different ways Maxwell and Giuliano express something of the pull and mystery of Sicily, the first an entranced, honest, highly intelligent but slightly baffled outsider, the second the embodiment of the enigmas of power in the island. Giuliano divides opinion to this day. In some quarters he is viewed as a Robin Hood figure, in others as a psychopathic killer. He was both. He was driven into the world of banditry after killing a policeman who stopped him while he was involved in an operation which was branded as illegal smuggling only in the desperate conditions of post-war Sicily. His public and private personae were formed of disparate elements: the ambiguous Sicilian view of law and of those who disregard it, an idiosyncratic personal religious sense which caused him to give his victims time to make their peace with God before he shot them, a very Sicilian devotion to his *mamma,* Latin-lover glamour which entranced a Swedish journalist who came to interview him but stayed to become his lover, and finally involvement in complex, self-deluding maneuvers to make Sicily independent or else the forty-ninth of the then forty-eight states of the USA. Independence offered him the only prospect of amnesty, and he converted his gang into the EVIS, the Voluntary Army for the Independence of Sicily. The wider independence movement involved politicians and the mafia, and Giuliano found himself enmeshed in a web spun by men more unscrupulous and devious than him. He was killed in Castelvetrano in the most mysterious circumstances, with the police mendaciously claiming responsibility for gunning him down after he had in fact been murdered by his cousin. He has featured in cinema twice, once a serious analytic film by Francesco Rosi and later in grotesquely misguided work entitled *The Sicilian,* based on a novel by Mario Puzo, directed by Michael Cimino and with Christopher Lambert playing Giuliano.

Even Giuliano's most fervent apologists cannot absolve him from guilt and responsibility for the massacre at Portella della Ginestra, unless the claim that he was the dupe of the mafia and politicians counts as an excuse.

This lonely plain is the gathering place for an annual First of May rally-cum-feast by people from the nearby villages of San Giuseppe Iato and Piana dei Greci, and in 1947, following the unexpected success of the left-wing parties in the elections to the Constituent Assembly, there were special reasons for trade unionists and peasant activists to celebrate. However, Giuliano's men were lying in wait in the mountains above and as the procession arrived, they opened fire on the unarmed, defenseless men, women, and children in the plain below. There was no shelter and when the firing stopped eleven people were dead and thirty-three injured. The place, Sicily's Glencoe, is isolated and beautiful in its own way but has the haunting feel which conscience or imagination attributes to a spot where crimes against humanity have been committed. Maxwell was appalled at the crime, but he found the whole story of Giuliano gripping and indecipherable and became an unashamed, perhaps naïve, apologist for the bandit leader. He was not the first honest man to flounder in the swirling waters of Sicilian politics, where currents and counter-currents ebb and flow in accordance with forces invisible on the surface. When he was on trial, Gaspare Pisciotta indicated the network of treachery and double-dealing surrounding and involving Giuliano when he produced a statement which became famous: "we were a single body, bandits, police and mafia, like the Father, Son and Holy Spirit."

Those who have ventured into the Palermo hinterland will almost inevitably have an interest in mafia matters, since the attraction of violence, especially in a far-off land of which we know little, even more especially when accompanied by an arcane code, is for many people irresistible. Such people may wish to visit Partinico, which became the home of Danilo Dolci (1924-97), social reformer, poet, author, and anti-mafia activist. In the 1950s Dolci was one of the most famous men in Europe. His activities drew the admiration of Albert Camus and Bertrand Russell, but although tenaciously opposed to the mafia he fell foul of the political and judicial authorities who were at worst complicit with Cosa Nostra or at best preferred to hush their activities up. It was Dolci and not the mafia bosses who ended up serving time in jail. He invented the "reverse strike," which saw unemployed men work without pay in building the dam at San Giuseppe Iato. Dolci was a charismatic, saintly figure endowed with an innocent vanity, and he spoke with charming, unself-conscious conceit of his part in constructing the dam and so revolutionizing local agriculture.

However, saints are awkward companions and Dolci aroused bitter hostility among some people who would gladly have been his allies. He improved conditions of life for ordinary people, but he did not eliminate the mafia. No one has.

There is no danger in venturing further inland to Corleone, the town which gave its name to the mafia chieftain in Mario Puzo's novel and which has been the birthplace of some of the most brutal mafia killers, but also of some of the most heroic anti-mafia activists. Curiously, Corleone has produced more saints canonized by the Catholic Church than any other town in Sicily, and some of its churches, especially the cathedral which dates back to 1382, are interesting, but no one pretends that these are reasons visitors are drawn to the town. There is no eerie feel to the place except for those with over-active imaginations, although the slightly sinister dominating castle on the hilltop does its best to provide it. There are now two anti-mafia museums, one in the town hall and the other a fascinating ethnographic collection set up by the parish priest. Wealth confiscated from imprisoned mafia bosses is now being redeployed in welfare projects.

POETS AND ECCENTRICS

Another road out of Partinico leads to Alcamo, which is near the temple at Segesta and whose place in mafia history was guaranteed by the activities in the 1960s of the smuggler and psychopath Vincenzo Rimi. But let us try to ignore the mafia, not because it is a negligible force but because not all Sicily is mafia. Alcamo is a pretty town celebrated for many reasons. The name demonstrates its Arabic origins, but for literary historians it is associated with Sicily's first poet after classical times, known only as Ciullo (or Cielo) d'Alcamo. His one extant work is a dialogue piece in which a man tries to seduce a young woman. Cielo (heaven) might be a prissy rewriting of Ciullo, which is an archaic dialect term for "prick." The town has no problem is using the more forceful form to designate the central piazza. It has a galaxy of churches which attracted stucco sculptors including the great Giacomo Serpotta, whose allegorical statues of the Virtues adorn the Badia Nuova (New Abbey), and the lesser known Vincenzo Messina, whose best work can be seen in the midst of the Baroque extravaganza of the Church of Santi Paolo e Bartolomeo (Saints Paul and Batholomew). Local spirituality is also expressed by the sweets in the form of *minne di vergini* (virgins' breasts) which were once produced by convents but are now on general sale. The enormous fourteenth-century castle in the center has the towers, high turreted walls, mullioned windows, and paved inner courtyard which made it virtually impregnable. It has been tastefully recycled as a thriving arts and community center. A couple of miles outside the town is a rival castle, Calatubo, a ruined Arabic structure which rises in solitary majesty on a spur of rock.

Back on the coast to the east of Palermo, Bagheria has been celebrated since the eighteenth century for its eccentric inhabitants but deserves recognition today for more recent talents. It was the home of Sicily's greatest artist of modern times, Renato Guttuso, a life-long communist whose realist depiction of Sicilian life was always touched with a vein of lyricism. There is now a gallery devoted largely to his work in the eighteenth-century Villa Cattolica, once an aristocratic summer residence. The choice is curiously appropriate since for all his Marxist convictions Guttuso enjoyed the good life. The writer Dacia Maraini was taken to Japan by her father when still a small child, but her tender years did not stop her being imprisoned there in a concentration camp during the Second World War. Her mother was Princess Topazia Alliata di Salaparuta, a Sicilian aristocrat, and on her release Dacia and her family returned to Bagheria. Some of her novels, notably the 1990 *La lunga vita di Marianna Ucrìa* (translated as *The Silent Duchess*) are set in the town. The silence of the duchess derives from her childhood experience of rape and violence by her noble uncle whom she was later compelled to marry. Dacia Maraini also wrote *Bagheria* (1993), a short autobiographical account of her upbringing in the town. Bagheria seems to maintain a tenacious hold on the imagination of its creative spirits, so many of the films of Giuseppe Tornatore such as the Oscar-winning *Cinema Paradiso* unfold in the town. He also allowed his intellect and imagination to wander round the place in the epic film, *Baarìa,* the dialect name by which the town is known to its inhabitants.

Unusually for a Sicilian town, Bagheria has no ancient past. It was chosen in the eighteenth century by the Prince of Butera, whose name was given to the main street, as a suitable spot for his summer villa. Over the entrance the words *O corte adio* (Farewell, oh Court) can still be deciphered, and presumably these grand words indicated a disgust with the folderols of courtly life. Other noble families followed suit, establishing in Bagheria either their principal residence or their summer retreat. For that reason the town contains some very fine Baroque villas which once stood in their own parks or surrounded by orchards or olive groves, but the town has expanded wildly and these palaces, mainly in Via Butera and Corso Umberto, need to be sought out among the unregulated, unlovely modern office and apartment blocks.

The most curious of Bagheria's palaces is Villa Palagonia, celebrated for the grotesque statues which stand atop the walls surrounding the villa. It has attracted interest and has aroused contrasting reactions ever since Prince Ferdinando Gravina had it built in 1715. Patrick Brydone made the trip out from Palermo and wrote that the prince had

> devoted his whole life to the study of monsters and chimeras, greater and more ridiculous than ever entered into the imagination of the wildest writers of romance of knight errantry.
>
> The amazing crowd of statues that surround his house appear at a distance like an army drawn up for its defence; but when you get amongst them... there is not one made to represent any object in nature; nor is the absurdity of the wretched imagination that created them less astonishing than its fertility... he has put the heads of men to the bodies of every sort of animal and the heads of every other animal to the bodies of men. Sometimes he makes a compound of five or six animals that have no sort of resemblance in nature. He puts the head of a lion to the neck of a goose, the body of a lizard, the legs of a goat, the tail of a fox... This is a strange species of madness and it is truly unaccountable that he has not been shut up many years ago ... the seeing of the regiment of monsters by women with child is said to have been already attended with very unfortunate circumstances; several living monsters have been brought forth in the neighbourhood.

The French painter Jean-Pierre Houël visited the villa in the 1780s, a decade after Brydone, and was revolted by the sight of the grotesques, which he compared unfavorable to the wooden statues on the Pont Neuf in Paris: "You see confused here all the creatures of the skies and sea, men, quadrupeds, birds, fish and plants which grow in the most varied climes, brought together here without taste or harmony." Goethe too visited the place and although he was left bemused and disconcerted he could not resist writing at length about "the madhouse," noting that "the Prince has

Grotesque statues on a wall surrounding the Villa Palagonia, Bagheria

given free rein to his passion for deformed and revolting shapes, and it would be paying him too great a compliment to credit him with the faintest spark of imagination."

The complaint of lack of imagination is odd, and a generation accustomed to the surrealist art of De Chirico or Dalí will find it easier to cope with the prince's wild fantasies. Many of the statues have gone but a sufficient number remain to give some sense of the prince's bizarre fancies. Some are fairly tame depictions of musicians and strolling players, others supposedly vengeful caricatures of his wife's lovers, and these stand alongside dwarfs with bodies that could have come from sculptures on Easter Island, monsters with curly tails and rows of ferocious teeth, grumpy seated females, a horse with hands, and flying things that exude menace. This is a wonderland of whimsy, with a touch of captivating bewilderment.

Some contemporary historians of architecture suggest that the statues in the gardens are the least interesting part of the villa. Entrance to the villa is by a grand, double set of stairs arranged in front of a cleverly curved façade, and the whole garden-and-villa complex is enclosed by a circular wall which is oddly reminiscent of Bernini's colonnade at the Vatican. The walls and ceilings of the inner rooms are elaborately decorated with frescoes of mythological scenes, and the ballroom is embellished by a mirrored ceiling and inlaid medallions whose portraits may or may not depict members of the family. The family's sense of humor once ran to inviting guests to sit on cushioned seats which concealed prickly spikes.

All that remains of Solunto, one of the three principal Phoenician settlements in Sicily, stands slightly to the north of Bagheria, on a promontory dominated by Mount Catalfano. It was founded in the fourth century BC and around the middle of the second century, in the course of the Punic Wars, it was conquered by the Romans. It was finally abandoned in the second century AD, but puzzlingly the Arabs later found it necessary to knock down what was left. Excavations began in the nineteenth century and many of the finds are in the museum in Palermo, although there is an *antiquarium* beside the entrance. The ruins cover a wide area and some houses have original mosaics. The purpose of what seem to be public buildings is often obscure, since early archaeologists saw them through the prism of the Greek or Roman structures with which they were more familiar. The Phoenicians plainly had developed a sophisticated system of waterworks and there are cisterns even in individual residences.

Termini Imerese lies further to the east on the coast road, in the shadow of Monte San Calogero. The name comes from the Latin for baths, but the original settlement was Carthaginian and its main attraction for the Roman conquerors was its waters, since wherever they went the Romans were always drawn to a place which could be made into a spa. The waters, apparently slightly but harmlessly radioactive, are still taken for their curative qualities. The town is divided into two sections, the upper part containing the main civic and religious buildings, and the lower section around the port housing the town's offices and commercial quarters. The cathedral was built in the late fifteenth century, and from the adjacent piazza there is a splendid view of the port and coast stretching towards Cefalú. There is a Roman amphitheater and the civic museum is housed in an ex-hospital and late medieval building. The items it contains are said to be of mainly local interest, but since they are Greek, Roman, and Phoenician, this is hardly a parochial museum. Some of the exhibits come from the nearby Greek colony of Himera, modern *Imera,* which was the site of the battle where the Greeks defeated the Carthaginians in 480 BC. Signs to the battlefield are a challenge.

The Madonie mountain range, to the right on the road to Cefalú, contains some dramatic scenery and several intriguing towns such as Polizzi Generosa, which was given the right to call itself "Generous" by Frederick II. There are two towns called Petralia, slightly over a mile apart, Petralia Sottana (Lower) and Petralia Soprana (Upper). The towns probably date back to Greek and Roman times, became strongholds of Arab power, were occupied by the Normans, and then dominated for centuries by noble families of Spanish origin. Further to the east Gangi is an intriguing place, disputed by a succession of noble families and with an astonishing array of churches monasteries and palaces. Its remoteness made it a center for brigands and in 1926 it was literally surrounded and besieged in medieval style by Cesare Mori, the so-called "iron-prefect" appointed by Mussolini to root out the mafia. Other villages in the vicinity are denominated Lombard after the peoples who came to Sicily in the wake of the Norman Conquest. However, the main attraction of this district is the regional park itself with its woodlands, wildlife, springs, hills, and cool refreshing air. On the far side of Cefalú in the direction of Messina lies the even larger regional park of the Nebrodi mountain range, where the lush vegetation, the cool climate, and the lakes will challenge any notion of a Sicily scorched by the pitiless sun.

CEFALÙ

On the coast the most significant place between Palermo and Messina is the magnificent town of Cefalù, the site of the third of the island's great Norman cathedrals. It is impossible not to be enchanted by the historic center with its maze of perfectly preserved streets and alleyways, all snuggling under the beetling high crag which dwarves and shelters the town. At the top of the rock, there is Saracen cistern, the ruins of a medieval castle, and an entrance porch which is all that remains of an ancient structure believed on poor authority to be a temple of Diana. Those who manage the grueling climb will be rewarded by a magnificent view. The town also has beautiful beaches and the combination of historical interest and contemporary amenities means that it has become one of Sicily's main tourist resorts.

The town also boasts Roman Baths and the Osterio Magno, once believed to be the residence of King Roger although now thought to be of a later date. The nineteenth-century Baron Mandralisca embellished the

269

town whose life he dominated. He became protagonist of Vincenzo Consolo's historical novel *The Smile of the Unknown Mariner* (1976), which is set at the time of the arrival of Garibaldi and has been regarded by many as a riposte from the left to *The Leopard*. The title was taken from a painting by Antonello da Messina which the historical Mandralisca bought and which is now the prime item in the museum named after the collector. Another remarkable exhibit is a vase from the fourth century BC depicting a fish vendor and a customer having what appears to be a disagreement. The baron's chief interest was in collecting sea shells and there are upwards of 20,000 examples on display, but these will be of interest only to specialists in the science of malacology. The man himself is buried in a grand tomb in Santa Maria della Catena (Our Lady of the Chain).

Cefalù also holds an interest for those susceptible to the charms of the occult or the outlandish fringes of human behavior and misbehavior. Aleister Crowley, known variously as "Beast 666," or "the king of depravity" or more simply as the "wickedest man in the world," took up residence in 1920. He planned to write a biography of Mussolini but his dedication to the project may be doubted. With his faithful followers he established on the outskirts of the town the so-called Abbey of Thelema, a name originally taken from one of the novels of Rabelais who gave his imagined community the slogan, "Do what you wish." And Crowley did. The abbey was in fact an unpretentious villa, and its associations make the local tourist office unsure whether to advertise or conceal its presence. It is uninhabited and the walls are scrawled with etchings of demons, giving rise to probably well founded tales of satanic rituals. Townspeople still talk of shepherds coming across naked girls tied to rocks in the countryside, and certainly female disciples were branded with the "mark of the beast." Things started to go wrong in 1923 when a follower named Raoul Loveday died, perhaps while taking part in some bizarre ceremonial. The activities of the group were exposed in sensational headlines in the pages of the *Sunday Express* and caused a scandal in both Britain and Italy. Mussolini's patience ran out and he expelled Crowley but his stay in Sicily provided material for stories by several Sicilian writers.

The origins of modern Cefalù are Norman, even if the name comes from the Greek. Its rise to prominence dates from 1131 when the Norman King Roger II began building the cathedral which he dedicated to San Salvatore, (The Holy Savior). Legend has it that the king was caught in a

Sea bathing in the shadow of the great Norman cathedral at Cefalù

storm at sea and swore an oath that if he were delivered safely he would build a great church near the spot he landed. His intention was to make the church the mausoleum of the Norman monarchs, but his successors did not respect his wishes.

From the piazza below, the architecture of the cathedral is impressive but perplexing, and no one has ever satisfactorily explained why the two flanking towers are not identical. There are three graceful arches between them, the central one with a circular top and the lateral ones pointed, and above them are two layers of differently designed arcades. The architecture was an Arab-Norman collaborative venture. Construction began in the 1130s, but the cathedral was consecrated only in 1267 so, unlike Monreale, building took place over an extended period. The windows in the towers are spaced differently and the vaults added at a later date, so the design may have been rethought over time. However, there is an inscription inside which states that the mosaics were completed in 1148, decades before the mosaics in Monreale.

The basic design of the interior is the Latin cross, with a nave and two aisles lined by sixteen ancient Roman columns. The last figure on the column in the left aisle, an enigmatic portrait of a man holding a vase with two heads painted on the side, has traditionally been called King Roger. The twin thrones of king and bishop are positioned facing each other on either side of the altar, and the sanctuary itself is raised five steps above the body of the nave, a positioning whose symbolism is obvious. Everywhere in Norman ecclesiastical architecture spiritual meaning combines with reminders of the reality of power. On the wooden ceiling it is just possible to detect traces of early paintings, whose features are impressive but their impact shrinks in the face of the sheer majesty and power of the mosaics. These are not as extensive as in Monreale but are as magnificent in craftsmanship. The most remarkable is the mighty Christ Pantocrator, one hand raised in blessing and the other holding a Bible with characters in Latin and Greek proclaiming him as Light of the World. The Virgin Mary occupies the central place beneath the Godhead, as theology deems appropriate, with archangels on both sides and the apostles arrayed on a lower tier. The adjacent walls are adorned with mosaics of Old Testament patriarchs and prophets as well as Christian saints.

Another important landmark for Sicilian spirituality is to be found at Tindari, on the heights of a headland further along the coast towards Messina. It was once an important Greek settlement, whose ruins include a well-preserved theater and are slightly apart from the modern town. Tindari is famed as the principal place of pilgrimage in Sicily. Although pilgrimages take place all year round the largest gathering is on 8 September, the feast of the Birth of the Virgin. The object of veneration is the Black Madonna, a miraculous statue of the Virgin Mary of probable Byzantine origin, originally kept in a sanctuary which was destroyed by the Algerian pirate Barbarossa in 1544. The chapel which replaced it was, judging from images, an impressive and pretty structure but in the late 1960s the then bishop judged it inadequate and had it demolished. The 1960s were everywhere a low point in architectural taste and the modern, lavish, grandiose, and swaggering basilica the bishop had built is frankly appalling. The icon is kept in a case above the altar, but curiously the reproduction of it on the mosaic on the ceiling shows the Madonna as white.

Chapter Eighteen
THE AEOLIAN ISLANDS
A VOLCANIC ARCHIPELAGO

One final stopping point may be permitted, not on mainland Sicily but on the offshore Aeolian Islands. No one has a bad word to say about them, so a visit will be for many people the ideal way of relaxing after an exhausting tour round Sicily. The unanimous judgment is that the islands are all *bellissime* and that the islanders will ensure visitors are initiated into the quintessentially Italian art of the *dolce far niente.*

The Aeolians now attract and live on mass tourism. Anyone arriving on the islands on the ferry from Milazzo, Messina, or Palermo may think they are in a Sicilian Majorca without the sandy beaches, for the beaches here are pebbly. The town of Lipari, the largest in the archipelago, has all the noisy, frenetic activity associated with mass holiday-making on

View of the Aeolian Islands, once visited by Odysseus and home of the King of the Winds, and now a favored holiday resort

Mediterranean coasts. On the quay are wide-boys offering rooms or cheap hotels, touts hawking trashy mementoes, hawkers beside the gangway proclaiming the rival claims of other islands in the archipelago, and pushy salespeople offering bargain excursions to quiet beaches, with the chance to see erupting volcanoes by night thrown in.

Not all the islands offer the same fare, and Lipari is certainly the brashest. In any case tourist fare is not all the Aeolian Islands have to offer. They are all of volcanic origin and appear to have been inhabited since the fifth or fourth millennium BC by peoples emanating from all corners of the Mediterranean. They were no backwater even in prehistoric times and excavations suggest they were home to rich, flourishing, enterprising peoples who engaged in trade with countries around the Mediterranean and even as far afield as Cornwall. The islands were rich in obsidian, a natural substance which is a derivative of volcanic ash and which was much in demand as a cutting instrument before harder metals were known.

The islands were finally colonized by the Greeks and consequently were drawn into the struggles with the Carthaginians as well as into the wars between Siracusa and Athens. They have figured in poetry and myth as well as history, and were the habitation of creatures that have their being in that hazy borderland between history and fantasy. Critics have puzzled over Homer's description of Lipari as "the floating island of Aeolus." Odysseus put in here after his bloody encounter with the Cyclops and it was here he met Aeolus, a kindly king and lord of the winds, the man who gave the archipelago his name. Aeolus made Odysseus a present of a goatskin filled with the appropriate winds to take the wanderers home to Ithaca, but it was opened prematurely by crewmen who thought it contained treasure. This action caused a storm to blow up and divert the ship away from Greece back to Aeolians, whose ruler was not pleased to see them again. The winds in that part of the Mediterranean can still be ferocious, perhaps a sign of the king's enduring displeasure. In later times the Aeolian Islands attracted the attention of the Romans, Byzantines, Arabs, Normans, and Spanish during their period of rule in Sicily.

There are seven islands making up the one volcanic archipelago: Lipari, Salina, Vulcano, Panarea, Stromboli, Filicudi, and Alicudi, each with individual qualities and characteristics. Lipari, the largest and most important, has the richest history and has been inhabited since Neolithic times. Some of its beaches are white with dust from the pumice quarries, a commodity still mined on the island. It was a brutal business and many of the miners contracted dreadful pulmonary diseases. The continuity of history revealed by the layers of architecture in some buildings is remarkable. The Baths of San Calogero are on the west of the island and although the hot springs are now named after a Christian saint, some part of the construction can be traced back to the early Mycenaean age, and others to the Romans who built their own baths there. The town of Lipari contains well preserved walls built in the second millennium BC, strengthened by the Greeks in the fourth century BC and by the Spanish rulers in the sixteenth century AD. These last fortifications surround the castle-citadel, a generic name given to the walled zone which overlooks the town and its port area and the central point for inhabitants over millennia. Access is via a gate built by the Normans but there are remains from the Bronze Age as well as of the Greek acropolis. The cathedral, dedicated to San Bartolo, is Norman while the Church of the Addolorata (Madonna of Sorrows) is a medieval structure with later Baroque altarpieces.

The castle also houses the Aeolian Archaeological Museum, spread over several different pavilions but whose main collection is in the former Archbishop's Palace. It may come as a surprise to discover that this museum not only has a display of items found in highly professional excavations in all the islands in the archipelago but also is one of the richest and best presented historical museums in Italy. The skilfully decorated ceramic work, vases, funerary urns, and general pottery show the superb standards attained in ancient times by artists who are anonymous but who can be associated with a definite, individual body of work. The "painter of Maron" created some memorable images such as a delicate portrait of a languid Dionysus with a female nude alongside, glancing over her shoulder in his direction. The so-called "painter of Lipari," active in the third century BC, was responsible for almost one hundred vases. He was clearly an artist of the highest caliber who would not have been out of place in Renaissance Florence. All his figures are female, portrayed in various poses, and if experts insist that these works have some unattainable religious significance, the casual visitor will be struck by the realistic naturalness of the women portrayed.

A separate pavilion is devoted to the biggest collection anywhere of the theatrical masks employed for tragedy, comedy, and the satyr shows of classical Greek theater. These masks cover the two-hundred-year period when Greek theater was at its highest point and include portrayals of actual characters from plays by such great playwrights as Sophocles and Euripides. Their historical importance cannot be over-emphasized and the craftsmanship is breathtaking. These small terracotta masks were not created for use in production but as funeral offerings to the god Dionysus, whose cult was widespread in these islands and who was the god of theater as well as of wine.

Salina is the second biggest of the island chain and provided the set for Michael Radford's charming 1994 film *Il postino,* which dramatized the story of the friendship between the Chilean poet Pablo Neruda who was exiled there and the island's postman. The island's name comes from the salt pans which are spread around the island, and since there are no fewer than six volcanoes here it is no surprise that it is noted for its rich vegetation. A stay will be made more pleasant by the supplies of *malvasia,* a delicious sweet wine which is now produced in other parts of Sicily, but whose grape is native to Salina. In the pretty village of Santa Marina a museum commemorates the many emigrants who left the island, often for Australia.

STROMBOLI

Stromboli was the Mecca of international gossip-columnists in 1950, fortunately before *paparazzi* had been invented. Roberto Rossellini was directing a film simply entitled *Stromboli* with Ingrid Bergman in the starring role, and the two fell in love. The couple were execrated as adulterers by bishops and politicians, especially in America, but the scandal enhanced the island's profile. It has its own perfectly conical volcano which is described as having "permanent eruptive activity," and this too adds to Stromboli's pulling power. It is a friendly pet of a volcano, they all say, not like Etna, and at night it frequently performs its own pleasing routine of shooting tongues of flame into the sky and causing the sea at points round the island to bubble under the impact of its submarine gases. The attractive houses are built with lava and pumice stone, and the town's cathedral was constructed in the seventeenth century by the Spanish rulers of Sicily, who kept a base on Stromboli to provide defence against pirate ships.

Vulcano was known to the Greeks as the island of fire and is formed by four volcanoes, only one of which, Fossa di Vulcano, is in any way active. The last eruption was in 1888 and was so spectacular that the

The *Raging Passions* were not just in the film script, but ignited the lives of director and star

Scottish engineer James Stevenson, who had invested heavily in the island, fled, abandoning everything. It is safe today to make the climb to the crater, but it is a bracing walk so some people will prefer a more relaxing plunge into the sulphur-rich mud of the hot-water springs near Porto di Levante.

Panarea, the smallest of the islands, has several archaeological sites which prove the existence of trade with communities in the Aegean from the earliest times. The island has a different kind of treasure in the form of two shipwrecks, both which can be seen from the surface, a Roman ship under the sea near Basiluzzo and a British ship near the rocks at Lisca Bianca. These are a delight for snorkelers. There are five miles of coastline, which goes a long way to explaining why Panarea has acquired a reputation as the most fashionable of the Aeolians, a fact demonstrated by the yachts of the wealthy and the powerful docked in the harbor. It has no real roads or street lights but does have robust little electric taxis. Alicudi and Filicudi are the other islands, each quite distinctive. On Alicudi the only real road goes along the coast so the main means of transport are by either boat or donkey, as was once the case all over Sicily.

Envoi

JOURNEY'S END

MESSINA AGAIN

Messina was the beginning and is the end of our circular tour. As ever, Patrick Brydone had the appropriate words. "I had still a great deal more to say both of the Sicilians and their island, and shall leave them, I assure you, with a good deal of regret."

The first and last view of Messina from the ferry, the Church of Christ the King, built in 1937 as a burial place for casualties of the First World War

Further Reading

GENERAL

Barolini, Helen, *A Circular Journey*. New York: Fordham University Press, 2006.

Blunt, Anthony, *Sicilian Baroque*. London: Weidenfeld & Nicolson, 1968.

Borgese, Giuseppe Antonio, *Una Sicilia Senza Aranci*. Rome: Avagliano Editore, 2005.

Brydone, Patrick, *A Tour Through Sicily and Malta*. First edition, 1773; edition consulted, Dublin: United Company of Booksellers, MDCCLXXV.

Collura, Matteo, *Sicilia Sconosciuta*. Milan: Rizzoli, 2000.

Cronin, Vincent, *The Golden Honeycomb*. London: Rupert Hart-Davis, 1954.

Diolé, Philippe (translated by Alan Ross), *The Seas of Sicily*. London: Sidgwick & Jackson, 1959.

Dummett, Jeremy, *Syracuse: City of Legends*. London: I. B. Tauris, 2010.

Goethe, J. W. *Italian Journey*. London: Penguin, 1970.

Jannelli, Lorena and Longo, Fausto, *The Greeks in Sicily*. Verona, Arsenale Editrice, 2004.

King, Russell, *Sicily*. Newton Abbot: David & Charles, 1973.

Lawrence, D. H., *Letters, 2 volumes*. London: Heinemann, 1968.

Lawrence, D. H., *Sea and Sardinia*. London: Heinemann, 1968.

Lewis, Norman, *In Sicily*. London: Jonathan Cape 2000.

Maggio,Theresa, *Mattanza*. New York: Penguin Books 2001.

Maupassant, Guy de, *Viaggio in* Sicily. Palermo: Pomopress, 1991.

Maxwell, Gavin, *God Protect Me from My Friends*. London: Pan Books. 1958

Maxwell, Gavin, *The Ten Pains of Death*. London: Longman, 1959.

Miller, Arthur, *Timebends*. London: Methuen, 1987.

Miller, Arthur, *A View From the Bridge*. London: Penguin, 1998.

Militello, Fabio and Santoro, Rodo, *Castelli di Sicilia*. Palermo: Kalos, 2006.

Olivastri, Valentina, *Sicily*. Oxford: Clio Press, 1998.

Phelps, Daphne, *A House in Sicily*. London: Virago Press, 1999.

Pratt, Michael, *Nelson's Duchy, A Sicilian Anomaly*. Staplehurst: Spellmount, 2005.

Robb, Peter, *Midnight in Sicily*. London: Harvill, 1998.

Rosselli, John, *Life of Bellini*. Cambridge, Cambridge University Press, 1996.

Servadio, Gaia, *Motya, Unearthing a Lost Civilisation*. London: Victor Gollancz, 2000.

Taylor, Mary Simeti, *On Persephone's Island*. Harmondsworth: Viking, 1986.

Tomasi, Gioacchino Lanza, *I luoghi del Gattopardo*. Palermo: Sellerio, 2001.

White, Jonathan, *Italy: The Enduring Culture*. London: Leicester University Press., 2000.

Williams, Tennessee, *The Rose Tattoo*. London: Secker & Warburg, 1954.

SICILIAN WRITERS

Alexander, Alfred, *Giovanni Verga*. London: Grant & Cutler, 1972.

Battaglia, Letizia, *Passion, Justice, Freedom: Photographs of Sicily*. London: Aperture, 1999.

Brancati, Vitaliano, *Opere 1932-1946*. Milan: Bompiani, 1987.

Brancati, Vitaliano (translated by Patrick Creagh), *The Lost Years*. London: Harvill, 1992.

Brancati, Vitaliano (translated by Patrick Creagh), *Bell'Antonio*. London: Harvill, 1993.

Consolo, Vincenzo (translated by Joseph Farrell), *The Smile of the Unknown Mariner*. Manchester: Carcanet 1994.

Consolo, Vincenzo (ed. Bouchard & Lollina), *Reading and Writing the Mediterranean*. Toronto: University of Toronto Press 2006.

Farrell, Joseph, *Leonardo Sciascia*. Edinburgh: Edinburgh University Press, 1995.

Gilmour, David, *The Last Leopard*. London: Quartet Books, 1988.

Maraini, Dacia (translated by Dick Kitto and Elspeth Spottiswood), *Bagheria*. London: Peter Owen, 1993.

Maraini , Dacia (translated by Dick Kitto and Elspeth Spottiswood), *The Silent Duchess*. London: Peter Owen, 1992.

Piccolo, Lucio (translated by Brian Swann and Ruth Feldman), *Collected Poems*. Princeton, Princeton University Press, 1972.

Quasimodo, Salvatore (translated by Jack Bevan), *Debit and Credit*. London: Anvil Press, 1972.

Sciascia, Leonardo (translated by Archibald Colquhoun & Arthur Oliver), *The Day of the Owl*. London: Granta Books 2001.

Sciascia, Leonardo (translated by C. N. S. Thompson), *Sicilian Uncles*. London: Granta Books 2001.

Theocritus (translated by Robert Wells), *The Idylls*. Manchester: Carcanet, 1998.

Tomasi di Lampedusa, Giuseppe (translated by Archibald Colquhoun), *The Leopard*. Glasgow & London: Fontana Collins, 1960.

Tomasi di Lampedusa, Giuseppe (translated by Archibald Colquhoun), *Two Stories and a Memory*. London: Penguin, 1966.

Verga, Giovanni (translated by D. H. Lawrence), *Little Novels of Sicily*. London: Penguin, 1973.

Verga, Giovanni (translated by D. H. Lawrence), *Mastro-don Gesualdo*. London: Penguin, 1970.

HISTORY

Abulafia, David, *Frederck II, A Medieval Emperor*. London: Pimlico, 2002.

Ahmad, Aziz, *A History of Islamic Sicily*. Edinburgh: Edinburgh University Press, 1975.

D'Este, Carlo, *Bitter Victory*. London: Collins, 1988.

Finley, M. I., *Ancient Sicily, To the Arab Conquest*. London: Chatto & Windus, 1968.

Follan, John, *Mussolini's Island*. London: Hodder & Stoughton, 2005.

Leighton, Robert, *Sicily Before History*. London: Duckworth, 1999.

Loud, G. A., *The Age of Robert Guiscard, Southern Italy and the Norman Conquest*. Harlow: Longman, 2000.

Matthew, Donald, *The Norman Kingdom of Sicily*. Cambridge: Cambridge University Press, 1992.

Mack Smith, Denis, *Medieval Sicily: 800-1713*. London: Chatto & Windus 1968.

Mack Smith, Denis *Modern Sicily after 1713*. London: Chatto & Windus, 1968.

Marino, Carlo Giuseppe, *Storia del separatismo siciliano*. Rome, Editori Riuniti, 1993.

Norwich, John Julius, *The Normans in the South 1016-1130*. London: Longmans, 1967.

Norwich, John Julius, *The Kingdom in the Sun 1130-1194*. London: Longmans, 1970.

Runciman, Steven, *The Sicilian Vespers*. Cambridge: Cambridge University Press, 1958.

Thucydides, (translated by Rex Warner), *History of the Peloponnesian War*. London: Penguin, 1954.

Trevelyan, Raleigh, *Princes under the Volcano*. London: Michael Joseph, 1972.

Whitaker, Tina, *Sicily and England*. London: Constable, 1907.

CUISINE AND WINE

Camuto, Robert, *Palmento*. University of Nebraska Press, 2010.

Johnston, Brian, *Sicilian Summer*. Sydney: Allen & Unwin, 2005.

Simeti, Mary Taylor, *Sicilian Food*. London: Grub Street, 1999.

MAFIA

Arlacchi, Pino (translated by Martin Ryle), *Mafia Business*. London: Verso, 1986.

Bonanno, Joseph, *A Man of Honor: The Autobiography of a Godfather*. London: Andre Deutsch, 1983.

Dickie, John, *Cosa Nostra: A History of the Sicilian Mafia*. London: Hodder & Stoughton, 2004.

Duggan, Christopher, *Fascism and the Mafia*. London: Yale University Press, 1989.

Falcone, Giovanni with Padovani, Marcelle (translated by Edward Farrelly), *Men of Honour: the Truth about the Mafia*. London: Fourth Estate, 1992.

Hess, Henner, *Mafia & Mafiosi*. London: C. Hurst & Co., 1998.

Lewis, Norman *The Honoured Society, The Mafia*. London: Collins, 1964.

Servadio, Gaia, *Mafioso*. London: Secker & Warburg, 1976.

Stille, Alexander, *Excellent Cadavers*. London: Jonathan Cape, 1995.

GUIDE BOOKS

Andrews, Robert & Brown, Jules, *The Rough Guide, Sicily*. London: 1999.

Duncan, Paul, *Sicily, A Traveller's Guide*. London: John Murray, 1992.

Hare, Augustus J. C. & St. Clair Baddeley, *Sicily*. London: Heinemann, 1905.

Kininmonth, Christopher, *Sicily*. London: Jonathan Cape, 1965.

Sharp, Lisa Gerard (ed.), *Sicily*. Basingstoke: APA Publications, 1993.

Touring Club Italiano, *Sicilia*. Milan: 2007.

Index of Literary, Historical, & Mythological Names

Index of Places & Landmarks